ROARS FROM THE
BACK OF THE BUS

Roars from the Back of the Bus

Rugby Tales of Life with the Lions

Edited by

STEWART McKINNEY

MAINSTREAM
PUBLISHING

EDINBURGH AND LONDON

First published in Great Britain in 2012 by
MAINSTREAM PUBLISHING COMPANY
(EDINBURGH) LTD
7 Albany Street
Edinburgh EH1 3UG

ISBN 9781845967758 (Hardback edition)
ISBN 9781845967833 (Trade paperback edition)

A catalogue record for this book is available
from the British Library

Printed in Great Britain by
CPI Group (UK), Croydon, CR0 4YY

1 3 5 7 9 10 8 6 4 2

ACKNOWLEDGEMENTS

I want to dedicate this book to the great game that gave me so much fun and friendship and to Stewart senior and Gladys, who made so many sacrifices.

I want to thank Siobhan McKinney for her secretarial skills and dedication to getting this book completed. Special mention should be given to the Blair Mayne Society and Derek Harkness, who provided the material, photographs and the copy of George Cromey's diaries; Peter Brown, the Blackheath archivist, whose exclusive historical material was invaluable; Cecil Pedlow, who allowed me to peruse his personal diaries from 1955; and Syd Millar, for his support and great selection of photographs, which brought back so many happy memories.

This book could not have been completed without the Lions contributors and the help of the following people: Jeremy Birch (Old Merchant Taylors'), Alan Wyn Bevan (Llanelli), Colin Johnson (Swansea), Colin McVicker and Moira McIlderry, Arthur McMurray, John Martin (Old Millhillians), Towbridge Juddians Rugby Club, Paul Dobson (rugby historian, South Africa), Frederick Humbert (rugby pioneer), Jan Matsaert (Windhoek), Mike Dams (Newport), Roy Bergiers, J.J. Williams, Ian McLauchlan, Sandy Carmichael, Peter Jackson (*Daily Mail/The Rugby Paper*), Mark Hudson (MBN Promotions), Ronnie Chambers (NIFC), Syd Millar, Willie Duncan, Jim Stokes, Andy Loughlin, Henry Edwards, Guy Richardson and John Feehan.

The last year has been very challenging for a variety of reasons and I would like to thank the following people who supported me through those difficult times: Mark Bromage, Tony Daly, Alan Hunt, Sean McManus, Michael Paul, Mannfred Toms, Maeve Kelly, David Devlin, Mervyn Elder, Joe and Norman McKinney, Jackie Hassett and Ian and Lizzie Sproule.

Of course, I owe immense gratitude to the Lions Trust, who helped sort out various ailments that plagued me and old injuries which came back to haunt me, sustained through my love of rugby.

At Mainstream Publishing, I would like to thank Bill Campbell for his faith in the project, Peter McKenzie, Graeme Blaikie, Ailsa Bathgate and Chris Stone.

CONTENTS

INTRODUCTION

The game against the Orange Free State was the closest the 1974 Lions came to defeat. The Free State players had prepared for months under the expert coaching of Nelie Smith. They understood, as we had destroyed every opposition scrum so far, the importance of matching us in that department. Their answer was to scrummage against a tractor.

It was a totally committed Orange Free State who faced the Lions, ready to die for their province. All afternoon they put their bodies on the line and with the help of a 'sympathetic' referee almost pulled off a famous victory. They killed the ball in the rucks but no matter how much we hammered and pummelled them, they stuck to their game plan and in injury time the body of their huge second row Stoffie Botha could take no more. His legs buckled like a punch-drunk boxer as the ambulance crew helped him off the pitch. One last scrum, Free State put in and the game was over. We rocketed them off the ball, Mervyn Davies picked up, fed Gareth Edwards who couldn't quite make the line on a diagonal run to the corner but J.J. Williams scooped it up to score: 11–9. I never saw a team play with such bravery as the Orange Free State that day and at the after-match function their battered pack looked as if it had gone 15 rounds with Joe Frazier.

Thirty-five years later I was back in South Africa to watch some of the games during the 2009 Lions tour. I was invited to a function in Bloemfontein before the game against the Orange Free State (now the Cheetahs), not realising it was a reunion of the side who had faced us in 1974. Stoffie Botha, who had reeled off the pitch before that fateful last scrum, was there along with the flankers, captain Jake Swart and Harold Verster and the hooker, Andre Bestbier (the huge one-eyed Johann De Bruyn was meeting up with them later). Unfortunately, three of the forwards had passed away – Rompie Stander, Martiens Le Roux and Ken Grobler. I was a little apprehensive at first – how might most folk react when faced with a bunch of guys who on your last encounter had tried to kick the stuffing out of you? Still, I swallowed hard and hoped they appreciated the skill behind the penalty I had kicked that made a difference in 1974 (only because Ian McGeechan and J.P.R. Williams had missed everything up to then and Willie John McBride had given me the kick as a last resort) – we're all lovers of the game, after all.

I needn't have worried. With the true hospitality and camaraderie that is unique to rugby football I was given a wonderful welcome and we were soon swapping 'war stories'. I remarked to Andre Bestbier that the last time I saw him he was sporting the best black eye I had ever seen and that Bobby Windsor was a dirty bastard. He laughed and said that Windsor wasn't responsible but the 'Mighty Mouse' Ian McLauchlan, and he was a dirty bastard too.

Syd Millar, in *Voices from the Back of the Bus*, stated that rugby once tasted can become addictive. I am still addicted to the game and the last time I spoke to that wonderful person, England and Lions number 8 Andy Ripley, three weeks before his death, he – as only Andy could – put it so simply: 'Stewart, rugby was a love story, the love of your team-mates, the love of the opposition after you knocked lumps out of them and the love of a great game.'

I know of no other game where you could have 80 minutes of pure attrition against your opposite number, search him out in the clubhouse and have a pint with him and revel in the physicality of the recent afternoon. I don't know if the modern professional player has the time or inclination to indulge in post-match rituals, but if not, they are missing out on a very special friendship, as rugby friendships are for ever. Character and characters were created on the rugby pitch, an amazing arena for displaying skill and courage, where committing assault – if well-executed – received applause.

Rugby football! Yes, Mr Ripley, it was a love story. Even after 55 years of participation, I still adore the game.

The rugby I first played in 1957 would be unrecognisable to the modern aficionado. As the game has evolved, gone are the three/two/three scrum, the striking hooker, the clump lineout, the compressed lineout, the throwing-in wing, the dive-passing scrum-half, the spinning maul à la France), the classical crash tackle, the dribble, the dynamic New Zealand-style ruck, the drop and place kicking at goal from the mark, the three-point try, the four-point drop goal and – most importantly – kicking directly to touch from outside the 22 and the offside line from scrum and lineout.

As the beauty of the old game fades, the beauty of the modern game emerges and long may each generation enjoy 'their game'.

INTRODUCTION

As I fast approach three score years and ten, just as the rotten summers of childhood have disappeared in my mind and I recall the sunny ones, I now only remember the winning games I played in. I can vividly recount France v Ireland in Paris in 1972, but the terrible defeat in 1976 is totally erased. However, I will never, ever, forget the fun and friendship I have enjoyed through partaking in the game.

At Andy Ripley's memorial service at Southwark Cathedral in 2010, full of nostalgia and red wine kindly supplied by the one and only Terry O'Connor (the oldest living rugby correspondent, ex-*Daily Mail*) and surrounded by rugby folk from all over the world, a lot of them friends from my era, I agreed to compile another book, a follow-up to *Voices From the Back of the Bus*. This book is not a history of the British and Irish Lions; rather it is a collection of stories, long past and recent, many of which have been gleaned from archive material, personal letters and diaries as well as anecdotes recalled by 60 years of Lions players, which show the colour and the calibre of men who play this fabulous game.

1

TOURISTS OF THE NINETEENTH CENTURY

A.E. Stoddart
Inaugural Australia and New Zealand tour 1888
England 1885–93, 10 caps

The Original Superstar

Arguably one of the finest all-round sportsmen ever was A.E. Stoddart, the only man to have captained England at both cricket and rugby. Born in South Shields in 1865, he played cricket for Hampstead, Middlesex, the Gentlemen and England. He scored 215 not out for Middlesex v Lancashire in 1891; 151 for England v MCC at Lord's in 1887; and 485 for Hampstead v Stoics in 1886 (at the time the highest individual score on record). His highest county score was his last innings – 221 v Somerset in 1890. Stoddart never believed in coaching. He said 'if a game was within one, it would come out'.

In 1888, Stoddart, who had previously been on cricket tours to Australia along with two entrepreneurial promoters, Alfred Shaw and Arthur Shrewsbury, arranged a rugby tour to Australia and New Zealand although the Rugby Union refused to give it official backing.

The team departed for the tour on 8 March 1888 and returned on 11 November, having played 35 games, winning 27, drawing 6 and losing 2. To the fury of the Rugby Union, 18 extra games under Aussie Rules were played, mainly in Victoria, to raise money for the promoters. The Corinthian spirit so admired at this time had been ignored. Perhaps they should have stuck to Union games, as their results in the Aussie Rules matches resulted in only six wins and a draw out of the eighteen games played.

Stoddart, in particular, was extraordinarily quick at developing mastery even in these exhibition games, especially popular in places like Victoria where there was scant rugby available to watch. He became extremely popular with the colonials because of his remarkable skill in both codes, and he was the undoubted hero of the tour. Stoddart adapted quickly to the 'foreign game' and excelled at it, impressing the Australian crowds

13

with his speed and skills. The whole team performed well, but had the RFU sanctioned this tour, doubtless no such matches would have ever been played.

Rumours circulated that players of this predominantly English side had been paid expenses for clothes and suchlike. The returning players were made to sign an affidavit that they had not received pecuniary benefit from the tour, and there the matter ended. The only player to admit to it, Jack Clowes (Halifax), was declared a professional by the RFU and banned.

At the beginning of the tour, the captain, Bob Seddon, was drowned in a boating accident on the Hunter River, and Stoddart took over the captaincy with great flair and aplomb. He became secretary of the Queen's Club and lost his money at the outset of the 1914–18 war, when he sadly took his own life.

The Times
Tuesday, 6 April 1915

SUICIDE of MR A.E. STODDART

A GREAT CRICKETER

PLAYER IN TEN RUGBY 'INTERNATIONALS'

We regret to announce that Mr. Andrew Ernest Stoddart committed suicide by shooting himself with a revolver on Saturday night at his residence in St. John's Wood.

Stoddart's name will always live as one of the really great players of cricket and Rugby football – the only man who has ever captained England both in a Test Match and a 'Rugger' International. Born at South Shields in 1863, he was in his prime as a cricketer in a great heyday of cricket popularity – the late 'eighties and early 'nineties. Middlesex, the Gentlemen, and England – he did great work for all. It was as a batsman that he was most famous, and a beautiful bat he was, scoring fast in the old-fashioned, attacking style, with all the shots, drive, cut and glance, and yet with quite a sound defence. He could hit balls of all paces and all lengths, and he dearly loved a duel with a fast bowler.

Among his most famous innings were 215 not out, against

Lancashire at Manchester in 1891, and 151 for England against the MCC at Lord's in 1887, when he and Arthur Shrewsbury raised the total to 266 for the first wicket. In 1886, for Hampstead against the Stoics, he played an innings of 485 — at the time the highest individual score on record. He was a great favourite of the Lord's crowd in the palmy days of Middlesex cricket, when his friend Mr. A. J. Webbe was captain of the side, and truly did Mr. Norman Galo write of him :– 'When Stoddart makes her hum up at Lord's.'

VISITS TO AUSTRALIA

In Australia his name was a household word, and his happiest recollections were of his Australian trips. He paid four visits to Australia – in 1887, 1891, 1894 and 1897 – on the last two occasions taking out his own team. He was a fine field, and a well-known professional once said to him:– 'Mr. Stoddart, if you had been a professional you would have been a great bowler.' But he was a much better bowler than many people imagined: In 1899 – his last full season – his batting average was 52.

Brilliant as he was at cricket, he was equally so as a three-quarter; his play at Blackheath, when he was captain of 'the Club' for some years, and for England was a household word. Between 1886 and 1893 he played in ten Rugby internationals, and would certainly have played in more but for the fact that in two of the intermediate seasons England, owing to a dispute with the other unions, had no international matches. He was fast, full of resource, and a splendid kick. It was a memorable drop kick that he made against a gale of wind that, giving Middlesex victory over Yorkshire by a goal to four tries, led to the rules of the game being altered. At that time a goal counted more than any number of tries.

Stoddart never believed in coaching. He never paid much attention to coaches himself, and he was a great example of a born player of games. One of the kindest of friends and most sympathetic, he was always encouraging to and thoughtful for the young player and his loss will be widely missed.

THE INQUEST

At the inquest held at Marylebone yesterday Mrs Ethel Stoddart said that last year her husband had to give up his secretaryship of Queen's Club on account of bad health and nervous breakdown, and had done nothing since. He was a temperate man but lately had been depressed, and said that life was not worth living. Last year he was treated for an attack of influenza and a sea voyage was arranged for him, but it did not take place. Lately he had been very moody. He was in financial difficulties and lost all his money through the war, and that had preyed on his mind and worried him.

Late on Saturday night he took a pistol out of his pocket, laid it on the table and said he was tired of it all and was going to finish it. The witness advised him to wait until they could consult their friends the next day. She picked the pistol up and they had a slight struggle for it, but she gave it back to him after having found it was unloaded, and took from him a full box of cartridges. He then put the pistol into his pocket and later went to bed. Before midnight she went to his room and saw him in bed. There was blood on his cheek. She called for help and then found that he was dead. There was no smoke in the room, and no report had been heard. Lately he had been forgetful and irritable, and even when she had rustled a paper he asked her not to do so, saying it would drive him mad. It was afterwards discovered that he had another box of cartridges in his possession.

Isabel Dalton, a friend, also said Mr Stoddart was moody and restless. He was happy at home but had had a good deal of money trouble. The witness was called by Mrs Stoddart on Saturday night, and saw him in bed with a revolver in his right hand. She had heard no report, and was certain that his mind was affected by his troubles.

Dr Lindsey Saunders, of Maida Vale, said he was called late on Saturday night. Stoddart had a bullet wound in the brain on the right side, and the bullet was found embedded in the skull on the opposite side of the head. The heart was enlarged, as was usual in the case of athletes, and the lungs showed commencing pneumonia, which would increase despondency owing to its depressing effect. Death was due to the bullet wound, which, in the opinion of the witness, was self-inflicted.

The jury returned a verdict of 'Suicide while of unsound mind.'

Harry Vassall
Administrator and British Team Selector 1891
England 1881–3, 5 caps

The First British Selector

Cambridge University has always provided a wealth of international rugby players. Robert Thompson followed in the footsteps of William Harry Thomas, the Welsh and Cambridge University forward, when he embarked on the 1891 tour to South Africa. The first overseas British tour of 1888 had not been sanctioned by the RFU and is often not recognised as an official Lions tour, so the South African Tests were in reality the first matches that allowed British players to be awarded international caps. In 1889, following the formation of the South African Rugby Board, the committee decided that a good way to encourage the game would be to invite a British side to visit, similar to the British Isles tour of Australia and New Zealand the year before. The notion developed into a fully sanctioned invitation, backed by Cecil Rhodes as guarantor against any financial loss the tour might suffer.

In all, 11 players from Cambridge made the trip: both full-backs William Grant Mitchell and Edward Bromet, the huge (6 ft 2 in.) three-quarter Randolph Aston who played every game and scored 30 out of the 89 tries of the tour, half-backs Arthur Rotherham and William Wotherspoon, and forwards Johnny Hammond, Edwin Mayfield, Clement Pearson, Aubone Surtees and William Henry Thorman. With the familiarity of varsity rugby they were joined also by Edward Bromet's brother, William, in the forwards and Douglas Marshall, 1891 Lion, his Oxford University team-mate and three-quarter Paul Robert Clauss. The remainder of the party was made up of the team captain, the experienced international Bill Maclagan, and Robert MacMillan, both from London Scottish, Howard Marshall (Richmond), B.G. Roscoe (Lancashire), John Harding Gould (Old Leysians), Froude Hancock (Somerset), Walter Jesse Jackson (Gloucester) and Thomas Sherren Whittaker (Lancashire). This was a tight squad of young men, four of whom were used to playing alongside each other.

The Rugby Union supported and approved the 1891 British Tour to South Africa. They believed that the amateur ethics had been flouted by the 1888 tour and they were determined that the situation would not arise again. A committee was formed and the most influential rugby figure of his day, Harry Vassall, was a member. A great innovator and forward thinker, his theories and ideals in *Rugby Football* (published in 1886) have merit today, as many of the principles still apply.

An extremely strong player, weighing close to 16 stone, Vassall was reported to have had an individual maul with a certain Charles Gurdon that lasted five minutes. He played in the formative years when the sides were reduced from 20 to 15 a side and saw the possibility of the game becoming much more attractive and skilful than the previous free-for-all shoving and wrestling match.

His coaching manual dealt with the development of the play, captaincy and the role of the full-back, three-quarter back, half-back and forward. Here, I include some examples of his thinking.

> The change from twenty to fifteen a side, which was started by club secretaries because of the difficulty of putting twenty men in to the field, was officially adopted by the Union in 1877, at the request of Scotland. A more open style of play naturally followed, which was so much appreciated that the laws were soon altered to suit it by insisting on the ball being put down immediately it was held; and this led to the increase in the number of three-quarter backs, first from one to two, with two full-backs and then to three, with one full-back in other words, three-quarter back became the main line of defence against the rush of opposing forwards.
>
> Meanwhile the advantages of passing the ball were becoming apparent, and a system of short passing, amongst the forwards only, was brought to a considerable pitch of perfection by Blackheath and a few other clubs, but it was not until 1882 that the Oxford team took up a suggestion made by Mr A. Budd in a magazine article, and developed the modern system of long, low passing to the open by both backs and forwards alike with such success that they kept an unbeaten record for nearly three seasons against the best clubs in the country.

The captain's role was paramount when there were no coaches in the game.

> After thoroughly mastering all the laws, our captain must next make up his mind as to what style of play he means his team to adopt, and by personal instruction, both on the field of play and off it, he must see that his men fully understand that style and carry it out in all its

details. Of course his selection of a style may be limited by the traditions of his club, if those traditions are sound, in which case he will be wise not to attempt more than the introduction of any modifications which seem to him necessary, or again by the capacity of the men at his disposal. It is his business to get out of his men absolutely all that they are worth, and a great deal can be done, by skilful education, with what looks like poor material at the start; but it is no use to adopt a style for which his men are physically unsuited. And here we may remark that it is of the utmost importance that the captain should have the unfettered selection of his team whenever such a course is possible. At schools, universities, and any other places where there is a large field to select from, this rule should be absolute, and we must trust to the pressure of public opinion as a guarantee against unfair selections.

Granted, then, that the captain's power is practically absolute, after deciding on what is to be the dominant style of his team, he must see that they are able to adapt their style to any emergencies that arise owing to variations in the weather, or the strength and style of teams opposed to him. If, for instance, he has adopted the long-passing game he will probably find it useless in wet weather, and must make his men dribble instead.

If he is playing four three-quarters and finds his eight forwards are swamped by the opposing nine, he must make his extra three-quarter go forward. If, when playing against a strong wind, he finds his backs unable to check the attack of his opponents, he may sometimes be justified in playing an extra man behind for the time, provided that the forwards can spare the man; or if his team are accustomed to playing an offensive game, he may have to make them adopt defensive tactics, such as keeping the ball tight in the scrummage, or punting it constantly into touch for a while; but we hope that no captain will ever make his team adopt the tight game as their regular style of play.

The object of the game is not merely to avoid being beaten, but to win the match, and to get as much enjoyment out of the process as possible. Defensive tactics are quite justifiable in special cases, but we should be very sorry to be a member whether forward or behind of a team whose ambition was to make a draw of every match, or at most to win by a dropped goal with luck.

Full-back tackling:

There is one elementary rule about tackling under all circumstances, and that is, to go at your man low to aim at the hips and not at the shoulder. In the latter case the tackler can always be shoved off and the try is a certainty; in the former case, provided the tackler knows the right moment to go for his man, he is certain to hold him and the ball. But how he knows the right moment is a mystery which we have never been able to understand.

We can only suppose that it comes by instinct to some and not to others. It is easy enough to learn to tackle as a forward, where you can go at your man with a rush, but it is quite another matter to stand the last man on your side, and to feel that you must bring the runner down at all costs. Some backs seem to exercise a sort of fascination over you, and you feel bound to run into their clutches. We have a lively recollection in this respect of the play of A.S. Taylor of Cambridge, and we believe that others felt much the same about H.B. Tristram of Oxford.

Three-quarters:

Coming next to the three-quarter backs, the captain has to settle how many of them he means to play. Since the introduction of the open passing game the orthodox number has been three; but Cardiff and a few other clubs have played four with such success as to make it an open question whether the odd man is of more use as a ninth forward or as a fourth three-quarter.

Supposing that only three are played, the next question to be decided is which of them to put in the centre, and which on the wings. In our opinion, the best player of the three should always be in the centre – mere sprinters will do for the wings, if nothing better can be secured; but the centre must have a head on his shoulders, as he is the man who has not only to bear the brunt of the attack, but also to give the wings their openings, and sometimes to win the match himself by dropping a goal. To fulfil these requirements he must throw himself without hesitation on to the ball at the feet of the opponent's forwards when they are dribbling down upon him, a task which is not half so difficult as it looks, if done fearlessly.

In wing three-quarters, on the other hand, pace is the first essential, because they should be the chief try-getters in the team. Their principal work consists of getting into position in the open for receiving passes from the centre, and sometimes direct from the halves, and then running as hard as they can run. In this way sprinters, pure and simple, have often earned for themselves great reputations; but a real player will make much more out of the post than the best sprinter.

He will allow himself to be run into touch or tackled by the last of his opponents, as the sprinter so often does, but will pass back again whilst still engaging the attention of that last man, and so make a try a certainty for his side. Many a glorious chance of winning a match has been thrown away by wings holding on to the ball just too long, in the hopes of getting through themselves.

Half-backs:

The whole machinery of the passing game breaks down unless the halves are smart and unremitting in starting passes; therefore, if a captain has no better material to start upon, he must try forward after forward at the post, until he finds one who is quick on to the ball, and quicker still in getting rid of it. The first mark of a good half is that he gets the ball when it comes out of the scrummage oftener than his opponent.

Forward:

The work of the forward can be suitably divided into two branches, play in the open and play in the scrummage. It is given to very few to be equally good at both; but as every player, however good he may be in the open, has to go into scrummages whether he likes it or not, he can at least learn not to spoil the play of the genuine scrummagers; and as every scrummager has to make a show in the open, he can learn to follow up and to tackle, even if nature has not intended him to shine in the finer arts of passing and dribbling.

Supposing, first, that the passing game is adopted, forwards must remember that a series of passes is hardly ever brought to a successful issue without their aid. It is true that the half-back will start the passing whilst the scrummage is still breaking up, but directly they can free themselves from the scrummage, it is their business to spread out over the ground at some distance from one another, so as to be ready to take up the passing as soon as the three-quarter gets into difficulties with his opponents.

Regarding scrummage work:

It must not for a moment be supposed that shoving is all that is wanted. It is a great thing no doubt to get the first shove, and for that reason forwards cannot be too quick in packing; but scrummage work had been of late years reduced to such a science that mere shoving will be of very little avail against a team of skilled scrummagers. Most teams have recognised leaders in the scrummage such as J.G. Walker of Oxford, Gurdon of Richmond and many others, who keep careful watch over the whereabouts of the ball; the usual plan nowadays being to keep it just behind the first row of legs, so as to retain command of it until the opponents have been worked off it to one side or the other, when with a final effort the scrummage is 'screwed' or 'swung' and the team breaks away with the ball at their feet.

It may perhaps be considered that we have already sketched out sufficient work to occupy most of a forward's time; but there still remain the duties of tackling any and every opponent who happens to be in possession of the ball, of following up every kick-off and kick-out, and of marking his man at every lineout, with which to fill up his spare moments. It will thus be inferred that no one can hope to be a good forward who is not in good training. We are no advocates for stopping a man's beer or his pipe, we do not want the training of an athlete preparing for a race, but we do hold it to be the imperative duty of every member of every team, however humble, to keep in good condition.

No doubt some men are much more favourably situated than others for getting regular exercise; but every man can find time to use light dumb-bells and clubs, to indulge in an occasional bout of boxing and wrestling, and to go for a sharp walk varied by occasional sprints in the evening after his work.

Tom Crean
South Africa 1896, 4 caps
Ireland 1894–6, 9 caps

Brother in Arms, Brother-in-law

At the height of the Battle of the Somme, as the artillery shells exploded around him, Tom Crean calmly lit a cigarette and stood up to attend to the injured and the dying. From the deeper shelter of the trench, his commanding officer lambasted him as a fool. 'I forbid it,' the general fumed. 'You'll most certainly be killed if you attempt to reach the forward line. You'll be no earthly use to us if you are killed. I order you to stay here.'

Crean, a giant of a man with a will strong enough to match any badge of rank, was unperturbed. His men were dying, he explained. He was their medic. He would go where needed. 'It's written that I'm to die in my bed,' he said. 'My boys need me. Go I must.'

There is a vigorous, uncomplicated, almost schoolboy heroism to the tale of Tom Crean and how he came to win Britain's highest award for valour. Irish rugby's greatest star at the close of the nineteenth century, Crean set his fate by remaining in South Africa after a 1896 tour. At heart, Crean was an adventurer, and wild Africa seemed to offer far more than a doctor's life in Dublin. The most dashing player of his generation, Crean admitted that his early life consisted of wine, women, song and rugby.

'Tom Crean would have been a rich man if he'd been born a hundred years later,' suggests Gavin Mortimer in *Fields of Glory*, an account of how sports heroes fared on the world's battlefields. 'A talent such as his would have been rewarded handsomely by professional rugby union . . . Crean, however, would have hated professional rugby.'

Tom, at 6 ft 2 in., was a fine sprinter, a decent middle-distance runner and a determined force in a rugby scrum. He won nine caps for Ireland, his looks and fearsome appetite for action generating 'a raging, tearing, rampaging, terrible opponent,' one contemporary recalled. 'His six feet of brawn, handsomely proportioned, his fair hair and his always laughing face gave him the semblance of a Greek god or an outsize naughty cherub.'

He was also a very strong swimmer and in September of 1891 when swimming with a group of fellow students he and another saved an arts student called William Ahern from drowning off Blackrock, Co. Dublin. So at the age of 18 he won the first of his medals for bravery when awarded the Royal Humane Society's medal for saving a life at sea.

The strength of Irish rugby was reflected in the Anglo-Irish team selected to tour South Africa in 1896. Tom was one of nine Irishmen selected. Seven – Crean, Louis Magee, J. Sealy, L. Bulger, A.D. Clinch, A. Meares and R. Johnson – were internationals, the last having played in 1893. They were joined by Jim Magee, a brother of Louis, and the as yet uncapped Trinity student C.V. Boyd. Tom played in all four Tests, scoring a try in the second. Tour captain Johnny Hammond played only seven of the twenty-one games. It was said the real captain was Tom Crean.

Yet for all his sporting gifts, the rugby pitch seemed too small to accommodate Tom Crean's talents. In South Africa, the pioneer spirit appeared to match his mood and when the tour finished he stayed on, working in the Johannesburg Hospital and playing for the Johannesburg Wanderers club. War proved to be both the making and the ultimate downfall of Tom Crean. He was still in South Africa when the Boer War broke out, and he enlisted as a trooper on the side of the British in the Imperial Light Horse, becoming the brigade's Medical Officer in 1901. He immediately became a regimental favourite for his irreverent approach.

One story tells amply of Crean's panache. Working as a general practitioner, he was outraged when a pushy patient burst in on him as he stood shaving. Crean, dressed only in a vest and with a shaving brush in his hand, roared at the man for his lack of manners. 'Your face is a cruel one,' he told his intruder. 'It needs hitting. Will you fight me?' When the man ran, Crean followed him, laying siege to the would-be patient's house. He eventually retired from the scene, his dignity protected by a borrowed jacket, wrapped around him like a kilt.

Tales of Crean's army life are legion. One tells of how he acted as Cupid for a tongue-tied soldier friend and was eventually sent with a diamond ring to seal the match. He returned with no bride and no ring. 'I've saved you,' he told his friend. 'She's a withered crone, of no intelligence, and I've decided she's unworthy of you.'

Shocked, the soldier stood speechless. Crean offered his explanation for the ring's absence and the mysterious sight of a small truckload of alcohol that arrived with him. 'I knew your heart would be breaking with sadness,' he said, 'so I sold the ring and I've come to help you drown your sorrows.'

On 18 December 1901, at the Battle of Tygerkloof, Tom won his Victoria Cross when he successfully attended the wounds of two soldiers and a fellow officer under heavy enemy fire. He was wounded in the stomach and arm during these encounters and was invalided back to England where he made a full recovery. On 13 March 1902, King Edward VII presented him with the VC and he was made an Honorary Fellow of the Royal College of Surgeons of Ireland in the same year.

He became a popular figure on the social circuit. In 1905, he married Victoria, the beautiful daughter of a Spanish don. They lived comfortably and well, but Crean clearly hungered for action. When the First World War broke out, he enlisted after a week and set sail for France. Tom rejoined the Royal Army Medical Corps and served with the 1st Cavalry Brigade. Wounded several times and 'mentioned in dispatches', he won a Distinguished Service Order in June 1915. In February 1916, he was promoted Major and commanded the 44th Field Ambulance, British Expeditionary Force, in France.

The grim impersonalities of war in the trenches quenched what remained of Crean's lust for adventure. This was no hero's war, where strong character could prevail against adversity. Instead, he daily witnessed senseless massacre. The trenches were not his idea of the military life, and his exit from them – sent home with diabetes – he found dispiriting.

The years before his death in 1923 brought a tarnished final chapter to Tom Crean's gilded life. He began to spend too freely and was plunged into debt. He struggled to maintain his Mayfair practice and was taken to the bankruptcy courts. The adventuring was over, and Crean died at only 49, a shadow of the free spirit he had once been. He died in bed. His boast to a Somme general had come ironically true.

Only four rugby internationals were awarded the Victoria Cross and three of them came from Wanderers. Tom Crean was one.

The Dublin-born man is buried in St Mary's RC Cemetery, Kensal Green, London. His VC can be seen at the Army Medical Services Museum, Keogh Barracks, Aldershot.

For 'rugby theme' stamp collectors, it is interesting to note that the South African Post Office launched their third stamp issue – 'Angels of Mercy', in a series commemorating the Anglo-Boer War on 1 August 2000. They produced a set of two stamps – one of the Rev. Kestell, a Dutch Reform Church minister who served with the Boer Commando, and the other of Capt. Thomas Crean VC.

With special thanks to archivist Willow Murray and rugby historian Paul Dobson, Cape Town.

Robert Johnson
South Africa 1896, 2 caps
Ireland 1893, 2 caps

An Intrepid Wanderer

Robert Johnson, who played with Crean at Wanderers and on the South Africa tour of 1896 when he was 24 years of age, was another rugby player to be awarded the VC. Originally from Kilkenny, like Thomas Crean he stayed on in South Africa when the tour was over and played rugby for Transvaal.

He enlisted in the Imperial Horse Brigade and won his VC at Elandslaagte on 21 October 1899. His former team-mate, Crean, attended to him after he was injured under heavy fire at point-blank range. Capt. Johnson was not a man to cross or mess with. Continuing to charge at the enemy along with Capt. Charles Herbert Mullins, also mentioned in the citation for the VC, they enabled a flanking movement that secured their position and decided the outcome of the battle. Capt. Charles Mullins was a brother of one of Johnson's team-mates on the Lions tour three years earlier.

One can only speculate about the parallels of combat on the pitch and the camaraderie and allegiance later displayed when fighting in the Second Boer War. Rugby featured strongly in Johnson's family; two of his brothers also represented Ireland at the game. It would appear that bravery and loyalty developed through rugby readily transferred to the battlefield. Apart from the VC awarded to him, Robert Johnson also received the Queen's South Africa medal and bars and the King's South Africa medal for his service following his roles as Commandant at a concentration camp at Middelburg, Mpumalanga, in 1902 and as Eastern Transvaal District Commissioner, 1903.

Discipline and determination continued to dominate Johnson's later life as he joined the Prison Service on his return to Ireland in 1911 when he turned 40. He became Commandant of the POW camp at Oldcastle 1914–15, and was appointed Governor of His Majesty's Convict Prison at Maryborough, Portlaoise, in 1915, before returning to Oldcastle in 1916. In 1918 he was appointed a Resident Magistrate. He returned to Kilkenny in later years and that is where he died.

Alexander Findlater Todd
South Africa 1896, 4 caps
England 1900, 2 caps

An Early Performer

In 1896, Alexander Findlater Todd, son of a wealthy wine merchant, set sail for South Africa to play on the rugby tour that would keep him away from home for three months. The trip not only provided him with great contacts for the family business, but he was travelling with Thomas Crean and in 1902 would marry his sister, Alice Mary Crean.

His letters home, a selection of which follows, show the lifestyle of those who could afford to travel in those days and they provide great social commentary on the period. He wrote often and gave frank observations on South Africa, which was not much more than frontier country at the time, very much like the Wild West in places. These Tourists knew how to have fun – wine, women and song often the backdrop to their training schedules. Yet, despite the high jinks of youth and the privilege of position, Alexander Findlater Todd was another young rugby-playing man who gave his life for his country when he died of injuries resulting from wounds inflicted during the action of the British assault on Hill 60 at Ypres Salient in 1915. He had survived the Boer War although wounded in action during that campaign too.

By Alexander Findlater Todd (22 years of age):

6 June 1896 – on board the Union Steam Ship *Tartar*

As we are arriving at Madeira tomorrow morning, I thought perhaps you would like to hear from him [*sic*]. So far everything has been first rate and the sea is somewhat like a millpond; the consequence is that everybody is extraordinarily cheerful; in fact such has been the case ever since we started. Among the first class passengers, there are very few of the latter besides the twenty odd of the team. Only about half a dozen of us were badly afflicted, your affectionate son *not* being among their number, though after oversleeping himself rather badly and not waking up until well inside the Bay of Biscay, it took him rather a long time to get up; nevertheless, his internal arrangements have in no way suffered, judging by the heated appearance of the stewards who run about for his 'wittles'.

Sports were started yesterday afternoon, of course, and everyone felt fit and strong, and some surprising talent was shown, the 'present scribe' distinguishing himself from all competitors by the number of times he missed the pail. I have always heard that being on board for a long voyage rather tends to make one sentimental, but the Steamship Company didn't look after us in that respect, as I don't think there are more than two unmarried ladies in our part, and they seem pretty full up with acquaintances already.

14 July

As I suppose you have already seen in the papers that we arrived all safe here, you are no longer anxious. Our boat missed the homeward bound mail by two hours; in fact we passed it almost within speaking distance a few miles out from the Cape. So again if you wrote out by the mail I left, I shall most probably get your letter about a few hours after this leaves. In my last epistle I recounted the meagre events of the voyage to Madeira. We all went ashore there and walked up an enormous hill with the sun between 90 and 100, and consequently arrived at the top several pounds lighter than we started, but we consoled ourselves with the idea that it was 'good for training', and came down in about ten minutes from the top in a toboggan, the recognised method of progression there, where all the streets are cobbles worn smooth as glass. Then we sampled the wine and fruit of the country and walked about under palm trees, picking bananas and tropical orchids.

Against Cape Town Clubs I managed to score the second try of the tour; hooray for Taymount, that is fourteen points to nine. After the match we came to the conclusion that three weeks on board ship, lying on one's back, coming after a hot English summer (including items such as May week festivities) is not conducive to good training. In the last ten minutes I would gladly have changed places with a corpse; the papers gave us rather a slating next day, but how on earth did they expect us to get fit. Everybody thinks we did well to win at all, as the others are much better than any London team bar Blackheath, and had been training for five weeks for us. I think five weeks training is better than two days at it.

On Sunday, after going to early service, we drove out to a lovely place called Hout Bay; about fourteen miles out from the town, and had a sort of picnic. Mr Barney Barnato [mining entrepreneur] turned up just as we finished lunch. Another celebrity in the form of Melton Prior, the war artist of *The Graphic*, was there also. That just reminds me that we came out on the *Tartar* with Captain F.E. Younghusband, one of the first two men to get to Chitral and who has explored all sorts of unheard of places; he was an awfully nice little chap – he's been sent out here to discover the truth about Jameson [British colonial statesman Leander Starr Jameson]. We also made friends with a millionaire on board named Bertram, who owns a place called Bertram's Township, practically inclusive of half of Johannesburg.

On Monday we drove out to Cecil Rhodes' place where Miss Rhodes took us in hand and showed us all over the house, a lovely old Dutch mansion right under the shadow of Table Mountain. Rhodes is not here now, as he's watching the Matabele war, so she has invited us to lunch out there tomorrow. (We're doing ourselves pretty proud with our millionaire acquaintances, aren't we?)

In the afternoon we played our second match, against the Suburban teams, the first being against the Town teams, and won by a goal and a try (8 pts.) to nil. It was one of the hardest games I've ever played, especially as one of our men, Mackie, got his nose broken and had to go off for about ten minutes. But he came round afterwards and finished the game. The ground was even harder than before, and we've lost square yards of skin between us.

In the evening we (one or two of us, I mean) were asked to perform at a smoker [a room set aside for smokers]. I consented with the other songsters as we thought there would only be about 40 or 50 people present and no formality. Judge of our horror when we're taken to a place larger than the Queen's Hall in Regent Street, with the best part of a thousand people there, and told that that was the smoker. We were after thinking that we had been directed to the Albert Hall or a Handel Festival by mistake, but in we walked, being directed to seats at the top end. We walked up, the whole place rising and cheering like mad, and to think that we'd got to *sing* to them on a raised platform. I wished my boots had been sizes larger so that I could have sunk into them and disappeared, but it was not to be and we had to go through with it.

Last night, feeling sore and out of sorts, I was asked round to a meeting of the Orols Club (it corresponds in a way to the Savage Club, London) in order to meet Mark Twain, who has just completed a tour round the world. They gave him a book of photos and the old chap made an awfully good speech in reply. Then blow me, if they didn't make me sing again; my inside was all topsy-turvy and I never thought I should get through it, especially as it ended up on top A, but I managed it somehow and then went to bed and dreamt of foghorns and steam whistles.

July – Grahamstown

I don't think any of you are great letter writers at home. I think I am creating a record, having written home every mail so far, as well as from Madeira.

We had an awfully good time at Port Elizabeth, an awfully good dance among other things. They also gave us an evening performance of *The Mikado* by amateurs, which was distinctly good although Ko-Ko, the chief man, had a shocking cold; yet it was the best amateur theatrical show I was ever at. After the performance we went behind the scene, pulled up the curtain and had an impromptu dance, which must have looked rather funny.

The day after next there was some shooting, but I didn't go as I was quite done up after the ball the night before, and should have had to do with two hours' sleep, which was hardly good enough. At the Ball, the show of beauty was much better than before, likewise the dresses, but about the latter I don't know much. The supper, done by five energetic ladies, was just immense and the lady and her mother whom I took up to it were blessed with fairly healthy appetites and drinkitites, so I got enough to keep going on. My opinion of colonial dancing has not deteriorated one bit; they knock the homeborns into fits. One old sportsman we met here gave us ½ doz. ostrich feathers each, and as he said that if we wanted any more we could have them at trade price, I did a small deal; if you want any more you had better write and let me know, as there is no import duty and these enthusiasts out here practically give them to us.

On Tuesday last we played the Eastern Province XV and won by three goals and a try to nil, although we played badly.

On Thursday we played South Africa and simply sponged up the non-existent puddles with them, although we only won by one goal and a try. Their forwards were laid out absolutely flat several times, although they were heavier than we were. It was the finest forward game I've ever played.

On Friday morning we came on here after a miserable railway journey from 11.50 a.m. to 7.30 p.m. and have got into a beastly hotel where there is no water to be had for baths. Grahamstown seems a very nice place but not much in the hotel line.

20 July – Kimberley

After sending off your letter I went to lunch with the rest of the team to Cecil Rhodes' place near Cape Town which I described to you in my last letter. Miss Rhodes, his sister, presided and gave us a very good spread, with Veuve Clicquot '89 to drink. It was a good job that we had an hour or two to spare after lunch before playing.

The third match took place the same afternoon against the Western Province XV and, after a tremendous tussle, ended in a draw.

The same evening we embarked on the train for Kimberley, and after two nights and a day spent in smoking &c. managed to arrive here on Friday morning. The same afternoon we were taken to see the big Bultfontein and Premier mines, and managed to spoil all our hats and bruise our noddles in going through the low working tunnels. There's really very little to see in one of these diamond mines except a lot of dirt-covered natives digging and shovelling. The earth-decomposing machines are much more interesting, especially an electric revolving cylinder which is full of strong magnets and picks out all the diamonds with a smallish amount of rubbish which has to be sorted out afterwards by hand. In the sorting they find millions of tiny garnets and green stones too small for setting up and consequently worthless.

Kimberley is mostly built of very rusty, discoloured, corrugated iron. The land is as flat as a pancake and about six inches deep in dust.

The football ground has absolutely not one blade of grass on or near it; it is exceedingly flat which is a good point (its only one). Before playing they have to put a sort of harrow on it which scrapes up the hard surface to a depth of about six inches and then they water it.

We beat Kimberley, or rather Griqualand West, by 11 points to 9, so we have only lost a lot of skin so far, nothing else.

27 July – Bunton's Grand Hotel, Port Elizabeth

As you may perceive from the above heading, we are still on the travel round. This is about the nicest place we have been to yet, and is distinctly English in every way; our journey here from Kimberley was awfully dreary as we started on Thursday afternoon about 4.30 or 5.00 and didn't get here till 9 o'clock the following night, merely three hours late.

We had a day's buck-coursing at Kimberley on the open veldt or prairie, and had some rather good sport. The buck were mostly a kind of small antelope and go like the wind; we weren't allowed to ride as we had a stiff match on the next day, so our energy was confined to carts from which there wasn't much to see after the first few seconds unless the buck ran in a circle. We had to get up at six in the morning which came rather hard as we had had a dance the night before and didn't get to bed till the small hours. The ladies of Kimberley aren't much to look at, my first three introductions being ladies of distinctly mature age, consequently relegated to the after part of the programme when I was a mile or two away from the scene of the dance. Still the people here are about the best dancers I have ever seen.

The Griqualand West return match was looked forward to by the townspeople as a good thing for the local team, as they had kept in good training whilst we had had picnics, dances, hunting &c. but unfortunately for them we played a great game and won easily by two goals and two tries to nil, which they didn't like at all.

We went down to the big De Beers mine and saw the natives working for the diamonds a thousand feet below the surface; the passages are made for people about 4 ft 9 in. or 5 ft high and we walked about three miles along the various levels; I was rather cute so got behind a man about the same size as myself, and whenever I heard his head bang against the top I forthwith ducked mine, and so escaped concussion of the brain. It was so hot that I must have lost nearly six pounds, and my clothes were nearly dropping off me when I came up. We also went and saw about £500,000 worth of diamonds, cut and otherwise, of all colours, black, green, blue, orange, white, pink &c. the best being bluish white and a dark orange one. We were each presented with a pocketful of small garnets which I am afraid aren't of much value, but useful curiosities.

A gloom has just fallen on us as Roger Walker, our Manager and President of the English Rugby Union, has just had a cablegram to say his eldest daughter is dying, so he's off home, poor chap. He lives in Pangbourne.

17 August – Rand Club, Johannesburg (the Club I am writing
from has an entrance fee of £100!!)
My last letter was from Queenstown, where we had horrid weather
and had nothing to do but sit in a smoky little sitting room all day
and look at one another.

We started away from there at 9.30 on Sunday night and arrived
here at Johannesburg on Tuesday morning about 11 o'clock, just
about sick of the journey.

We had a fair sample of Johannesburg prices at Breakfast on
Tuesday morning, as after gaily eating half a dozen cheese sandwiches
we were informed they were only 1/-, and a large bottle of beer 4/-!
Thank goodness most things are paid for us here.

I got my money up here at last, having to wire Cape Town for it.

This place is simple marvel considering that only ten years ago
there was exactly one house here in the middle of a desolate prairie
– it's far and away the biggest place in S Africa, and they've got
everything here that it's possible to have.

Yesterday we drove out to Doornkop where Jameson had his
fight; it's about 15 miles from here and is the most one-sided position
imaginable. The Boers were all behind rocks and had all Jameson's
men against the skyline. Of course we all went trophy hunting; one
or two managed to get cartridges, but the rest had to be content
with horses' shin bones &c. It was awfully interesting (especially
when we got left behind on the veldt and had to walk eight miles to
the station).

We played the Diggers on Wednesday and beat them by seven
points to nil (one goal from mark and one try). The ground is *just the
road* with most of the stones taken off.

On Sunday we played the Transvaal, supposed to be our hardest
match, and beat them by three goals (one penalty) and a try to one
try (16 points to 3). We were told that if they won, the Dutch would
consider it another international victory, so we bucked up a bit.

For the match today there are only ten able-bodied men, four
crocks and one invalid playing for us!

2 September – Royal Hotel, Cape Town
I missed the last mail by a few minutes, owing to mistaking the time;
that's the very first opportunity I've missed for three months of
writing to you, and I feel very good indeed just now. This is the last

letter you will have from me from these parts, as I arrive a week after it in good old England again, and I shan't be sorry either. We're all just about played out now, having played nineteen matches and travelled ten thousand miles in ten weeks. The day I sent my last mail to you we played against Johannesburg town and could only with the greatest difficulty manage to raise 15 men to take the field; in fact one had fever all the morning before playing, but we won easily all the same.

We also won our return matches with Transvaal and S Africa. In the last match, quite unknowingly, I did a neat bit of gallery play, as I got a try and got winded at the same time and learnt afterwards that it happened within about 20 yards of my favourite partner at a dance the night before. I think it was rather neat as I was unconscious of the fair lady's presence. I shan't forget that dance in a hurry; there were about 450 to 500 people there instead of 300 and I had 26 dances down on my programme; that holds the record for the tour so far. Johannesburg people are absolutely the most untiring lot in their hospitality that I ever hope to come across. From nine in the morning till midnight they did us as proud as they could; they never left us, they wouldn't allow us to pay a thing – dances, dinner, concerts, native war dances, mines, picnics, tennis parties, drives, theatres, variety entertainment, in fact absolutely everything to make us enjoy ourselves, and they did their best to keep us fit all the way through and never forced us to do anything we didn't want to, if it was bad for training.

Going back to Kimberley, which someone described as the 'last place God made', was just too awful after Johannesburg. We won our two matches there against Cape Colony and S Africa again. We've only got two more matches now, and we want a rest badly.

You'll see me a week after the arrival of this letter; we sail on the *Mexican* on 9 September.

Fixtures and Results: 1896 Tour to South Africa

11 July	Cape Town Club	Cape Town	Win	14–9
13 July	Suburban Clubs	Cape Town	Win	8–0
15 July	Western Province	Cape Town	Draw	0–0
18 July	Griqualand West	Kimberley	Win	11–9
22 July	Griqualand West	Kimberley	Win	16–0
25 July	Port Elizabeth	Port Elizabeth	Win	26–3

28 July	Eastern Province	Port Elizabeth	Win	18–0
30 July	South Africa	Port Elizabeth	Win	8–0
1 August	Grahamstown	Grahamstown	Win	20–0
4 August	King Williams Town	KWT	Win	25–0
6 August	East London	East London	Win	27–0
8 August	Queenstown	Queenstown	Win	25–0
12 August	Johannesburg-Country	Johannesburg	Win	7–0
15 August	Transvaal	Johannesburg	Win	16–3
17 August	Johannesburg–Town	Johannesburg	Win	18–0
19 August	Transvaal	Johannesburg	Win	16–5
22 August	South Africa	Johannesburg	Win	17–8
26 August	Cape Colony	Kimberley	Win	7–0
29 August	South Africa	Kimberley	Win	9–3
3 September	Western Province	Cape Town	Win	32–0
5 September	South Africa	Cape Town	Loss	0–5

Rev. M.M. Mullineux
South Africa 1896, 1 cap; Australia 1899 (Captain and Manager)

Player, Captain and Manager

The Rev. M.M. Mullineux was born in Salford, Lancashire, on 8 August 1867. A diminutive man, weighing only 10 st. and standing 5 ft 4 in. tall, in 1896 he played half-back in J. Hammond's British team touring South Africa. The Rev. Mullineux must have savoured touring because he then organised, captained and managed the 1899 tour to Australia. He was the only captain of a British side who never played for his home country. After defeat in the first Test (3–13 in Sydney) he stood down for the Gloucester and England forward Frank Stout.

As a manager he was scathing in his remarks regarding the breaking of the rules by the Aussies. Some things have not changed: whinging Poms and cheating Aussies.

> *The Australian*, 26 August 1899: English v. Australian Rugby
> Football; Strong Comments by the Reverend M. Mullineux
> (Organiser and Captain of the Team of English Footballers who
> have been Touring the Colonies)
> When the English footballers were entertained at dinner by the
> Metropolitan Rugby Union at the conclusion of their last

representative match in this colony, their captain, the Reverend M. Mullineux, had a few words of manly, straightforward advice to offer to his hearers and to footballers generally. The reverend gentleman came out here under the auspices of the English Rugby Union, for the purpose of popularising the game, and, according to the manner in which he found it played in Sydney, it is very evident that there was good reason for dissatisfaction on the part of the Englishmen, who are under obligations to their own union – with which ours is affiliated – to see that the rules were strictly observed in every respect. In view of the comments which were made on both sides, and particularly by the visitors, a representative of the *Australian Field* sought an interview with Mr Mullineux. That gentleman was staying temporarily with friends, and had only just returned from the match against Great Public Schools, in which he had acted as referee – to the unbounded satisfaction of all who witnessed his performance – but, despite the fact he was tired, wet and muddy, he found time to talk and explain his views.

In the first place, it must be clearly understood that the visitors, in commenting on the play they were met with in Sydney, did so purely in the interests of the game. They were in the advantageous position of victors, and in finding fault they cannot, therefore, be suspected of a desire to make excuses for any shortcomings of their own.

Mr Mullineux made that very clear two or three times during the conversation, and was most anxious that it should be fully understood that he had but one object to serve – the promotion of a better spirit in the ranks of the representative footballers of this colony.

'There is a great deal too much pointing in the game,' is the prime basis of the complaints. 'I am here more or less as the representative of English Rugby football,' said Mr Mullineux, 'and I think it is my duty to speak against anything which the English Rugby Union would not approve or acknowledge as good sport. There are deliberate breaches of the rules which ought to be put a stop to. The points to which I refer more particularly are:-

'Pushing a man at the lineout instead of going fairly for the ball. The habit is a very bad one to practise. It may be sharp, but it is not football. Here is the development of it: On the lineout, A and B are Australians; they each push an opponent away, and thus make way for C, another Australian, to come through. That is not football, and Mr Corr stopped it in two or three matches in which he was referee.

'When tackled on the ground, some Australians, instead of playing the ball fairly between themselves and their opponent's goal line, push it back, with their hands, among their own forwards. They seem to think that is very smart forward work. It is a very bad practice, and is not the game.

'In the Test match at Brisbane, in the lineout on the Australian line, the ball, instead of being thrown out fairly, was thrown hard against an Englishman's legs, with the object of it rolling over the line and being touched down by an Australian. This allowed the Australians to kick out from their 25 instead of having a scrum in their own line. That is not in the spirit of the game at all.

'In the scrum they will put their elbows or their hands in an opponent's face to hamper his actions. That is not play, and, although I am told the Australian remedy is to bite the offending hand, we have not yet acquired habits of cannibalism.

'Also, when a scrum is breaking up, they will hold an opponent back, and prevent him getting clear.

'Perhaps the meanest system of pointing we came across was calling after an opponent for a pass. They will call after him by name, and in the excitement of the game it is difficult to stop to recognise a voice when so called upon, and a pass frequently results with the opposite effect to that anticipated by the man passing. That occurred very often. It may be very clever according to some lights, but it is unfair and low. Such a plan would never be resorted to in England, and should not be tolerated here.'

Those are the main points in detail which Mr Mullineux takes exception to, but at the same time he speaks very freely of other very reprehensible practices.

'We have played the game fairly and in the proper spirit on all occasions,' he says, 'and if we have, in the heat of the game, brought up appeals which have been wrong, it has been done in all honesty. We object to a very prevalent habit of appealing and saying things merely for the purpose of fooling the referee – if he can be fooled. That sort of thing is so very marked, and is done with such apparent skill, that one is almost led to think that they must hold committee meetings, or something of that sort, for the purpose of arranging the points they will try to work.'

The Englishmen were also much surprised at the frequency of free kicks in the game, as played in Australia, and they are at a loss to understand the great tendency to question the decisions of the referee, and also to indulge in purely speculative appeals. This all shows a very bad spirit in a game which should be played for the sake of the sport and the sport only – it is not honest play.

Much of the meaning of the comments indulged in by Mr Mullineux and his colleagues may, perhaps, be summed up generally in the expression that they conveyed to the interviewer an idea that the visitors regarded the practices of some of the players they had met in the metropolis of this colony as the result of either ignorance or wicked knowledge. Whichever it may have been, it is in the interest of a good manly sport that they should be exposed and suppressed without any delay. 'Football,' said Mr Mullineux, 'is a game in which you are put so much upon your honour that only by a recollection of what is due to a man of honour, and by insisting upon such a recollection, can resort to dishonest practices be prevented. In football there is so much takes place that a referee may not see clearly, and so many points may be worked unfairly, that if a player is not going to act honourably he had far better be excluded from the game altogether. In cricket it is a very different thing. That game is necessarily so very open that not only the umpires, but every player and every onlooker, practically, can see all that goes on, and there is not the same temptation to an unscrupulous man. If football is not played fairly and honourably it is not worth playing.'

In the country matches, and in that against the Schools, there was an absence of trickery, and a good spirit of true sport about the game as played by the opponents of the English visitors, and, although there may be some differences as to the interpretation of the rules, the Englishmen are clearly of opinion that the tone of footballers who were picked to play against them in the provinces was of a much higher order than that found in the metropolis. Mr Mullineux does not tar the whole of our metropolitan players with the same brush, and freely declares that he met some very fine fellows among his rivals. The Englishmen made many friends among those they played against, and are no more reluctant to award credit than they are to protest against practices which are calculated to ruin the true Rugby game. Some of the play which they saw was of a very high order, and Mr Mullineux makes no secret of the fact that he and his comrades learnt many valuable things. It was an all-round source of gratification, too, to notice that in the last Test match there was less pointing than had been the case on previous occasions, before the English captain's complaints were so much discussed.

The conversation turned upon the various causes of decadence in such games as football. The Rugby game, according to the English Union, is only able to maintain its high class as an amateur sport by the total prohibition of anything approaching payment or reward for services rendered. 'Matches for prize badges, cups, etc.,' said Mr Mullineux, 'are not allowed under our regulations, and it has been necessary on some occasions, when a patron of the game has wished to signalise a great victory by presenting medals, to obtain the permission of the union before they could be accepted. When Northumberland won the county championship an example of this was afforded. Wherever cups have been brought forward in England it has had a tendency to spoil the game, but, as opinion was divided between the South and the North, Yorkshire has started the Northern Rugby Union, where they are allowed to pay players for their loss of time. Under the rules of our union no player is allowed a farthing over the actual railway or other travelling expenses and the bare cost of his hotel while away from home for the purpose of playing. There can be no allowance for incidental expenses.'

Upon this point Mr Mullineux expressed indignant surprise and much incredulity when told that our clubs in Sydney – many of them – were in the habit of paying men, not only for loss of time, but for their allegiance throughout a season. He could not think that such a thing was done without the knowledge of the union, or that his team had been asked to play against paid members of the clubs affiliated to the union. 'Our union in England would certainly be very much annoyed at anything of that sort, and would not permit us to countenance it.' Mr Mullineux has evidently not known all that has gone on in the contest against the team he brought out, and possibly the bare and positive assertion now made, that men are paid in the Rugby clubs in and around Sydney, will lead him to make an investigation. He will not have very far to go for proof, and, as a preliminary, might very reasonably inquire in to the extent of the authority given to some of the New South Wales players who went to Queensland, how far they were supposed to journey when they left Sydney, and what conditions appertained when they went beyond the limit which was originally laid down for their trip.

Because I was once a teacher in Eltham, Kent, Mullineux's later life is of particular interest to me as he taught in the Royal Naval School, Eltham, after becoming a curate in the parish of St Andrew, Mottingham.

He became Chaplain to the forces in the Boer War until 1902 and was Chaplain to the Royal Navy 1902–07. He subsequently completed a spell as Chaplain for the Missions to Seamen in Stewart Street, San Francisco, a notorious part of the city, before working his passage to New Zealand when the 1914–18 war broke out and becoming Chaplain to the New Zealand Forces, serving in France before being discharged back to England in 1919.

The British War Medal, Victory Medal and Military Cross were all awarded to the Rev. Mullineux. On 16 September 1918, when he was 51, the Supplement to the *London Gazette* read:

> Rev. Matthew Mullineux New Zealand Chaplain, Dept., for conspicuous gallantry and devotion to duty. During two days' hard fighting, when the medical officer had become a casualty, early on the morning of the first day, he took charge of the Regimental Aid post, dressed the wounded and superintended their evacuation. The Regimental Aid post was subjected to very heavy high explosive and gas shell fire for twelve hours and but for his skill and excellent dispositions, serious congestion would have occurred. His untiring energy and cheerful service in providing comfort for the troops under most adverse circumstances were of the greatest value to all ranks of the battalion.

Following his distinguished war service, the Rev. Mullineux continued to provide a practical and spiritual role for those seeking to locate the graves of rugby dead. Based in St Barnabas Hostel, 3 Rue des Mavoobaux, Calais, his efforts for those to whom he offered hospitality and guidance soon became known as the St Barnabas Pilgrimages. It is ironic that St Barnabas should be so closely identified with the work of Rev. Mullineux, as Barnabas, stoned to death and privately interred by his kinsman, John

Mark, revealed his sepulchre in a dream to Archbishop of Constantia in 478. Graves, and finding them for poor families, became a compulsion for the Reverend.

The St Barnabas hostels were a small organisation. They offered tours to Flanders, the Somme and Ypres in 1923 and Gallipoli and Salonika in 1926. *St Martins' Review* by Ian Hay states:

> Last Palm Sunday St Barnabas organised a great pilgrimage of their loved ones at their own expense, and to whom the possibility of such a comforting excursion had seemed beyond the range of human hope. But in Flanders they duly found themselves, nearly a thousand strong, fulfilling their incredible dream. St Barnabas had raised the money for the trip, chiefly from other pilgrims better endowed, who were only too glad to acknowledge their duty in the matter; St Barnabas had collected them from their homes all over England and Scotland, conveyed them overseas, and directed each little group to its proper cemetery, with all the gentleness and privacy possible; then gathered them together and brought them home again, soothed and uplifted by the imperishable memory of a proud inscription set over a reverently tended grave.

Even in Canada, Rev. Mullineux was renowned, as the St Barnabas hostels worked with the Canadian Red Cross Society and Toc H (named after Talbot House in Poperinghe where thousands of men found refreshment for body, mind and soul in 1915). The *Toronto Saturday Night* refers to Rev. Mullineux MC as 'that splendid ex-army Chaplain and worker for the soldiers and their friends who is so well-known in Canada'. It also says:

> Over 2,500 applications were received from poor persons who had never visited the graves of their sons, their husbands and their fathers, and never could do so unless the visit was arranged for them and paid for them. The Rev. M Mullineux organised the pilgrimage, which alas could take less than 900 . . . It would be hard to think of anything better organised.

By 1927, Rev. Mullineux, having ensured every known grave had been visited, made a final pilgrimage to the Menin Gate at Ypres, a memorial to the soldiers who fell at the Ypres Salient and who have no known grave. He continued his work for the St Barnabas hostels until 1932, when he was 65 years old – retirement age.

However, he took up the position of Vicar of Marham in 1934 and held this until his death in 1945, when his body was discovered in a lodging house in London having been poisoned by carbon monoxide (coal gas), self-administered while the balance of his mind was disturbed. In the *Eastern Daily Press*, 20 February 1945, the day after the inquest into his death, a report says: 'Evidence of delusions from which he suffered, alleging crimes against himself which were completely unfounded was given at Hammersmith inquest yesterday.'

That his life should end in such distraught circumstances when he endeavoured to ensure so many could find the resting place of their fallen heroes is an unfair irony. Following his suicide, as with anyone else who died similarly in those days, there would not have been a large funeral. His death notice in *The Times* read:

MULLINEUX. On Feb. 13 1945 suddenly in London. Matthew Mullineux MC late Vicar of Marham and the beloved 'Padre' and founder of the St Barnabas Pilgrimages 1920–32. No one knows where his grave is, an unkind final chapter in this man's life, when he invested so much energy in making sure others could find the graves of their war dead.

2

WARS ON AND OFF THE PITCH

Cherry Pillman
South Africa 1910, 3 caps
England 1910–4, 18 caps

The Talented Tactician

Despite his amazing influence on rugby, there is little documentation on the career of Cherry (Charles Henry) Pillman. Billy Millar, the Western Province flank forward who captained South Africa in the last two Tests of 1910, noted, 'The visiting team was a powerful one, much better than its ultimate record (played 24, won 13, drawn 3 and 8 lost) suggests.'

Millar, born in 1883 and a member of the 1906 Springbok tour to Britain, had to wait until 1910 to win his first cap against the visiting British. He led the Cape Colony to a substantial 19–0 scoreline over the visitors and captained the Springboks in the second Test, when the Tourists, inspired by the exceptional Cherry Pillman, levelled the series with an 8–3 win. He retained the captaincy for the third Test, when he led the magnificent fightback of the Springboks to win the decisive encounter 21–5 and secure the series.

'What a remarkably erratic lot this British team was,' he noted, mentioning full-back Stanley Williams, centre J. Ponty Jones, winger Jack Spoors, scrum-half George Isherwood and forwards Harry Jarman, Phil Waller, W.R. Tyrrell, Robert Stevenson and Jim Webb among the excellent visiting players. However, he identified the 'outstanding brilliance' of Pillman as the deciding factor in the second Test: 'I assert confidently that if ever a man can have been said to have won an international match through his unorthodox and lone-handed efforts, it can be said of the inspired black-haired Pillman I played against on the Crusaders' ground on August 27, 1903, when the "Rover" played as fly-half, mark you not as forward.'

This roving role revolutionised the perception, and execution, of a wing forward's performance, which up until then had been limited to tight play with lots of pushing and shoving.

Unlike many other British players, South Africa's hard ground suited Pillman, a hard-muscled, rangy athlete who played for Blackheath. The 21-year-old England wing forward had won the first of his 18 caps earlier in the 1910 season against Scotland and became the leading personality of the tour. So supremely skilful and versatile was the 6 ft 3 in. tall player that he was able to play fly-half in the last two Tests, and return to perform his wing forward position for the last match of the tour against Western Province.

Dr Danie Craven simply said that Pillman, '. . . must be looked upon as one of the originators of what became known as the loose forward'. One could speculate what might have been had Pillman made an appearance in the first Test, missed due to injury. Although not a recognised kicker he completed the tour as the leading Lions scorer with 67 points – 6 tries, 3 penalties, 18 conversions and a drop goal.

From his obituary 20 November 1955:

> Even at school he showed himself a natural player of ball games, exceptionally fleet of foot and equally quick in thought. He developed into the most accomplished wing forward, as that type of player used to be called, English Rugby ever produced. No one, perhaps, anywhere in the world, has excelled him in his own capacity, while his versatility and knowledge of the game were such that he could figure with credit in almost any position on the field. During his playing days he never exceeded 13 stones in weight, which may seem dangerously light nowadays, but no one who saw him play against the South Africans of 1910 – who ranked as giants even then – would ever question his ability to distinguish himself in any company. No opponents ever appreciated his ability more than the Welsh.

Not only was Pillman a wonderful player, but we must remember his contribution to the game as a thinker and strategist. Through university rugby he may well have been influenced by the innovative Harry Vassall. Many of his ploys and tactics are still relevant to the game 100 years later. He kept confidential diagrams and tactics for the 1910 team.

Combined attack.

Forwards might occasionally watch back practice.

Forwards like 3/4s in open — passing, kicking, running & dribbling

Out of touch — through yourselves or back to 1/2 or 3/4 or out at another forward, feet or kick.

S.H. touching but 2 own forwards well out. Our wing faulty & marking bad on Sat: right out in their 1/2. Manoeuvre for vacant spot, when own 1/2 has throw.

Kick out & off. — when you kick either across for own men to pick up ball or long to corner flag.

When they kick — try to attack on open side — receiver must not go too much round or (1) his own men get bored (2) they get time to get across ∴ back up closely and behind, forwards (Edwards). Forwards might line a bit more across. Contra, when they kick out, don't let them go round but don't leave too open a spot anywhere.

Kick across — watch kicker and go up with him. If you are offside. Spread across for penalty kick at goal, you may score from a bad kick.

For free kick or mark all are onside, or referee whistles.

Play to the Score. — If behind in points & time is short, take all risks — don't kick to touch.

If leading by more than 5 pts & time is very short, you may "sit" on your score by kicking to touch. But don't "sit" on too little or you may be beaten.

Attack is generally the Best Defence.

Cohesion & Combination. — In the 'scrum' keep tight till you have heeled the ball or they are wheeling or are heeling.

Occasionally shove opponents straight over their line

Combination by voice.	Never let the ball bounce, if possible – one can run to it – Never have a misunderstanding, let the one with the better chance of catching the ball say 'right'. In backing up, Saving etc say 'right' or 'with you on right' ie if backing up properly ie with no opponent between you & holder of the ball
Combination in dribbling	Always have a man on each side of dribbler and always _one_ a yd or two behind – also for a ball that bounces _or_ is to be caught by one of your men backing up. Use instep or side of foot when dribbling. Go hard and fast.
Combination by Eyes	Have a 'bird's eye' view of the field and the positions of opponents and comrades – You will then be able to see the weak spot & attack there.
Forwards	Combine in Scrum – push together as _one unit_ 8 men at 11 stone = 88 stone pushing together will beat a Scrum of 100 stone if 2 or 3 of opponents are not quickly packed _or_ don't push together. Front row get under opponents. 3rd row flankers, get straight in for a wheel, not so much inwards. 3rd row should not 'heel', but ~~generally~~ gently touch ball to ½, with outside foot or walk all don't stop pushing till ball is out if ball stops in 3rd row over the ball

Combined Defence.

Be prepared to thwart all the varieties of
attack, which you adopt yourselves. E.g. if
you can attack by running round after a
'kick out' so can they, if an opening is
given them — so block them.

Touch lines — Guard your touch lines & leave no open spots.
In own 25 — keep ball near touch — don't run across goal.

'Cover' — This means back up in defence behind
not only for collaring but also for (1)
Saving or picking up (always pick up rather
than save, if possible) (2) for protection to a
catcher, who may miss ball or have kick
charged down.

Support full back — not only for tackling — nor only when he runs up
but also when catching, one might be back
to help him.

Their Saving — when they save, pin the man to the
ground, don't let him get up.

Marks — if men are right on you, make a mark or
out of touch from a knock on — never tire your forwards
by bringing them back unnecessarily.

Feint — never be done by a feint — see ball actually leave
man's hands before going on to next man. i.e. throw yourself at full back

Tackle — Duck when a yd or ½ yd from man & go hard & low from
waist downwards — if possible before, watch his eyes.

Kicking — should be to touch for safe defence

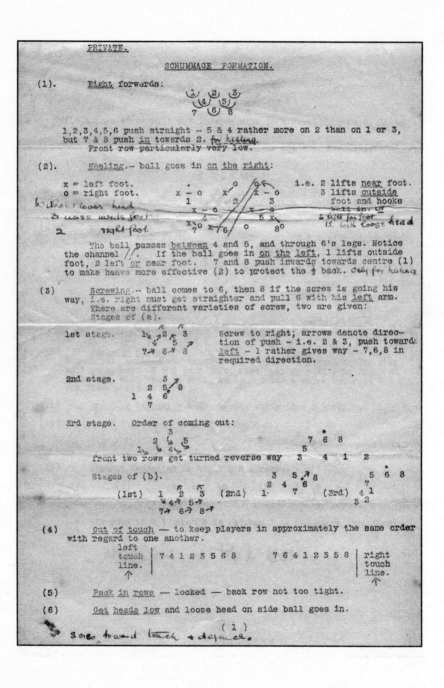

PRIVATE.

SCRUMMAGE FORMATION.

(1).   Eight forwards:

1,2,3,4,5,6 push straight — 5 & 4 rather more on 2 than on 1 or 3, but 7 & 8 push in towards 2. *for heeling.*
Front row particularly very low.

(2).   Heeling.— ball goes in on the right:

x = left foot.   i.e. 2 lifts near foot.
o = right foot.   3 lifts outside
without looser head   foot and hooks
3 uses inside foot   ball in. or
2   right foot.   2 lifts far foot
                                                  is with loose head

The ball passes between 4 and 5, and through 6's legs. Notice the channel //.   If the ball goes in on the left, 1 lifts outside foot, 2 left or near foot.   7 and 8 push inwards towards centre (1) to make heave more effective (2) to protect the ½ back. *Only for heeling*

(3)   Screwing.— ball comes to 6, then 8 if the screw is going his way, i.e. right must get straighter and pull 6 with his left arm. There are different varieties of screw, two are given:
Stages of (a).

1st stage.   Screw to right; arrows denote direc-
                              tion of push - i.e. 2 & 3, push toward:
                              left - 1 rather gives way - 7,6,8 in
                              required direction.

2nd stage.

3rd stage.   Order of coming out:

front two rows get turned reverse way

Stages of (b).

(1st)   (2nd)   (3rd)

(4)   Out of touch — to keep players in approximately the same order with regard to one another.
left
touch   7 4 1 2 3 5 6 8   7 6 4 1 2 3 5 8   right
line.   touch
                                                   line.

(5)   Pack in rows — locked — back row not too tight.

(6)   Get heads low and loose head on side ball goes in.

(1)
Screw toward touch & defence.

(7).   Seven forwards.- e.g.,

1,2,3 push straight, 5,7 inwards with left shoulders, 4,6, ditto with right shoulders.   Feet of 5 and 7:

left

x   right not x o, i.e. level
  o

" of 4 and 6:

x   not x o, i.e. level.

1 and 2 go in together, then 3 who binds them together, then 4 and 5 who lock on 3, then 6 and 7 who push on 3.

(8)   Heeling.

x = left foot.   1 & 2 lift inside feet, ball goes through 3's legs open wide.
o = right foot.

1 & 2 have legs sloping back and get as low as possible, with foot for hooking ready.

(9)   Out of touch.

left touch line.   4 1 3 2 5 6 7   6 7 4 1 3 2 5   right touch line.

(10)   Screw to right.
3 gets ball between his knees - 6 & 7 close up straighter to stop ball going out. 1 & 2 push left, rest push or pull 3 in required direction; when free he drops ball.   3 for a screw looks on 4 & 5 and loosens 1 & 2.

(11)   Break up laterally, i.e., divide scrum into 2 portions.

(12)   6 and 7 get back to help backs, e.g.:   1   2
                                                   4 3 5
                                                     6 7

(13)   Another formation is the South African:

    (a)   or   (b)

i.e. the same as N.Z., but 3 in (a) and 1 in (b) comes into front row.

(2)

1910 Newspaper Reports, The Natal Mercury

Newport hold the record for the highest number of players from one club selected for a British Lions tour, with seven being selected for the 1910 tour to South Africa: Stanley Williams, Mel Baker, Reg Plummer, Jack Jones, Tommy Smyth (captain), Phil Waller and Harry Jarman.

However no one is quite sure if the tour captain, Tommy Smyth, was actually on Newport's books or registered with Malone in Northern Ireland for 1910. As the tour took place over the summer, he could have been with Newport for the 1909–10 season and with Malone for the 1910–11 season. Both clubs claim him as a 1910 player, but there is no available archive material to clarify the situation. The Belfast-born medic lined up with fellow countryman and doctor William Tyrrell, along with a group of men, most of whom had professional backgrounds in law, finance and business.

Perhaps the prospect of being camped in tents aggravated the gentlemen's behaviour, which was reported in a local newspaper. During 1910, Durban was a growing port, still under construction, and had dirt roads with transport by rickshaws.

MONDAY, 25 JULY 1910

SCANDALOUS CONDUCT

Display of Hooliganism at

Durban

VISITING RUGBY TOURISTS 'NIGHT OUT'

Hitherto we have refrained from making any reference to the conduct of the Rugby football team at present visiting South Africa from the Old Country, out of deference to the wishes of a large number of prominent sportsmen in Durban. But as our Maritzburg morning contemporary has reluctantly taken the matter up, a representative at this journal, from inquiries made, can confirm the protest which the journal referred to has made against the visiting string. The 'Natal Witness' states:–

'We were told early in the week of certain highly discreditable incidents of which we said nothing in these columns pending careful inquiries as to their truth. We are now informed on the highest authority that the British Rugby team behaved on the night (Saturday week) after their match in Durban in a manner which was certainly not consistent with what we should expect from a body of gentlemen.' What actually occurred, notwithstanding the persons most aggrieved thereby have been extremely reticent on the subject, was a good deal of blatant rowdy-ism, extremely offensive to everyone subjected to it. The members of the team were courteously reminded by the proprietor of the hotel at which they were staying that, in addition to members of their own sex, the hotel was accommodating at the time about 150 ladies and children, to whom an exhibition of public rowdy-ism would be painful and alarming. The reminder passed unnoticed, and our Rugby guests proceeded on Saturday night to enjoy themselves in approved hooligan fashion by flinging furniture about and smashing nearly everything they could lay their hands on.

The proprietor of the hotel at which the visitors put up while in Durban, informed our representative that in view of the reported conduct of the team before their arrival in Maritzburg, he thought he would not be wise in allotting them quarters, particularly as he had living on the premises an extremely large number of ladies and children, and that the 'dormitory' for the visitors would be on the balcony. The proprietor of the hotel informed the Chief Constable of a message received from a certain Maritzburg hotel where the Tourists had been staying, and that official said that he would have men ready to step in if necessary but he pointed out that this might lead to a free fight. Eventually the proprietor thought that tents might be erected in some part of the town for the accommodation of the visitors, but it was felt that this would not be agreed to, and eventually the publican took the risk . . . and is now a sadder and wiser man.

Following upon the match the team visited the Ocean Beach Rink, and some having imbibed not wisely but too well, we learn that one man wanted to fight, and attempted to distinguish himself in several directions. Unfortunately, for him, according to all accounts, he met his pugilistic Sedan by tackling a sailor, in West Street.

The party returned to the hotel at a late hour, and proceeded to turn the private bar into a low-class canteen. One gentleman staying at the house, was, it is stated, insulted by having beer poured over him and one 'gentlemanly' footballer gained distinction by cutting his hand in smashing glasses wholesale. The landlord managed to pacify the most rowdy by taking them to supper, and, in the interim, he had the bar closed. But the behaviour on the balcony when the crowd turned in was not calculated to edify, for at an early hour on the Sunday morning the party commenced to throw wicker chairs and other articles over on the street, and one ill-fated traveller in a passing rickshaw was deluged with water by a 'funny' member of the party. Eventually, however, peace was secured, but though reflection may follow dissipation, not one of the Tourists suggested that the proprietor of the hotel should be compensated for the damage which their reprehensible conduct had occasioned. So far he has not made a claim, but we understand he is communicating with the managers of a certain Maritzburg hotel with a view to having the matter brought to the attention of the South African Rugby Union, and that in the event of the compensation due not being paid, a vigorous protest will be lodged with the English Football Association.

The point need not be laboured, for enough has been written to indicate that from visitors, as from local sportsmen, fairplay is not only required in the field, but also in private life – above all from those representatives of a sport which holds a prominent place in the country they represent.

THURSDAY, 28 JULY 1910
Bad Manners

In another column, we publish a letter from Mr J.M. Legate, proprietor of the Waverly Hotel, in which he takes exception to a report which has appeared with reference to the conduct of the Rugby football team in Durban. Currency was first given to a report of rowdy-ism by the *City* morning paper on Monday, with that wealth of exaggeration to which that journal is so very prone, and yesterday a return was made to the subject, with further gross exaggeration and an implied censure to the Durban people for a disposition to hush up the matter, and, of course, a pat on the back to the paper in question for exposing the conduct of the visiting footballers.

It is, of course, well-known that there was some disorderly behaviour the night after the match in Durban, but the description given in the *City* paper is a gross exaggeration. Where there are a large number of young fellows out on a kind of holiday, there are generally a few whose animal spirits get the better of their sense of good behaviour, and even Natal footballers, when visiting other places, have been known to be somewhat uproarious, and to indulge in horse-play, but no one has the bad taste to write up the matter after they have gone, as if a serious riot had taken place, and a lot of wilful and inexcusable damage done. If some of them forgot their manners, it is not for us, as their guests for the time being, to forget ours by not only publicly advertising their delinquencies, but to add to them by gross exaggeration and misrepresentation of the facts. The practical joking which took place is nothing very uncommon, and, if it was, perhaps, not to be commended, at least there was no injury done to anyone, and common courtesy to strangers ought to have been a safeguard against the circulation, in print, of sensational statements of rowdy conduct, which the visitors themselves may not see, and therefore not be able to reply to. If Rugby players offended against the laws of good conduct, the *City* morning paper has offended still more by forgetting that, after all, the team were our guests.

War Dead

Fourteen years were to pass after Dr Tom Smyth's tour in 1910 before a British and Irish team would visit the southern hemisphere again. Rugby players, like all young men from the British Isles, joined up to fight in the carnage of the First World War. Many never returned.

The prolific letter writer from the 1896 tour, Alexander Findlater Todd, was killed at Ypres in 1915, shot in the neck while in the trenches. The others who fell were Blair Swannell (Northampton 1899–1904), Major in the First Battalion AIF, during the Anzac Cove landing at Gallipoli, 25 April 1915, who knelt to show other soldiers how to aim better and was killed by a sniper; Royal Scots Fusilier Quartermaster Captain Charlie Adamson (Durham 1899), scored 136 points in 20 games, was killed in Salonika, Greece, 1918; Motorbike Dispatch Rider Sidney Crowther (Lennox 1904) was killed 8 October 1914 at Armentieres; 10th Battalion Tank Corps, Noel Forbes Humphries MC (Tynedale) was killed 27 March 1918 at Etables; Royal Navy David Bedell Sivright (Cambridge 1903–04) died of an insect bite at Gallipoli 1915; 2nd Lieutenant, Black Watch, Eric Milroy (Watsonians and Scotland) on the Roll of Honour, was killed at

Delville Wood 18 July 1916; South Africa Artillery, Phil Waller (Newport and Wales 1910) on the Roll of Honour, was killed in Arras 14 December 1917; Lieutenant John Edward Raphael (Old Merchant Taylors' and England 1910 Argentina), 18th Bn. King's Royal Rifle Corps died of wounds received at the Battle of Messines Ridge, 11 June 1917; and Johnnie Williams (Cardiff and Wales 1908) 38th (Welsh) Infantry Division died in the first few weeks of the Battle of the Somme, in the taking of Mametz Woods, 12 July 1916.

Stories abound about how later in the war, rugby players who defected to rugby league were denied mention on their former union club's roll of honour for those who had fallen in battle. One such 'casualty' of politics is Fred Perrett, who might have been selected for further Wales matches but turned professional at the end of the 1913–14 season, joining rugby league team Leeds RLFC. Perrett's league career was cut short by the outbreak of the First World War. He joined the Welsh Guards and served in France from 19 February 1916. He was subsequently commissioned as a 2nd lieutenant, and transferred to the 17th Battalion of the Royal Welsh Fusiliers with seniority from 27 June 1917. He was seriously injured and died of his wounds in a casualty clearing station a month after the Armistice. He is buried at Terlincthun British Cemetery at Wimille in France. Perrett is often left out of lists of the Welsh international war dead due to his supposed defection to the professional game.

A notable survivor (he died in 1968), and one who played in the famous Christmas Truce match, was William Tyrrell, a member of the 1910 British Tour of South Africa. In the First World War, he served in the Royal Army Medical Corps (RAMC) on the Western Front and was mentioned in dispatches six times. He received the DSO and Bar, the MC and the Belgian Croix de Guerre. While serving as Medical Officer in the 2nd Lancashire Fusiliers in 1915, he was buried by an exploding shell and experienced temporary shell shock. He drew on this experience when he participated in a War Office Committee of Enquiry into the causes and effects of shell shock in 1922 and stated that it was his belief that shell shock was primarily caused by a 'repression of fear'.

William Tyrrell: Lieutenant, Royal Army Medical Corps, promoted to Captain on 1 April 1915, later Temporary Lieutenant Colonel, RAMC, DSO Gazetted 1 January 1918, and bar, Gazetted 26 July 1918: 'For conspicuous gallantry and devotion to duty when in charge of a line of evacuation. He worked continuously for six days, and it was due to his gallantry, organisation, and energy that touch was maintained so efficiently with the brigades, and many casualties evacuated. He displayed great courage and coolness throughout, and inspired those under him by his fine example.' (*London Gazette*, July 1918)

William Tyrrell is mentioned in Stanley Weintraub's *The Christmas Truce,* where his diary entry for 25 December 1914, when he was the Medical Officer attached to the 2nd Battalion, Lancashire Fusiliers, is quoted: 'Germans send in a party and white flag. Our *B. F—I* of a sentry brings one in without blindfolding him and of course he had to be made prisoner.' Lt Col. William Dacre, Royal Army Medical Corps, wrote in his diary in April 1915:

> We played the 4th Division at footer and beat them. It was a famous match and a great number of old internationals were playing. The Gloucester County line were in the 5th Gloucesters and did great work. Tyrrell, the Irish international, was playing against us and Poulton captained our side.

Referenced in *Forgotten Voices of the Great War*, Private Alfred Bromfield of the 2nd Battalion, Lancashire Regiment (*sic*: the 2nd Battalion, Lancashire Fusiliers, 12th Brigade, 4th Division) comments on the opening of the Second Battle of Ypres on 22 April 1915:

> While we were doing this [firing rapidly into a cloud of chlorine gas] the rifles were getting hotter and hotter with the continual fire. Fat was pouring out of the woodwork and the muzzles were beginning to extend. Then an Irish medical officer named Captain Tyrrell, realising that we needed help, got out of the trench and ran along the back with a can of oil in his hand, pouring it on our rifles as he went by. We'd stop firing just long enough for him to splash a drop of oil on the bolt. All we needed was the bolts to work perfectly, and he managed to get right along the trench.

During a gas attack on 2 May 1915 during the Second Battle of Ypres, the 2nd Lancashire Fusiliers were at Shell Trap Farm. In B Company, a little to the east of the Farm, the medical officer, Lt W. Tyrrell, ordered the men to use a wetted rag over their noses and mouths to protect themselves. In the confusion that had ensued following the warning of gas, much of the available water in the trench, and the tea that had just been prepared, was spilled and Tyrrell immediately urinated on a rag and urged the men nearby to do the same. The natural ammonia in the urine gave added protection against the gas and at least B Company were able to stand to arms as the gas reached them. Tyrrell is reported to have been 'more than a hero' on that day and took full part in the defence of the line when the enemy infantry finally appeared.

1924 Souvenir Programme of the British Rugby Tour

This is the front page of the 1924 souvenir programme for the visit to South Africa. I think the article says it all – the war, how welcome the players are, etc. This was the first tour for 14 years.

OUR VISITORS

As in every other country, Britain's Rugby suffered through the war. Young players who were on the doorstep of international honours never realised their ambition in this great game, because of the 'greater game' in France, in Mesopotamia, Gallipoli, and Egypt. The passing of time, however, is healing the wound, and British Rugby today is practically back to its pre-war standard. In some respects it is said to be superior to what it has ever been before. The backs at command may not be men of such dominating personalities as, for instance, Kenneth MacLeod, the 'drop-kick king' of Scotland; J.G.G. Birkett, of the Harlequins, who was capped 21 times for England; R. Poulton Palmer; A.D. Stoop, of England; W.J. Bancroft, of Swansea and Wales; Percy Bush, of Cardiff; Ponty Jones, of Pontypool; Gwyn Nicholls, of Cardiff; or Dicky Owen, of Swansea; but what were at command are sound, if not quite so brilliant in individual bursts and penetrative thrusts.

Regarding the present-day power of the forwards in Britain, it is said, and we hold rightly so, that never in the history of the game overseas has forward play been of such a high standard. It is what is called 'modern forward play.' It has revolutionised the game in the Mother Country. It has made it much more spectacular to watch; and it is said that it is converting those people who went over to Soccer back to their old love. The new cult in forward play was really brought about because of the ravages of the war and the consequent deficiency in three-quarter play. Owing to the failure to get the right rhythm among the backs, which led to disconnected back play, the forwards were forced to develop a style which in reality converted them into an attacking force on scientific lines. They found that dribbling, allied with handling and passing, could be safely practised among them. The result was that passing and handling became an important match-winning factor, and so today we have these British forwards, who are now with us capable of carrying out brilliant passing movements, which at one time was held to be the exclusive rights of the backs.

It is a new style, which has won thousands of converts. It has made the game much more enjoyable to watch, as is conclusively proved by the fact that Twickenham, the headquarters of the English Rugby Union, which can house 40,000 people, is no longer big enough to house the crowds in international encounters.

T.N. Brand
South Africa 1924, 2 caps
Ireland 1925, 1 cap

Bozo the Mascot

T.N. Brand, the team mascot, was known by the nickname Bozo. The tradition now is for the team mascot to be given to the first team to beat the Tourists. Cove Smith's side lost their first game to Western Province (Town and Country), so God only knows what fate befell T.N. Brand – the mind boggles!

Brand was to play for Ireland against the 1924–25 All Blacks in Dublin in his only international. He died in an act of bravery saving a friend in Poole harbour in 1938.

> REFUSED TO ABANDON HIS FRIEND
> HOW MR. NORMAN BRAND DIED
> 'DON'T WORRY ABOUT ME'

The tragedy in Poole Harbour on 9 June, when Mr. Thomas Norman Brand, formerly of Belfast, lost his life, was described at the inquest at Poole yesterday. It was clear from the evidence that Mr. Brand was drowned through a heroic refusal to abandon a friend who was in danger, and whose life he helped to save.

A verdict of 'accidental death' was returned.

Walter E. Tranchell, of Parkstone, said that he had been with Mr.

Brand all day. In the evening they met Mr. T. A. Denny, and at 10.30 commenced to row out to a yacht in Poole Harbour, which witness was looking after.

DINGHY OVERTURNED

'I was rowing the dinghy,' said Tranchell. 'One of the others, in reaching for a cigarette, lurched, and the dinghy overturned.

'It was so sudden and unexpected I cannot say what happened. We were all thrown in the water. We righted the boat but as soon as one tried to get in it went down again. We were shouting for help but we treated it as a joke, actually.'

Tranchell said that Denny was suffering from the cold, and Mr. Brand and he took turns at holding him and swimming the boat ashore.

'I told Brand to swim ashore for help, and said I would look after Denny but he refused to go. We heard a call from the shore but nothing happened.

'It was Brand's turn to hold Denny, who was unconscious. Brand was getting weaker and I said to him "What is the matter old man?" He replied "Oh nothing." I could see there was something definitely wrong with him, so I took Denny and told him to hang on.'

I CAN'T GO ON

Tranchell said that after a time Brand said, 'Don't worry about me old man, I can't go on any longer.' He was talking very quietly.

'I tried to hold on to both of them,' said the witness. 'Brand got weaker and when I let him go once he sank. I got him by the hand and tried to tie the men together. It was impossible. I let go of Brand and he sank. Two minutes later Denny and I reached safety.'

Trenchall added that they were rescued by people from the Harbour Club.

A brother of the deceased gentleman said he had been a good waterman and a swimmer. His health had not been good in the last six or seven years. Three years ago he broke a leg.

The jury expressed sympathy with the relatives.

Ronald Cove-Smith
South Africa 1924, 4 caps
England 1921–9, 29 caps

Life is a great gift and to obtain the best from it the personality of each individual must be broad-based and well-balanced. The character of each one of us is built upon the tripod of body, mind and spirit; evenly equated this gives us a balanced personality that is a beautiful and satisfying thing. Efficiency, success and ultimately even happiness are largely dependent upon health and those of us who can realise that real health is no mere matter of luck, but a positive constructive condition of life that can be achieved by a little extra trouble and thought, will soon find its pursuit worthwhile.

The object before us should be health, not as an end in itself, but as a means whereby our lives may be of better use to the community and greater joy to ourselves.

From *Health for Everyman* by Dr R. Cove-Smith (1937)

Maintaining the Corinthian Spirit

Dr Ronald Cove-Smith of Merchant Taylors', commonly and warmly known as 'Cove', was one of England's greatest rugby players. He captained his country seven times and the British Lions on their tour of South Africa in 1924. The first of his 29 caps, achieved whilst at Cambridge studying natural sciences tripos before going on to King's College Hospital as a medical student, set him up for further selections and a place in English rugby history. Between 1921 and 1929 he was effectively an automatic choice as either a front or second row forward in the scrum. He was a fundamental force in a great England pack, which included W.W. Wakefield (captain), J.S. Tucker, G.S. Conway, A.F. Blakiston and A.T. Voyce.

Cove and his contemporaries were tough, devoted players who were ruthless. Probably at no other time as during the 1920s in the aftermath of war were games played for game's sake, with fierce commitment but true to the amateur spirit. During this period, England won four Grand Slams and Cove captained England to its grandest ever Slam in 1928 as it included a win over New South Wales – the Waratahs – who were in effect Australia, against whom international caps were awarded. He played in more winning England sides (twenty-two) than anyone during that period and on the winning England side against Wales on no fewer than six occasions. He scored his only try for England against the 1925 All Blacks. It was the first score of a classic encounter, which England lost, and which also featured the unfortunate dismissal of the New Zealand captain, Cyril Brownlie. In 1924, Cove-Smith led the British Isles tour, during which the moniker 'The Lions' was attached to the team.

Renowned coach Frank Sprage, a former OMT (Old Merchant Taylors') player of the era and *Sunday Telegraph* schools rugby correspondent, wrote:

> Some matches naturally stand out most vividly in the memory. There were the two Christmas tours of 1926 and 1928, on both of which we beat Gloucester and Bristol on successive days. The narrow victory over Bristol in 1928 I shall always think of as 'Cove's game'. He played like a man possessed and completely dominated, both verbally and physically, the three or four internationals in Bristol's team. He also found time to give the referee some very useful advice. The game was played in foul conditions of mud and rain and several times the ball was buried beneath a pile of bodies, close to or over our line. With a local referee, which was customary in those days, these situations would normally have resulted in the award of a try to Bristol. But before the referee could get the whistle to his lips, Cove somehow extricated himself from the pile-up and ordered a five-yard scrum. The referee was prompted to agree and I can still hear the thud of Bristol boots going into Cove's ribs.

Cove remained fit and active almost until the end of his life in 1988. When he was in his early 70s, a burglar made the mistake of entering the Cove-Smith residence in Maida Vale in the dead of night. The intruder was so firmly dealt with by the master of the house (and locked in a cupboard) that he was thankful when the police arrived to take him away. He certainly chose the wrong house.

Cove was a non-smoker, teetotaller and practising Christian. But he was no ascetic and did not indulge in any moralising or pontificating as many with his triumphs and successes might have been tempted to do. In fact his modesty, his natural charm and gentlemanly behaviour endeared him to all who knew him. It was sometimes overheard that he was a 'dirty player', probably sour grapes from an unfortunate individual on the opposing team who experienced Cove's ferocious tackles. Not that he ever travelled without his little black bag, and anyone could avail himself of a stitch or two to repair local damage, in the dressing-room surgery. He patched up injuries he caused and, of course, those he didn't.

Giants are often gentle and kind. These aspects of his character conspicuously governed his personal aversion to smoking and alcohol, which in no way modified his care for those occasionally suffering from excess. At a match in Bristol, Sam Tucker was hooking and performed some act which incurred Cove's disapproval, who then addressed a few curt words.

'Sam, don't do that.'

To which the England hooker meekly replied, 'Sorry, Doctor.'

Ivor Jones CBE
New Zealand and Australia 1930, 5 caps
Wales 1924–30, 16 caps

First Test British Isles 6 New Zealand 3, 21 June 1930 in Dunedin: 'Then Jones came away with the ball and set off up field. J.C. Morley (Newport) ran with him and as Jones was taken by Nepia, he flung the ball to Morley on the half-way. The little wing galloped for the corner and scored the winning try amid great excitement as Cooke failed by a yard to get him.'

Second Test British Isles 10 New Zealand 13, 6 July 1930 in Christchurch: 'Eight minutes from time, Jones dashed through the opposition and made a brilliant opening for C.D. Aarvold (Cambridge and England), who ran 40 yards to score under the posts.'

Third Test British Isles 10 New Zealand 15, 26 July 1930 in Auckland: 'Just on time Jones picked up in the loose and ran from half-way. He passed to Aarvold who scored a runaway try between the posts.'

Old-Fashioned Flair

Ivor Jones is considered by New Zealanders as the finest wing forward ever to tour their country, a fantastic accolade when one reflects on the sterling play of Bill McKay in 1950, Haydn Morgan (1959), Ronnie Lamont (1966) and John Taylor (1971).

Ivor Jones played for Loughor before joining Llanelli in 1922. By day, he worked the furnaces at Bynea. It was an era of extreme hardship and to succeed, Ivor had to make many sacrifices. His playing career spanned 17 seasons. He captained the 'Scarlets' for nine seasons and led them against the 1926 Maoris, 1927 Waratahs, 1931 Springboks and 1935 All Blacks. As a player, apart from his obvious commitment to the game, he was also a very skilful dribbler of the ball and a creative runner at a time when such skills were not generally recognised in an open-side wing forward. Constantly at hand to intimidate the opposing outside-half and ever present to pass on scoring opportunities when they came, he played 522 games for Llanelli before scarcity of work drove his family to Birmingham to seek employment. After retiring from the game he became a successful administrator and served as Chairman of the Welsh Rugby Union during the 1968–69 season.

H. O'H. O'Neill
New Zealand and Australia 1930, 5 caps
Ireland 1930–3, 6 caps

Sacrifice Your Studies

Below is a copy of the letter that Lions forward Henry O'Hara O'Neill received whilst a student at Queen's University, following his request to take leave of absence for the 1930 Tour to Australia and New Zealand.

QUEEN'S UNIVERSITY,
FACULTY OF AGRICULTURE,
WELLINGTON PLACE,
BELFAST
21 February 1930

Sir,

I am desired by Sir Edward Archdale to refer to your letter of the 20th instant, asking the Ministry to sanction your acceptance of an invitation received from the British Rugby Football Union to take part in a tour of Australia and New Zealand during the period of April to October of this year.

The Ministry is prepared to agree to the proposal, provided that on your return in October next you are prepared to complete, at your own expense, the final year of your degree at the University, and sit for the final Degree examination.

I am to add that in view of the fact that you will be leaving for

Australia in April next, the final instalment of your scholarship will not be paid.

I am, Sir,

Your obedient Servant,

(Signed: G.S. Robertson)

Sir Carl Douglas Aarvold OBE, TD
New Zealand and Australia, 5 caps
England 1928–33, 16 caps

Here Comes the Judge

Sir Carl Douglas Aarvold is one of the great English players who went on to fight in the Second World War and was honoured with an OBE for his war service. He served in the Royal Artillery as a Lieutenant Colonel.

Obituary, *The Independent*, 28 April 1995

There have been few more elegant rugby players in the typically English style more recently associated with Richard Sharp and David Duckham than Carl Aarvold. The long stride, flair for an opening and other more prosaic qualities were evident from an early age and became appreciated by all who saw him.

As a centre three-quarter Aarvold played in four winning Cambridge University teams against Oxford during the 1920s and won sixteen England caps as Captain between 1928 and 1934.

He toured with the British Lions to New Zealand and Australia in 1930. Because the Tour Captain, Doug Prentice, realised he was not good enough to make the team and Vice-Captain, Wilf Sobey, was injured, the captaincy in New Zealand fell to Aarvold. The first Test in Dunedin was won 6–3 and that was the last Test won in New Zealand until Ronnie Dawson's side won the last game in Auckland in 1959.

A critic of the day, Townsend Collins of the *South Wales Echo*, wrote: 'He knew the theory of centre play, varied the tactics cleverly and could make brilliant runs from which other men scored, testimony to his judgement. He also had a fine kick and his defence was adequate.'

Sir Carl Aarvold became an Old Bailey Judge from 1964–75. In 1965 the Kray twins were up before him for demanding protection money from a Soho club owner. They were acquitted, but four years later sentenced to life for murder.

Lions Military Players

The 1930 Lions were a side brimming with military personnel. Joe Kendrew and Tony Novis were members of the Royal Leicestershire Regiment.

Novis was an extremely fast winger and top scorer on the tour. He captained England in 1933 when Kendrew became pack leader. Kendrew was highly decorated, being awarded the DSO four times. In 1963, he was appointed Governor of Western Australia and made a Knight Commander of the Order of St Michael and St George (KCMG). Novis was awarded the MC for his actions at Sidi Barrani in Palestine, where he was wounded in the hand and neck.

George Beamish, the great Irish forward, served in the RAF from 1923 to 1958, rising to the rank of Air Marshal. He was responsible for getting a little bit of Irish green on the Lions kit as he led a delegation to express his dissatisfaction that Ireland's colours were not represented. The green turnover on the socks has been a feature of the kit since 1938.

Henry Rew was a sterling prop forward who played in the four Test matches in New Zealand. He was sadly killed at El Alamein aged 34 on 11 December 1940.

Brian Black, a place-kicking back row forward, played in the five Tests and died over Wiltshire on 29 July 1940 when an officer in the RAF.

George Cromey
South Africa 1938, 1 cap
Ireland 1937–9, 9 caps

The Diminutive Minister

The 18th of May 1938 was busy in the life of the diminutive Irish out-half George Cromey. His day began selling his Austin car. Later, he was licensed as a Presbyterian minister at the Chapel of Assemblies in Belfast before rushing to catch the Heysham boat to meet up with Sammy Walker (captain), Blair Mayne, Bob Alexander and Harry McKibbin, all British and Irish Lions from Ulster en route to South Africa.

I don't know if the 1938 team were a religious team, but George was well supported in South Africa when he preached at various churches. Indeed, Rev. Cooke arranged a Sportsman's Service in the Sea Point Congregational Church, Cape Town, on Sunday, 18 September. The team attended and the Mayor of Cape Town read the sermon. Mr Cooke, the minister of the church, handed George 31 shillings for conducting the service. George was amazed and reluctantly accepted the fee, which was a godsend – if you'll excuse the pun – as he was about to withdraw £2 from the manager, Major Hartley, to buy presents.

George was especially well supported by Elfred Jones, Haydn Tanner and Harry McKibbin. They paid visits to churches of many denominations and sometimes Major Jock Hartley read a lesson. Blair Mayne, probably on his final warning of being sent home, had taken to the sarsaparilla (root beer) for two weeks and promised to attend church to hear George preach. The Rev. Cromey, only a minute into his address, heard loud snoring – Blair had obviously returned to something stronger than sarsaparilla the night before and had fallen asleep, as George put it, 'On the ample bosom of the large lady in the pew beside him.'

Diary of a Tourist

I am incredibly grateful to have had access to George Cromey's diaries, courtesy of the Blair Mayne Society, as they reveal not only personal reflections as entries but also show how the squad spent their time on board ship during the initial 19 days travel to East London via Cape Town and Port Elizabeth. I include some excerpts below to show some of their life on board ship passing time with training and embracing a unique opportunity for bonding with fellow players.

Friday, 20 May

Up early. Luggage down in hall. Bus brings us all to Waterloo Station. Train 10 a.m. I suddenly find I have left my ticket in my bag (locked in luggage van). Hectic search. Almost held up train but found at last. All well. On boat at 12. Harry (Harry McKibbin) and I share cabin 185. Great boat. (*Stirling Castle*). Lunch on board in our honour. What a feast for a start. Photographs and explore ship. Later unpack. Dinner 7.30. No dress for first evening. *Stirling Castle* a floating palace. Bed early. Wrote some letters and posted before boat left Southampton. As we left Southampton, three people were found to have stayed on board by mistake (not having heard the horn). A small pinnace came and took them ashore. We passed the Isle of Wight and the Needles, where we dropped our pilot.

Saturday, 21 May

Up early 7 a.m. Breakfast 8.30. Again a huge feed. During the morning, played quoits, deck tennis, putting, then down to gym – a posh place with electric horse, bicycles. Then a swim in the warm seawater baths. Great! Beef tea 11 a.m. Lunch 1 p.m. about 7 or 8 courses. I read in afternoon. Afternoon tea 4 p.m. We had a team meeting at 5 when Major (Jock) Hartley addressed us and gave us instructions. All very good. Dinner at 7 p.m. Dress all laid out ready. What service! After dinner played a crossword game of Harry McKibbin's . . . and so to bed.

Today we were in the Bay of Biscay. Weather perfectly calm but dull. All the chaps are very decent and we are getting to know each other very well. It is grand fun.

Sunday, 22 May

7.30 Tea, fruit and biscuits. Breakfast 8.30. This is a glorious day. Very warm. Divine Service at 10.30 a.m., most of our chaps were there (about 21). Church of England service. We passed two sailing vessels today. I read some and talked to one of the other passengers. I think of all at home this Sunday. Clocks put back two hours since we left home. Very hot sunshine today. I read quite a lot. At night an orchestral concert on board.

Monday, 23 May

Another grand morning. At 7.30 I got up and did some gym then a bathe, and breakfast. Wrote and posted about a dozen letters. We trained at 11 a.m. John Unwin took us for PT; very good. Another bathe and dinner. Photographs. We passed the Deserted Islands and drew into Madeira at 1 p.m. (dinner). Madeira is inhabited by Portuguese. Houses (all red roofs and scattered for most part a field apart for fruit growing). We were driven in cars right up to about 2,000 feet up. Very hot climate. Roman Catholic Church (very beautiful) where Emperor Karl, father of Archduke Otto, was buried in exile. Then tea and descent again. We go for a drive in bullock sledge – 1/- each for ½ hour. Roads made of small neatly-fitting pebbles and feel very smooth in a vehicle. The inhabitants are swarthy, Spanish-like at first very unattractive. We visited a linen embroidery place where we were told the linen came from York Street. Back to the ship at 6 p.m. Little boys diving for pennies. Forty small boats crowding round sides, selling embroidered cloths, casks of wine etc. (hurl up rope to purchaser and pull purchase up in basket – money coming down in return). Madeira a very interesting place but we were almost glad to get away. We saw many young recruits in uniform, who we heard, were to sail this week for the Spanish War – poor chaps. Most people on the island seem poor. All come begging round the Tourist. As you travel by car, youngsters throw flowers in to car and ask for penny. One or two gave us a 'present' of a flower when we were up the hill and before we left asked for a penny for the 'present'. Families vary from 12–18. Thickly populated.

6 p.m. On we go again from Madeira. Play Ping-Pong with Haydn (Tanner). Dinner. Bob Graves' birthday 'speechifying'. Game of 'KAN U GO' Elfred James, Bill Clement, Eddie Morgan, Harry (McKibbin) and I.

Tuesday, 24 May

Weather very hot. Passed the Canary Islands today (Tenerife). PT as usual at 11. In afternoon we lay about and read. I read most of P.G. Wodehouse's *Heavy Weather*. Committee for Sports appointed. Usual programme of eating and games. Sea, sea, nothing but sea all the time. After dinner played again. I commenced a 'diary letter' home. Bed at 10.30.

Wednesday, 25 May

Again very hot. Warmer each day. Feel tired this morning. PT as usual but getting harder because of the heat. Great to have a dip now in pool.

Read in afternoon on deck (canvas covers overhead). I finished *Heavy Weather* and started H.G. Wells. At night played again after dinner with Bob Graves, Harry (McKibbin), Elfred Jones, and Haydn Tanner. Very good fun. Today we passed a steamer, first we sighted since Madeira. Got first snaps today (printed).

Thursday, 26 May

Some signs that we are nearing the Equator (we are to cross the Line tomorrow). Stewards and waiters all in white. During the day, we are all in white. Can do little training today. Have a great bathe. Glorious weather and heat terrific. Lie and sleep. See some birds today (swallows and seagulls). I beat Vivian Jenkins in 11 rounds of table tennis. Tonight clocks to go on 12 minutes. Today we got one guinea (for refreshments for past week). At night a dog race meeting. I looked in to see what was happening. Good fun. At 9 p.m. started my diary as usual. My weight is down to 9 st. 12½ lb. As a result I'm off training, I can't afford to lose weight.

Bed at 10 p.m. and read for a while. Finding Elfred Jones very nice. Having a marvellous time. Quiet. Time passing very quickly. Sea, sea, sea and sea.

Friday, 27 May

We didn't cross the Line last night. We cross tomorrow at 1 a.m. Very warm again today. My weight is down again so training is off. I played deck quoits and was beaten. Bob Alexander beat me at golf. Read a lot today. Photographs, I got some printed (costing 3/-). We passed a ship today. Having ice-cream at almost every meal. Two bathes today. Great. Lightning at night.

Saturday, 28 May

We crossed the Line during the morning. A good deal cooler today, a breeze has sprung up. I did no training but played some games and enjoyed a bath in the evening. Tonight a Fancy Dress Ball. Great craic. Jock Hartley as Scotsman – Bob Graves as Sheik, Laurie Duff – Mae West, Roy Leyland – a girl, and Charlie Grieve a parson. People on board are very nice. Quite a few Jews. Mr McKenzie a seaman, to be married in a few months. I started John Buchan's *Island of Sheep*, very good. Geoffrey Reynolds ill today and confined to bed.

Sunday, 29 May

I spent a beautiful quiet day today reading and thinking. I really enjoyed today. At 10.30 a.m. Divine Service in the Lounge, the Captain leading. But the service (Church of England) I thought formal and almost empty. Quite a fair turn out. In afternoon and evening I read. Elfred (Jones) talked for some time with Mr McKenzie (of Union Castle Line). Very nice. We saw some flying fish today. Small things like sardines. Lovely blue colour. Shoals of them. Fly like swallows. Orchestral concert at night which I did not attend.

Monday, 30 May

Still nothing around but sea, sea all the time. Training (light) at 11 this morning. Bathed as usual. Sea a bit rougher today. Ship pitching more. Read in afternoon and discussed tactics before tea. Prepare also for concert tomorrow night. At night a tape–cutting party. Hooked in. News today of an explosion in Belfast. First news we have from Belfast. Harry (McKibbin) sang tonight. Hit me with soap. Black eye.

Tuesday, 31 May

Getting much cooler now. Up till now I've been sleeping regularly after lunch (found it necessary). Today we played Monopoly instead. (Mrs Mathers won). In afternoon we saw through 'the bridge' of the ship. Very interesting indeed. Gyro compass and charts, alarms etc. Earlier we were in the engine room. Powerful engines and very large long shafts. At night Mr Rosenberg showed very good films of South Africa.

Wednesday, 1 June

Finals of all tournaments being played today. No training today. Ship rolling a good deal. We practised today for the concert tonight. Each country to perform, but Jock Hartley does think good enough. Some of us play Monopoly in afternoon. Very good ship's concert tonight after dinner. Conjuring tricks etc. Rose Alpen (opera singer) was outstanding, a most beautiful singer. All justly impressed. Afterwards I had a yarn with Mr Edmunds, a small South African doctor (Durban), hear very interesting things about the country. Vesey Boyle ill today.

Thursday, 2 June

Nearing Cape Town now. Ship still rolling and jolting. We had combined photograph today (with officers). Given kit bag and miniature ball today (also 3 lions badges) and our refreshment allowance. I have a bit of a headache which annoys me. Read a bit of *Five Men Go to Prison* (Ralph Straus). Getting near South Africa now. We had a team discussion at 4 p.m. today. Jim (Giles) outlined some 'tricks' then training. Some people leaving ship at Cape Town tomorrow and they do not dress tonight. We have two wires of welcome already aboard ship (by wireless).

Friday, 3 June

Wonderful welcome at Cape Town where we arrived about 6.30 a.m. At 7 a.m. Harry (McKibbin) and I dressing in our room when a press-man knocks and sketches us. He tells me 'Pat' (Bertie) Coulter is waiting for me outside. Hundreds of people on board to see us. Dozens of photographs taken: great fun all round.

Pat's very decent. He has come some distance to see me and is arranging for a day out sometime. I meet two ministers, all are very friendly and welcome us warmly. Mayor of Cape Town (Mr Foster). We get our first newspapers for two weeks. Cape Town is beautiful in the sun, new harbour costing millions. Table Mountain rising nearly 4,000 feet behind the city, sharp and steep. City of white houses and red roofs like Madeira, stretching for miles round the coast. We go ashore and see Cape Town Charlie (conjuror) juggling four balls – England, Ireland, Scotland and Belfast! Bob Graves meets Mr Layt (pronounced 'Late'). 'I'm Layt . . .' 'No,' says Bob, 'you're early!'

Meet many friends already. Tea in a café. Irish and Welsh airs and we sing. Lunch in City Hall. Hundreds there. Speeches broadcast. First mail arrives. None for me but a parcel at Post Office. Second mail arrives. Letter from dad which greatly relieves me.

We train on the Track (Hamilton's ground at Green Point). Very hot indeed – and it is winter here! A hot boiling sun. Have developed a very stiff neck overnight. I had it massaged. At night we go to the pictures in Cape Town at Alhambra, picture *Submarine D1*. We get a great reception there. Our arrival actually was given on the screen (only taken this morning and training pictures of the afternoon also) – wonderful.

Saturday, 4 June

Wake greatly refreshed. Headache etc. almost gone. In morning we train again, very strong sun indeed – like our hottest summer at home. I hear that the African Union has promised £13,000 for our tour. We are given a box of 50 cigarettes each and a map of our tour (Oil Company advertisement). This country is rugger mad.

Press cuttings etc. all very interesting. Photographs etc. I collect parcel of two collars I ordered per Albert Gardiner at home. Vesey Boyle still in bed. New passengers on board today, sailing up coast. Ground very hard in Cape Town. Not looking forward to a hard game on it. Can hardly believe this is Saturday. Sail again at 12 noon for Port Elizabeth and follow coast all round. I sleep in afternoon, as have a right headache from heat. Read. I really am enjoying this, tho' I think often of home now and what is happening there.

Sunday, 5 June

Steaming along the coast. A Mrs Evans (wife of Rev. Evans of Durham) introduced herself to me and asked me to call when in Durban. At 11.30 a.m. arrived at Port Elizabeth. What a reception. Hundreds of people awaiting us on quayside. A paper today estimates 2,000 people but I don't think so many. Short speeches. Major Hartley says a few words. In afternoon some go golfing and some on a picnic. We go on a short run into country and have tea there. Wonderful to see the 'veld'. Narrow roads – big cars – because of tax by weight (e.g.: 24h/p costs £7½).

We saw and photographed ostriches and a native in traditional costume and two others fighting with staves. What a sight! Harry and I mentioned church and we were taken to Hill Church (Rev. M Patterson). Just same service, same hymns and books as at home. Impresses one with the really widely scattered unity of our own church (7–8 p.m.). After church, straight to bed.

Monday, 6 June

Spent morning writing letters. Afternoon we trained at Crusader Ground (Port Elizabeth). Saw some strange sights (Mr Layt took me on a walk into town). Women with loads balanced on their heads. Signed autographs etc. Last night on board ship. Sail again at 5.30 for East London. Diary and packing, also try to finish *Five Men Go to Prison*. Bed early.

Tuesday, 7 June

Arrive in East London about 7 a.m. Up and shore at 8.30. Great reception. Indian representatives put wreath of laurel leaves round Jock Hartley.

Driven in the usual big cars to our hotel, a big new place (King's Court) a mile out of the town. Hotel is just down by the sea – a glorious spot. Almost immediately, 10 a.m., great reception in Town Hall. We were all paraded up on to the platform where we were cheered and welcomed. We sang MacNamara's Band. Then on to hotel where we unpacked and had lunch. We are becoming quite used to climate now and feel at home already. Trained in afternoon. Ground is turfed (hard – but not so hard as expected). After dinner we met a large body of local sportsmen in our hotel who entertained us (and themselves) with song and drink etc. The people here really, I think, take rugby too seriously – have everything discussed – cut and dried. I got two letters today, both from South Africa – from Pat Coulter and Willie McConkey.

Weather very sunny and warm. We are almost getting scared by the way these South Africans talk about their rugby.

And so George's diary continues, with entries about the matches and where they visited. One of the wonderful experiences of the 'long' Lions tour was the opportunity to sightsee areas of interest the colonialists were so proud to show. Every touring side to South Africa was fascinated by the wonders of the Cango Caves, the Kruger Park, the Victoria Falls, the mighty Zambezi, the Kimberley mines and de Beers and the ostrich farms. Likewise, in New Zealand, it was the Treaty House at Russell in the Bay of Islands, the Waitamo Caves and Queenstown at the foot of the Southern Alps. What wonders for young men to see.

In East London, 8 June 1938, the team took a bus drive around the countryside:

Absolutely great. Saw native huts and stopped at one. All the women ran away. We tried to photograph women carrying bundles on their heads but when the bus stopped, they all became shy and bit by bit broke into flight.

Thursday, 9 June

This morning we went on a run out towards an Anglican Mission Station. Saw the usual kraals etc. and at the Mission Station saw the schoolchildren. They sang Negro spirituals. Wonderful! We were all very deeply impressed indeed.

Sunday, 12 June

Today the East London people entertained us to a picnic at Bonza Bay. Most of the chaps went.

Tuesday, 14 June (in Kimberley)

After lunch we are shown about £150,000 worth of diamonds in de

Beers exhibition office. We see the £5 million cheque which brought about amalgamation. Handled a stone worth £1,000 and saw others (£2,000 each). These diamonds sparkle wonderfully.

Wednesday, 15 June

Harry and I go for a walk and are shown the Biggest Hole in the World – the old diamond mine in Kimberley. We threw, or tried to throw, a stone down.

Thursday, 16 June (in Cape Town)

At 10.30 a.m. train back from Kimberley to Cape Town – usual good send off. Country is monotonous but not without interest. We saw coasts today. Great stretches of wild, brownish coloured land – very dry looking. Small hills. We saw some block-houses built for defence of railway line in Boer War. We see also some places where battles were fought. We got out and walked at many stations. Read quite a lot today.

Sunday, 19 June

This morning a trip up the mountains has been arranged. Overnight train from Cape Town 20 June. Played cards until we arrived at Oudtshoorn. We passed some grand scenery today. We climbed among hills and through tunnels and mountain passes. Rain and mist. At one time passed through a cloud.

Tuesday, 21 June (at Cango Caves in Oudtshoorn)

In morning we are taken out by car to see caves – wonderful underground passages and chambers and formations of stalagmites etc. Pillars and shapes of peculiar formation – Cleopatra's Needle, Bust of Edward VII, Madonna and Child, Pulpit and Vestry, and others – The Chamber – a dark passage where we had to crawl for 30 yards or so into a black hole/bend two double, all electrically lit. Formations said to add an inch in a thousand years.

Wednesday, 22 June

This morning we were brought round ostrich farms and saw many interesting things. We saw three ostrich eggs. A boom would come if Paris etc. caught on to ostrich feathers. We saw through a tobacco-drying station. Feel quite tired with our walking all morning.

Thursday, 23 June

In afternoon we were taken away by car to Kammanassie Dam (near De Rust). Huge dam collecting water for irrigation purposes. Schoolmaster driving us tells us much about water etc. We return and have tea at Mayor's invitation then presented as a team with ostrich feathers each.

Friday, 24 June (train to Cape Town)

At 5 a.m. we wakened suddenly and Bob Graves found himself on the floor. The rest of us all felt a jolt, which nearly pushed me out of bed. Our train had crashed into another one at a small siding. Rail accidents are very common in South Africa. It might have been much worse. The engine was broken a little (cow-catcher).

Tuesday, 28 June (overnight from Cape Town)

All awake and fresh for another day's train journey. Very dry and dusty. Travelling mile after mile through Karoo — at one time level plains without a rise or hill as far as one can see, flat as a pancake — at another, winding through between mountains. Dotted everywhere, we see wells with their windmills. Water must be a tremendous problem. See Boer War stockhouses once again.

Tuesday, 5 July (in Kroonstad, Free State)

Another summer's morning. Had the choice today of bowls, riding or boating. We would have been shooting except that a drought destroyed the game some years ago. Harry and I play at bowls and then have tea at the river with two chaps who we are playing against tomorrow.

Sunday, 10 July (in Johannesburg)

Saw native war dance this morning. Not so hot.

Monday, 11 July

Harry and I had arranged to be rung up at 7.30 to visit the Crown Gold Mines. Unfortunately a mistake was made and were not wakened — we slept until 9 and missed it.

Thursday, 14 July

This morning we went to a dealer of animal skins (lion, leopard etc.). Harry and some others bought some.

Friday, 15 July

This morning we were taken over the diamond mines. We did not go down, but saw all the surface workings – very dusty – and were shown the native compound at the mines. Then the dog kennels where dogs are trained to guard the diamond field. The dogs performed some wonderful tricks – clearing a 10 ft carrier, walking a narrow plank, clearing a burning ditch, scenting out a single match hidden by a stranger and attacking a native.

Monday, 18 July (in Bulawayo)

About 27 miles out of Bulawayo, visited Matabo this morning. Rhodes' grave on a hillside of granite – World's View. For miles around nothing but little kopjes of granite and brush – stones perilously perched on top of one another. This place was a centre of fighting. Very dangerous it must have been for sniping etc. The grave of Cecil Rhodes (died 1902) is a very impressive monument. A simple chamber in solid rock in the centre of a ring of huge boulders lying on the granite 'Here lies Cecil John Rhodes'. The ground is consecrated and a burying ground for those who had 'deserved well of their country'. Two others are buried there – soldiers who died in service of country. Rhodes means a lot to the South African.

Monday, 25 July (in Salisbury)

Arrived at Victoria Falls station at 6 a.m. Up and off to beautiful hotel where we spent a lovely day. Noticed huge black cloud of spray over the Falls. We explored a little before breakfast. Having walked about 2 miles we enjoyed a hearty breakfast. Then we explored all the Falls under Basil Nicholson's guidance – across the bridge, down the palm grove and over into Northern Rhodesia where we had a cup of tea. Many snaps taken. Very hot but there is a strange quiet and peace. Rainbow always on the Falls when sun shining. We appreciate the fact that we are alone and free to go where we like. Feel dirty and tired after long, hot and dusty tramp so had hot bath before lunch. After lunch about half of us went up the Zambezi (about 7 or 8 miles) in a motor launch. We saw many crocodiles, by the way, basking in the sun. Landed on a small island where we saw many little monkeys. Water calm, sun hot. During the day we saw baboons quite frequently. Coming back from the river we visited the rainforest with waterproofs. We did really feel the impressiveness of the Falls – sat quietly and drank it all in. After dinner had a quiet walk in the grounds and seven of us sang songs under the stars. As I write, the Falls can be heard booming distinctly. A lizard is clinging to the window.

Tuesday, 26 July

There is a magical air about this place which silences me and makes me happy. I could stay here a long time. This morning we paid a visit to the village of Livingstone, about 7 miles from the Falls. Bus fare 4/- each provided. We spent a pleasant morning exploring the curio shop and about bought the place out.

Monday, 8 August

We were wakened at 7.30 this morning to get off at Nelspring. We are travelling light with only a small bag each. Breakfast at Nelspring and off by 9 in hired cars for the Kruger game reserve (38 miles away). We see a lot of wildebeest and other animals round Pretoria, giraffes, jackals, impala, steenbuck and sable antelope but we have not seen any lions yet. We had several runs round in the morning and then in the afternoon motored off to the hippo pool where we saw half a dozen hippo in the water. We did not see much – just head and backs, huge slimy-looking creatures. We are sleeping in little 'rondavels' tonight – good fun with Bill Howard, Russell and Bill Travers – ghost stories and lion 'frights'. Great to sleep in little round huts and hear the cries of wild beasts all around. Lovely moonlit night.

Tuesday, 9 August

Up at Pretoria Kop at 5.30. Black boy brought in coffee. Eddie and I got up – the rest of the camp is in motion already. By 6 a.m. we were on our way to Skukuza via River Road. We kept a look out as usual for lions; we missed them, but saw quite a crowd round the Kop and got photos quite close up. We saw the usual wildebeest etc. and some bushbuck. We arrived at Skukuza (32 miles). There we had breakfast. We set off immediately for Satara (55 miles). We at last caught sight of six lions basking in the sun under the tree. Great excitement – a lioness and lion and cubs. We drove through the usual old roads down into deep river gulleys. Saw jackals and plenty of impala, turkey buzzards, giraffes again. In afternoon drove back from

Satara, Basil sitting in front and Charlie and myself sleeping in back seat. Drove back in time for dinner. Camp on the bank of the river. Good fun at night. Later – a rowdy night. The chaps spent a couple of hours throwing water round each other. Luckily Charlie shut our window. Kept the rascals out. They dried themselves round the fire.

Wednesday, 10 August

Up at 5.30 and off again on our chase. Our beards have fairly grown. Early we struck lucky – three great lionesses came along the road. We, and about five other cars, watched closely. They padded along towards us without taking any notice and passed within two yards of our car. I think we have good snaps. We continued on our way to Crocodile Bridge. Saw many of the usual animals and some new ones. Later we saw two lionesses and in late afternoon while leaving the Reserve we saw two huge lions, one with a large hunk of meat and a vulture overhead in the tree. We also saw a leopard and giraffes etc. We arrived at 6 p.m. and bathed (some shaved). I went for a walk along dusty road. After dinner (a good one) we caught train for Jo'burg. Early to bed.

Sunday, 14 August (in Johannesburg)

We saw the Zulu dance. It was most interesting. Burning hot sun. On our way back we had a cup of tea.

Friday, 19 August (in East London)

After lunch a bus run up to Nahoon River where some man living in a beautiful, ultra-modern house entertained us to afternoon tea. He and his young daughter took us up the river in two motor boats.

Saturday, 20 August

After breakfast we watched the manoeuvres of a large whale just about 50 yards out at sea. Went for a stroll along to the point where we watched the waves shooting up in a cloud of spray.

Thursday, 25 August (in Burgersdorp)

11.30 taken off by car to Middleborough. It is quite a small town. We had lunch and reception, after which, we motored out to the Agricultural College where we watched sheep shearing. We inspected different breeds of sheep and saw experiments in cross-breeding.

Wednesday, 14 September (in Cape Town)

Some of us set out at 10 this morning to climb Table Mountain. Mountain covered with mist but we met two coloured mountaineers who took charge of us. We climbed right up. We had lunch in the hostel or hut belonging to the Mountain Club. Very cold. We lit wood fire. Started to pour and we set off in torrential rain at 2 p.m. to continue over the top. Soaked through. Splashing through streams etc. We continued happy as larks, singing and chaffing each other. I sat down in a stream without feeling it. At 4 p.m. we arrived at the car and returned to find Jock anxious. We popped into a hot bath. Felt as warm as toast after it all.

Harry McKibbin
South Africa 1938, 3 caps
Ireland 1938–9, 4 caps

After one cap for Ireland against Wales in 1938, the late Harry McKibbin CBE was selected for Sammy Walkers' 'Blue Lions'. He became a star on tour and played 13 of the final 15 games. He continued to serve rugby at committee level for the rest of his life and was President of the IRFU in our centenary year, 1974. I played with all his three sons, Harry (Jnr) and Alistair who both played for Ireland, and Roger who should have played for Ireland when I was at London Irish. His grandson Roger Wilson played at Northampton with distinction and returned to his Ulster roots for the 2012–13 season.

My Father

Harry's son, Harry McKibbin Jnr, told me, 'In 1938, my father was selected for the British and Irish Lions on the basis of one international cap. He arrived in South Africa just before his 23rd birthday and was one of the "babies", if not *the* "baby" of the touring party.

'Dad told us very few stories of his own exploits. He was that kind of guy – very self-effacing. But my brothers and I had, as children, almost devoured the old scrapbooks that my mother, just his girlfriend at the time, had collated, telling us of Dad's achievements on the field of play.

'What he did tell us was much more about the off-field adventures of him and his mates on tour. The most memorable of these, as with many of the others, concerned Blair Mayne.

'Lions tours in those days went on for much longer than nowadays.

Nearly every provincial side in South Africa, as well as teams such as the Combined Universities, were entitled to their "crack" at the visitors from overseas. They were there for quite a number of months and no doubt from time to time became a bit bored. Blair Mayne, certainly, clearly felt the need to liven things up a little.

'On this particular occasion, the Lions had arrived in a bit of a backwater somewhere in deepest South Africa and there was little to do. They played hard on and off the pitch. Dad felt in need of a little lie-down and went upstairs to his bed. Blair, who obviously wanted to play, was having none of this. Having knocked in vain to gain admittance, he put his mighty shoulder clean through the door and entered the room in that fashion. But he was not content with this. When Dad refused to come out to play, he proceeded to dismantle the room. Dad says he knew Blair was powerfully strong, but not even he had realised the extent of this until Blair had disassembled and then broken up almost every item of furniture in the room, leaving my poor father alone in a bed (untouched) and in a sea of what amounted to a pile of sticks, fit only to put on a house fire. Blair left the room quite calmly, content with his handiwork, only for the hotel staff to arrive and find my father alone in the room – and naturally getting the blame!

'In those days, of course, such matters were quietly hushed up. The repair bill was negotiated and quietly paid, and the Lions moved on . . . "*O tempora, o mores*", as the ancients no doubt would have said! (Oh the times, oh the customs.)'

Blair Mayne
South Africa 1938, 3 caps
Ireland 1937–9, 6 caps

Hankie

On 11 March 1938, Ireland and Wales met at Ravenhill. More than 28,000 spectators attended this Triple Crown decider. This was to be Blair Mayne's last international before he set off to become immortalised in the Second World War. Five of his Lions team-mates, Harry McKibbin, Vesey Boyle, George Cromey, George Morgan and Bob Alexander, played that afternoon and Wales, captained by the great Wilf Wooller, included Haydn Tanner and Bunner Travers. Wales won 7–0.

Just before half-time, a Welsh forward kicked George Cromey and at the next scrum Blair Mayne wreaked terrible retribution; amid the carnage a Welsh nose was broken.

Blair's mother and his sister Frances were among the crowd. He feared no man, but he respected and revered his mother and loved all his sisters. At half-time, Frances appeared at the touchline, sent by her mother, with a hankie. She summoned her brother. 'Mum says you've got to wipe the blood off the Welshman's face,' she commanded.

Blair set off to the Welsh huddle and wiped the blood from the bemused Welshman. 'Now,' he said, 'look up at the stand and smile at my mother or I'll break every bone in your body behind the changing-rooms after the game.'

A Force to be Reckoned With

On 12 March 1938, Ireland played against Wales at the St Helen's ground, Swansea, in front of 40,000 spectators. Blair played alongside six of seven other Irish players who were to be picked for the forthcoming tour to South Africa. Bob Alexander was injured but Harry McKibbin (debutant) Vesey Boyle, George Cromey, Bob Graves, Sammy Walker and George Morgan all participated in an 11–5 defeat by a Welsh side that included greats like Wilf Wooller, Hadyn Tanner and Bunner Travers.

It was during this game that Blair Mayne's freakish strength was demonstrated. An Irish rugby reporter of the time wrote:

> There was one incident in this match which I never saw on a rugby field before or since. That great fly-half, Cliff Jones, with one of his bewildering, jinking runs, pierced our defence and went over at the corner flag. Not content with that, Cliff continued to jink with the idea of grounding the ball under the posts. Unfortunately for him he encountered Blair Mayne en route.
>
> Blair gathered Jones in his mighty arms like a child, and to the astonishment and ill-disguised amusement of the Welsh crowd solemnly carried him to touch-in-goal and dumped him out of play! The Welsh players were so astounded by this feat of strength that they made no attempt to retrieve the situation.

Rooster

Modern-day South Africa boasts contemporary, state-of-the-art stadia, but this is only a recent development. The grounds on the Highveld used to consist of a small permanent grandstand, clubhouse and pavilion, and bank upon bank of seats constructed from scaffolding. At Ellis Park and Loftus Versfeld, these seemed to reach the sky. I remember crawling gingerly on hands and knees to the top of 120 rows on the eve of the decisive third Test in Pretoria in 1974 and wondering how anyone could relax and watch a game on such fragile seating. At the first Test in Johannesburg in 1955, 95,000 official spectators perched on the temporary stands (then a world record) while a further 10,000 gatecrashed.

When the 1938 Lions reached Ellis Park, the stands were still being erected by convicts from the local prison who also slept in a compound beneath the scaffolding. Blair Mayne, being curious, asked one of the convicts what his offence was to merit a prison sentence.

He replied, 'Stealing chickens, and I've received a seven-year sentence.' Blair immediately nicknamed him 'Rooster' and replied, 'I don't think you'll be doing seven years.'

That night, Blair, aided and abetted by Bunner Travers, returned with bolt cutters and clothes to replace the prison uniforms and released Rooster and a close friend. There was only one problem: papers in the clothes were traceable to the Tourists, and Rooster and friend were recaptured. I wonder how Major Jock Hartley, the Lions manager, explained that one. And Alan Thomas thought he had problems with Bobby Windsor in 1974 . . .

Durban Docks

The 1938 Lions were in Natal between 12 and 18 August. It was during this period that Blair totally drained the patience of manager Major B.C. (Jock) Hartley and assistant manager H.A. Haig-Smith, and but for the pleading of Sammy Walker about his importance on the field he would have been sent home.

In Durban on Saturday, 13 August, the Lions were beaten 26–8 by Northern Provinces and one evening before they left for Pietermaritzburg, Blair and Bunner Travers, the hard coal-trimmer from Newport, went to the rough pubs on the Durban docks dressed as sailors. It was a planned operation and by the time they returned to the Empress Hotel there were many bruised and bloodied bodies left by the quayside.

Then, when the team arrived in Pietermaritzburg to play Natal, Blair didn't just break the door of his room but absolutely trashed it and terrified the hotel manager who had come to view the wreckage.

Fresh Meat

Resplendent in their white dress suits, the 1938 Lions walked the short distance from their hotel in Cape Town to a reception when Blair Mayne noticed something much more interesting than another official function. Outside a bar sat some men with rifles and lamps. As a Bisley Class marksman, Blair's natural curiosity got the better of him. He broke away from his fellow Lions and soon his new friends invited him to join them, lamping for game.

George Cromey, rooming with Blair, read until three o'clock waiting for him to return. He gave up, turned his bedside lamp off and was just dozing off when Blair smashed the door down (he left a trail of broken doors throughout South Africa) and announced, 'I've just shot a Springbok.'

Cromey felt his blood run cold, but when he turned on the light there was Blair, cummerbund still intact, standing with a four-legged Springbok draped over his shoulders. 'Sammy Walker's been complaining the meat in South Africa isn't as fresh as at home,' he said. Off he went to Sammy's room, walked through his door and launched the deer at Sammy in bed. 'Fresh meat for you, Sammy.' Unfortunately one of the beast's horns spiked Sammy's thigh and he missed a couple of games because of the injury.

What to do now with the Springbok? Blair discovered where the manager of the South African team was sleeping, inched along a ledge and hung it on the railings outside his room with the message: 'A gift of fresh meat from the British Isles Touring Team.'

When the team assembled at 10 a.m. next morning to travel by car back to Durban, they were to board the *Arundel Castle* at 12.30 p.m. to sail back to East London to play Border. Blair Mayne was missing, but as the convoy of cars pulled up on the dockside who was leaning over the railings of the ship but the big Irish second row.

The management's intention was that Blair would not disembark at East London but continue on to Southampton on his own. Sammy Walker's diplomacy saved the day (again). The warning must have had a temporary effect, though, because George Cromey's diary entry for Saturday, 30 August, after beating Border 19–11, reads: 'Blair Mayne drinking a lot of lemonade and barley water – great!'

It's Sorted

Billy, Blair Mayne's father, had an expression when a problem was solved, 'It's sorted.' Blair used it too when he dealt with any difficult situation.

The 1938 side, who were the first team to be called the Lions, originally were to play 18 provincial matches and 3 Tests, although the side agreed to remain in South Africa and play 2 further games.

Because of his misdemeanours – Blair was always involved in some shenanigans or other, on and off the pitch – the management were seriously considering sending him home and probably tried to keep him busy and out of mischief by involving him in as many games as possible. As a result, Blair played with great distinction in 17 provincial games and 3 Tests.

Sammy Walker, the captain who probably knew Blair as well as anyone, used his influence with the management to keep him on tour. During one particularly dirty game, Sammy was felled and as he was regaining his consciousness, he spotted two stretcher bearers racing across the pitch. However, they didn't stop with him but continued a few more yards to where a South African forward was lying unconscious. Sammy looked up and Blair Mayne was standing over him. He winked and said, 'Don't worry, Sammy, it's sorted.'

He owed his captain one.

A Lion Rampant

Blair Mayne had been a member of Queen's University OTC (Officer Training Corps) during his student days and when the Second World War broke out he joined his local unit in Newtownards, the 5th Light Anti-Aircraft Battery SR (Special Reserve). But Blair thirsted for action and transferred first to the Royal Ulster Rifles and then the Cameronians. He transferred again to the 11th (Scottish) Commando and first saw action at the Litani River in Syria, where he was mentioned in dispatches for his deeds.

David Stirling had, at this time, formed 'A Special Service Unit' with the purpose of attacking specific targets behind enemy lines. He managed to persuade General Ritchie, Deputy Chief of Staff, that his unconventional tactics might succeed. A few days later he began to recruit, initially six officers and sixty other ranks, with the intention of attacking German airfields and transport lines. The unit was to be called the Special Air Services Brigade. Volunteers for the ranks were plentiful, but Stirling insisted that his officers would be of the highest calibre.

Stirling asked one of his first officer recruits, Eoin McGonigal, if he knew anyone who would meet his standards. McGonigal did indeed have a friend who would fit the bill. He had volunteered for the Commandos, had been mentioned in dispatches for his actions at the

Litani River and was an exceptional physical specimen who had played international rugby for Ireland and the British Lions. There was only one problem, said McGonigal — he was in prison awaiting court martial for striking a senior officer.

Stirling went to visit Blair Mayne in prison, who after initial suspicion agreed to join the SAS if strings could be pulled to secure his release. This was soon arranged and thus began the SAS career of one of the finest warriors in military history. I heard Jack Kyle, speaking in the Reform Club in London, refer to him as perhaps the greatest killer the world has ever seen, but he killed to save mankind from tyranny. Blair called it 'good killing'.

The first mission, after months of training in navigation, parachuting and sabotage, was an absolute failure. North Africa was struck by a dreadful storm and the objective of destroying a series of airfields was doomed by the elements. Only 22 of the 62 who had set out returned, and Blair took it very badly when he learnt that his great friend Eoin McGonigal had been killed during the raid.

The sceptics in military headquarters who had doubted the ability of the SAS from its inception pushed for its abandonment.

However, opinion changed when on 8 December 1941 two raiding parties, led by Mayne and Stirling, left their base at the Jalo Oasis, Libya, well behind enemy lines, in their specially adapted Willys Jeeps (fitted with twin Vickers K guns or 0.5 in. Browning heavy machine guns, armour plating to protect the gunner and driver, a field radio, spare ammunition, fuel and water) to attack the airfields at Sirte and Tamit. Stirling's raid was a failure, but Mayne's was an unmitigated success.

They came upon a hut as they entered the airfield unchallenged. From Mayne's account: 'I kicked open the door and stood there with my Colt 45, the others at my side with a tommy gun and another automatic. The Germans stared at us. We were a peculiar and frightening sight, bearded, unkempt hair. For what seemed an age we just stood there looking at each other in complete silence. I said, "Good evening." At that, a young German arose and moved slowly backwards. I shot him — I turned and fired at another six feet away, throwing hand grenades to add to the confusion. The exploding grenades lit up the airfield and we were as grateful as children on a Christmas morning moving from plane to plane, placing our bombs in the cockpits or petrol tanks.'

One plane had been overlooked and as there were no bombs left, Blair, with an immense feat of strength, pulled out the cockpit with his bare hands.

Although Stirling's group had failed, he was ecstatic when he learnt that Mayne's party had destroyed 24 aircraft. Two weeks later, Mayne revisited Tamit and this time destroyed 27 planes. Apart from the destroyed aircraft, the killings so far behind enemy lines were creating a climate of fear.

This type of guerrilla warfare was extremely dangerous, but Blair Mayne thrived on it. The medical officer, James, recounts, 'This sort of fighting was in his blood, there was no give or take about his method of warfare, and he was out to kill when the opportunity presented itself. There was no question of sparing an enemy – this was war, and war meant killing.'

Fellow SAS member Johnny Cooper recalled when he was in his 80s: 'I never saw him scared; he just didn't have the same sort of fear that the rest of us had. He didn't have a problem about his own safety – although he cared deeply about the rest of us – and it seemed that he accepted death as part of the job, and if it happened, well, it happened.'

An example of Blair's coolness and daring occurred in June 1942. Stirling had visited Benina airfield, in Libya, with great success the previous night and Mayne, in the banter, disputed Stirling's tally and suggested they should return for verification. The dare was accepted.

The pair appropriated a Chevrolet truck and set off into enemy territory with five others, including Cooper. The Germans, weary of the SAS activities, had nicknamed the man who led the raids 'The Phantom Major'. Stirling expected they would retrace their steps without too much trouble. However, the Germans had established a roadblock to prevent any further efforts by Phantom to breach their lines. When they met a heavily armed roadblock, Mayne was driving. 'This is it,' Cooper remembers thinking. 'The barrier extended right across the road in the form of barbed wire on trestles and there was no way to slip round. As far as we could make out from our shielded light, there were several Germans in obviously aggressive stance behind machine guns.'

A sergeant major drew near the driver's seat where Mayne sat with his pistol in his lap. As one of the Germans stomped closer, Cooper and the other four men in the back fingered their grenade pins. When he reached the vehicle, the German shone a torch into Mayne's face, who squinted and curled his fingers around the hidden gun.

'Password!' he barked.

Karl Kahane reacted and leaned forward from the back of the truck to harangue the German in his own language. 'How the bloody hell do we know what the bloody password is? We've been fighting the British for six bloody weeks. Now remove the bloody barrier and let us through because we're cold, tired and want a bloody bath.'

Staggered by the outburst, the German was convinced the group were his own people. He glanced at the driver and furrowed his brow – something didn't quite fit. He stepped closer to peer in at Blair Mayne's face and found himself staring down the barrel of the firearm Blair had raised. He gulped and looked beyond the gun – Mayne stared at the German with a cold and impassive gaze, displaying no distress, only an eerie detachment, before he smiled. The German became rigid with fear. He turned to his men at the roadblock and shouted out a guttural command. Boots clattered on the dusty road as they rushed to move the barricade and bade the party in the truck '*Gute nacht!*'

Next morning, they returned safe though somewhat bruise-mottled from the bumpy cross-country detour imposed upon them when they had been forced to escape a German armoured car that the roadblock had alerted.

Blair Mayne received his first DSO (Distinguished Service Order) in 1942 for his actions in the North African desert, where he single-handedly destroyed 100 enemy planes.

Blair took command of the First Squadron SAS in May 1943, as Stirling had been taken prisoner and was languishing in Colditz. After the desert war they embarked to Sicily and arrived on the beaches at Augusta on 12 July 1943, where, due to his actions, he received the second DSO.

A sad consequence of the Sicily Campaign was that Bob Alexander, top try scorer amongst the forwards on the 1938 Lions tour and team-mate of Blair Mayne for Ulster and Ireland, was killed on 19 July 1943 at Catania attacking the Simento River. He was a captain with the Royal Inniskilling (Enniskillen) Fusiliers. David Cole, a fellow officer, said, 'Bob passed me on the way . . . I wished him luck. He paused for a second and whispered with a smile, "It's suicide," and then went on.' Bob Alexander is buried at the Catania War Cemetery.

The Sicily Campaign lasted 38 days and the SAS landed on the Italian mainland at Termoli in October. They encountered dogged resistance from a crack German paratrooper unit and suffered heavy casualties. Twenty-one were killed, twenty-four wounded and twenty-three captured.

As the *Official History of the SAS* recorded: 'Mayne was reported to have conducted a minor war single-handed. He was observed to have killed twelve Germans early in the fighting . . . he seemed to have a charmed life but possibly some part of his "luck" was his amazingly quick reaction.'

At the start of 1944, all SAS units were recalled to Ayrshire to prepare for the thrust into France. Their headquarters were at a country estate in the village of Darvel and the exertions of commandos in training – climbing cliffs, parachute jumping, scaling mountains – all designed to build up supreme physical fitness, also developed hearty appetites. During their stay, the game on the estate was severely depleted, as were the contents of the wine cellar.

After the invasion of France, Mayne remained in England and directed SAS operations from HQ in Fairford, Gloucestershire, for two months. At least those were his orders. He kept disappearing and it was only in 1946 that it became known that he made many rogue undercover sorties to France, parachuting to meet intelligence agents and returning by small boats from Brittany.

In August 1944 he returned to set up attacks on the retreating Germans after the Allied landing.

He was awarded the third DSO for his inspirational work during the next month. The citation for this award ends: 'During the next few weeks he successfully penetrated the German and American lines in a jeep on four occasions in order to lead parties of reinforcements. It was entirely due to Lt-Col. Mayne's fine leadership and example and his utter disregard of danger that the unit was able to achieve such striking success.'

Blair Mayne's fourth DSO citation reveals just how determined and ruthless he could be. Part of his determination drew from his fury when he discovered his friend, Major Bond, who, on 9 April 1945, led B Squadron's armoured jeeps as part of the plan to fan out along two parallel roads in the Pappenburg region, had been shot through the head by German ambushers. Lt-Col. Mayne demanded the men in his jeep get out. He then revved the engine and raced at full throttle towards a house in the village where the Germans responsible were holed up. Dust, stones and debris clouded his approach and by the time the Germans realised what was coming at them it was too late. Blair tore the door from its hinges and began firing his tommy gun. His men heard the gunfire and subsequent screams of those inside. When it ran out of ammunition, he returned to his jeep, took his Bren and shoved two fresh magazines in his tunic pocket before he entered the second house, where he sprayed bursts of fire as he moved from room to room. Despite his rage, he remained calm enough to rescue wounded personnel, under intense and accurate enemy fire, cowering behind a jeep. One by one, he lifted them gently to his vehicle, reassuring them that they would soon be with medics.

Below is the full official citation that followed these events:

THIRD BAR TO THE DISTINGUISHED SERVICE ORDER
Lieutenant Colonel (Temporary) Robert Blair Mayne (87306)
DSO 1st Special Air Service Regiment, Army Air Corps

On Monday, 9 April 1945, Lieutenant Colonel Mayne was ordered by the General Officer Commanding, 4th Canadian Armoured Division to lead his regiment (then consisting of two Armoured Jeep Squadrons) through the British lines and infiltrate through the German lines. His general axis of advance was north-east towards the city of Oldenburg, with the special task of clearing a path for Canadian armoured cars and tanks and also causing alarm and disorganisation behind the enemy lines. As subsequent events proved, the operation of Lieutenant Colonel Mayne's force was entirely and completely successful. This success, however, was solely due to the brilliant military leadership and cool, calculating courage of Lieutenant Colonel Mayne, who by a single act of supreme bravery, drove the enemy from a strongly-held key village, thereby breaking the crust of enemy defences on the whole of this sector. The following is a detailed account of Lieutenant Colonel Mayne's individual action, which called for both unsurpassed heroism and cool, clear-sighted military knowledge.

Lieutenant Colonel Mayne, on receiving a wireless message from the leading squadron reporting that it was heavily engaged by enemy fire and the Squadron Commander had been killed, immediately drove forward to the scene of the action. From the time of his arrival until the end of the action he was in full view of the enemy and exposed to fire from small arms, machine guns, sniper rifles and panzerfausts. On arrival, he summed up the situation in a matter of seconds and entered the nearest house alone, and ensured that the enemy here had either withdrawn or been killed. He then seized a Bren gun and magazines and, single-handed, fired burst after burst into a second house, killing or wounding enemy there. He then ordered a jeep to come forward. He got into the jeep and with another officer as rear-gunner, drove forward past the position where the Squadron Commander had been killed a few minutes earlier, and continued to a point a hundred yards ahead, where a further section of jeeps were halted by intense and accurate enemy fire. The section had suffered casualties in killed and wounded owing to heavy fire, and the survivors were unable at the time to influence the action in any way until the arrival of Lieutenant Colonel Mayne. He then continued along the road, all the time engaging the enemy with fire from his own jeep.

Having swept the whole area very thoroughly with close-range fire, he turned his jeep round and drove back again down the road, still in full view of the enemy. By this time the enemy had suffered casualties and had started to withdraw. Nevertheless they maintained an accurate fire on the road and it appeared almost impossible to extricate the wounded, who were in a ditch near the forward jeeps. Any attempt at rescuing these men under those conditions appeared virtually suicidal owing to the concentrated and accurate fire of the Germans.

Though he fully realised the risk he was taking Lieutenant Colonel Mayne turned his jeep round once again and returned to try and rescue those wounded. Then, by superlative determination and displaying gallantry of the highest degree, and in the face of intense enemy machine-gun fire, he lifted the wounded one by one to the main jeep, turned round and drove back to the main body. The entire enemy position had been wiped out, the majority having been killed or wounded. The squadron, having suffered no further casualties, were able to continue their advance and drive deeper behind the enemy lines to complete their work of sabotage and destruction of the enemy. Finally, they reached a point 20 miles ahead of the advance guard of the advancing Canadian Division, thus threatening the rear of the Germans who finally withdrew.

From the time of the arrival of Lieutenant Colonel Mayne, his cool, determined action, and his complete command of the situation, together with unsurpassed gallantry, inspired all ranks. Not only did he save the lives of wounded but also completely defeated and destroyed the enemy.

Each one of his four citations reached the same conclusions when they described Mayne's qualities of superb, fine and brilliant leadership. They also mentioned his outstanding gallantry and great courage.

The DSO ranks just slightly lower in stature than the Victoria Cross and to gain that prestigious award while holding the junior rank of lieutenant made it an even more significant achievement. Only seven other men were to be awarded three bars to the DSO. The French people and their Government knew his worth and held Blair Mayne in very high esteem for his gallant and fearless conduct in helping to free their country from the Germans. They honoured him with the award of the *Légion d'honneur* and *Croix de guerre* on 5 March 1946 for his services. Those two great honours made him one of the most highly decorated Allied soldiers at the end of the Second World War.

Nearly 70 years on since the ending of the Second World War, a very large number of men and women, including 100 Members of Parliament, from all sides of the House, still feel very strongly that despite all of his hard-fought battles, undoubted bravery, outstanding leadership and incredible wartime achievements he was wrongly, and indeed shamefully, treated by the military and political establishment of the day. Although, in fact, it is highly possible that he had already earned his country's highest bravery award on many previous occasions, these people are of the firm belief that Lt Col. Robert Blair Mayne should not have had his citation downgraded but instead should been granted the award that he was originally cited for after his heroic and selfless deeds during the action near Oldenburg. (He was originally recommended for the VC and that it was stroked out and replaced with a recommendation for Third Bar DSO is clearly visible on the documentation of the time.)

Blair Mayne found it difficult to settle down to civilian life after the thrill and adventure of the war years. He was tragically killed in a car accident in his home town of Newtownards on 15 December 1955.

3

TRAINS AND BOATS AND PLANES

Lewis Jones
New Zealand and Australia 1950, 3 caps
Wales 1950–2, 10 caps

On a Wing and a Prayer

George Norton, the Irish full-back, had broken a leg prior to the tour to New Zealand and Australia, and Lewis Jones, the brilliant Welsh full-back who debuted against England in January 1950 at the tender age of 18 years 9 months, was selected as his replacement. And so . . . Lewis Jones became the first Lion to fly. He flew out to Los Angeles then south over the Pacific.

In an article by Dai Llewellyn, following a rare interview in February 2006 for the World Rugby Museum, Lewis Jones recalled: 'That year, 1950, was wonderful. When George Norton broke his arm [*sic*] I was called up to replace him. When I arrived at London Airport I looked out at the plane. It was a monster, a Boeing Stratocruiser. No doubt by today's standards it would be dwarfed by the Jumbos and so on, but to me it was huge. These days it's a journey that means 24 hours flying time to New Zealand. Back then it was somewhat different. It took four and a half days, with four or five changes of planes, to fly there. We landed in Gisborne on the east coast and my first game was the following day.'

The precocious youngster, on his first international appearance, created one of the greatest tries ever seen at Twickenham. Just before half-time, Murray Hofmeyr, the English full-back, dropped a kick short of the halfway line. Ordinarily, one would have expected Lewis to have safely kicked the ball into touch. However, astonishing everyone at rugby HQ, including his own team, the opposition and 75,000 spectators, he set off. The resulting try at the end of this daring move is as worthy of merit as that scored by Prince Obolensky in 1936 against New Zealand.

Quick to collect the ball, and scanning the area for the next best move, Lewis Jones noticed the England defence unhurried to reach the tackle area. Not only did this give him time to cross the advantage line, but in front of him a vast area of open, unprotected space gave him room to manoeuvre. Already the spectators had risen to their feet, anticipating something spectacular. Roars of encouragement filled the stadium, which spurred Jones on to dummy the opposition twice before he was finally tackled. Even then, he managed to hand on to Malcolm Thomas, who found Bob Evans distributing to Cliff Davies (Kenfig Hill and Cardiff), who claimed the try.

At the end of the match, the captain, John Gwilliam, and the boy wonder, Lewis Jones, were hoisted shoulder high and carried off the field by their ecstatic supporters. That score, which secured a win for Wales by 11–5 and eventually led to a Grand Slam, went down in the chronicles of rugby history.

Lewis Jones played for Llanelli for 2 seasons, breaking all club records when he scored 505 points during the 1956–57 season, before he swapped codes and joined Leeds, where he would stay for 12 years. At Stradey Park he was as much a hero as Albert Jenkins had been in the 1920s. It was this intrinsic ability to create the unpredicted, to captivate and entertain the crowds that personified the talent that was B.L. Jones – a true phenomenon.

Jack Kyle OBE
New Zealand and Australia 1950, 6 caps
Ireland 1947–58, 46 caps

In 2010, I was speaking to Phil Bennett the week before Ireland played Wales in Dublin. I asked him if he was coming over to the dinner for the IRFU Charitable Trust and he said he was for one reason – to meet Jack Kyle again as he loved to listen to him. I too have sat in awe listening to Jack deliver his speeches on a host of topics. In Dungannon one evening, although he didn't know it, he started to recite my favourite poem, Frost's 'The Road Not Taken'. I was most impressed. After the war was a period of golden years of Irish rugby, years of a Grand Slam and Triple Crowns. I wish he was a pundit on television today, as he makes the game seem so simple. There would be no such terms as territory management. Jack would prefer to talk about playing the game in their half or making 'a wee dart'.

No Insurance
On New Year's Day 1948, Ireland played France in Paris on the first leg

of the Grand Slam. The preparation stunned me. The Belfast contingent travelled by train to Dublin to meet up with their southern team-mates. They then travelled by boat from Dublin to Liverpool, an overnight journey. There was another train journey to London and from there to Dover to catch the ferry to Calais. From there, they took a train to Paris and had a 'squad session' on the eve of the game at the Folies-Bergère.

The 1950 Lions were the last team to travel by boat; a journey of seven weeks via the Panama Canal. Jack Kyle said: 'We travelled by boat because no insurance company was prepared to cover the party to fly, as they considered air travel unsafe. The last thing my old headmaster from Belfast Royal Academy, A.R. Foster (a member of the 1910 side), did was to present me with books on Irish history and poetry, as he said I would have plenty of time to read them on the voyage.'

Jack recalled how the Lions had a lineout inside their 25-yard line. 'We had practised shortening the lineout and the winger throwing the ball over the top. The ball was thrown over the top to me and I passed to Bleddyn Williams. However, it never reached him, as Lewis Jones entered the line between us to initiate a wonderful try. Lewis swooped up the ball and jinked through the opposition, sprinting towards the halfway line. Flair often partners fate and the field opened up in front of him. Free to run on unobstructed he glanced right to find Ken Jones predictably at his shoulder. Lewis kept on racing even when Bob Scott obstructed his path. Despite facing the finest full-back of the generation head to head, Lewis passed a perfectly timed ball to Ken Jones, at the New Zealand 10-yard line. Ken Jones executed an easy 45-yard run and score, leaving Henderson and Roper, the All Blacks three-quarters, watching in abject horror and surprise.'

Jimmy Nelson
New Zealand and Australia 1950, 4 caps
Ireland 1947–54, 16 caps

Eighteen of the twenty-two living Ulster British and Irish Lions attended a wonderful function in Belfast City Hall on 3 February 2012, organised by Ballymena Rugby Club. We were led in by that amazing rugby man from the Malone Club – Jimmy Nelson. A hard second row, he had the distinction of scoring two tries for the Lions against Australia in Sydney in 1950. He was a constant presence for Ireland during the golden era and continued to serve Ulster and Irish rugby for many years at committee level. He was Honorary Treasurer for 11 years and President of the IRFU in the 1982 season.

Puffed-Up Chests

Jimmy recalled: 'The 1950 tour to New Zealand and Australia was special for several reasons. It was called many things like "The Friendly Tour" and we were labelled the "Singing Lions" because of our jovial nature and being readily available to burst into song.

'Led by Karl Mullen, it was also the first tour played in red jerseys and we were called the British and Irish Lions. It was also the last time a tour party travelled by boat. We were on the steamship *Ceramic*, not a passenger liner but a cargo boat, and we were the only passengers, no women at all, which came as a bit of a shock. But having left the austerity of the immediate post-war years behind, we were intent on enjoying ourselves as best we could. Leaving sobriety and healthy eating behind, I'm sure everyone put on at least a stone in weight, despite our fitness regime on deck.

'Tommy Clifford was a Limerick slaughterman with a great sense of humour but very little money. Yet he was without doubt the best-dressed player on tour. He arrived with three enormous trunks at the docks, which came as a bit of a shock to the rest of us. Most of us had a small square case to carry on board, but Tommy had been kitted out by all the shopkeepers in Limerick and on arriving asked a porter to put two particular trunks safely in the hold, but to put one in his cabin.

'With his incredible appetite, in one sitting he went through the whole menu from start to finish, which took some eating as 32 courses were available. Not satisfied with that he brought a group of us back to his cabin, flung open his suitcase and amazingly out fell about a dozen massive fruit cakes, which we quickly scoffed. "Ah, me mother was worried I wouldn't get enough to eat!"

'Anyway, it took us a fortnight to reach our first stop at the Panama Canal, and as we were tying up, another ship came in from New Zealand with a lot of women on board. We got talking and then somebody came up with the idea that we should head to Kelly's nightclub in Panama, which was well known at the time. All told, forty of us marched down to Kelly's with two dollars each in our pockets. Dollars were very scarce then, but we didn't think much about it as we expected to be well received.

'We got a couple of tables together and ordered a beer apiece, but when it came to the bill, we hadn't enough money to pay for the first round, never mind another one. We sheepishly put all the dollars we had on the table to pay the waiter. He left and not long afterwards Kelly's owner arrived with three hairy bouncers to do whatever they had to do.

'But Scottish prop Grahame Budge shouted, "OK, boys, let's all stand up and stick out your chests." We all stood up in unison and no sooner had we done that than Kelly and his bouncers disappeared. Better still, we had free drink the rest of the night and we rolled back to the boat in a rather inebriated state. Perhaps we were still finding our land legs.'

Rhys Williams
South Africa 1955, 4 caps; New Zealand and Australia 1959, 6 caps
Wales 1954–60, 23 caps

Stellar Second Row

Colin Meads regarded Rhys Williams and Johan Claassen as the finest second rows he ever played against. Syd Millar reckons Williams was the best second row he ever played with.

It is difficult to compare players of different eras, but the giant from Cwmllynfell was a world-class forward who bettered the best of South Africa in 1955. In the process, he played for the Lions in ten consecutive Test games. He possessed physical and mental strength, technique, stamina, bravery, resilience, a 'never say die' spirit and the ability to influence others. His commitment was phenomenal.

Carwyn James wrote of him: 'Rhys Williams was that rarity among British locks, a world-class rugby player. Of all the positions in a rugby team, lock forward has been that in which British rugby has found it most difficult to match the forwards produced by South Africa, New Zealand and, in latter years, France. But as Colin Meads himself says, "Rhys Williams was a champion."'

Douglas Baker
South Africa 1955, 2 caps
England 1955, 4 caps

Douglas Baker was the last player from an English old boys' club to play for the Lions. His club, Old Merchant Taylors', were a first-class club in

1955 with a fine fixture list. I managed to trace Douglas in Australia and he was charming and only too willing to contribute. I can't wait to meet him if I manage to get to Australia for the next Lions tour.

A Welcome Sight

Douglas said: 'Whilst I was at school towards the end of the war, just outside London, I realised my sight was deteriorating. I could not read the writing on the blackboard from the back of the class. After investing in a pair of glasses, I felt much more secure. Though I enjoyed rugby at school, and afterwards, I felt disadvantaged by my inability to see clearly on the field.

'Some two or three years later whilst at university, I was lucky enough to be invited on a tour of Germany with the OU Greyhounds [University 2nd XV]. We played mostly against BAOR [British Army of the Rhine] teams and in conversation with one of the team members in Hamburg, he mentioned a firm called Campbell's who specialised in contact lenses. I quickly found my way there and purchased a pair off the shelf which fitted under eyelids and had the correct magnification. Ten pounds was a lot of money for a student then, but oh! So well worth it!

I only used the lenses for sport and they were with me when I was selected for the Lions tour to South Africa in 1955. I was understudy to Cliff Morgan at fly-half, so was unlikely to be selected for any of the Tests; however, I was considered as a "utility" player, having played in the centre and full-back.

'In SA, prior to the third Test in Pretoria (having won in Johannesburg and lost in Cape Town), I was on standby because of team injuries, myself included. The Monday before the Saturday Test, one of my contact lenses was unfortunately knocked off the mantelpiece whilst the hotel room was being cleaned, and trodden on. I couldn't play without them and was devastated. I spoke of my dilemma to Jack Siggins, our manager on the tour, who contacted the British High Commissioner based in the capital, Pretoria. Campbell's in Hamburg were called and a duplicate pair airmailed out to SA. Uncertain whether they would arrive in time for Saturday's match, the host officials kindly arranged for me to travel to Johannesburg each day to have a pair especially made for me.

'When Friday arrived, recovered from my injury, I was the proud owner of two pairs of contact lenses and to cap it all was selected as full-back for the third Test, which, incidentally, we won.'

Andrew Stoddart.

Thomas Crean.

Alexander
Findlater Todd.

Alexander Findlater Todd's tombstone.

Rev. M.M. Mullineux.

President of the WPRU Mr L.B. Smuts
and Cherry Pillman, 1910.

The Visitors and FPRFU at Redhouse, 1910.

'A Few of our
Rugby Visitors.'

Cape Times Weekly –
montage of
the 1910 Tour.

1924 team disembarking the boat at Southampton.

Cover of the 1924 Souvenir Programme.

Lions badge, 1924.

N. Brand as Bozo the mascot.

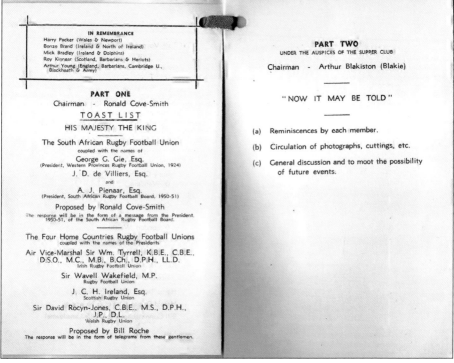

PART ONE

Chairman - Ronald Cove-Smith

TOAST LIST

HIS MAJESTY THE KING

The South African Rugby Football Union
coupled with the names of
George G. Gie, Esq.
(President, Western Provinces Rugby Football Union, 1924)
J. D. de Villiers, Esq.
and
A. J. Pienaar, Esq.
(President, South African Rugby Football Board, 1950-51)

Proposed by Ronald Cove-Smith
The response will be in the form of a message from the President, 1950-51, of the South African Rugby Football Board.

The Four Home Countries Rugby Football Unions
coupled with the names of the Presidents
Air Vice-Marshal Sir Wm. Tyrrell, K.B.E., C.B.E., D.S.O., M.C., M.B., B.Ch., D.P.H., LL.D.
Irish Rugby Football Union
Sir Wavell Wakefield, M.P.
Rugby Football Union
J. C. H. Ireland, Esq.
Scottish Rugby Union
Sir David Rocyn-Jones, C.B.E., M.S., D.P.H., J.P., D.L.
Welsh Rugby Union

Proposed by Bill Roche
The response will be in the form of telegrams from these gentlemen.

PART TWO
UNDER THE AUSPICES OF THE SUPPER CLUB

Chairman - Arthur Blakiston (Blakie)

"NOW IT MAY BE TOLD"

(a) Reminiscences by each member.

(b) Circulation of photographs, cuttings, etc.

(c) General discussion and to moot the possibility of future events.

Menu card for the 1951 Reunion Dinner for the 1924 Lions team.

1930 team sailing to New Zealand.

1930 Lions pack.

Lions badge 1930.

H. O'H. O'Neill.

Sir Carl Aarvold – fun golf.

R.C.C. (Clem) Thomas
South Africa 1955, 2 caps
Wales 1949–59, 26 caps

Clem Thomas, such a respected player and commentator on the game, died in 1996. He is another of the great Welsh personalities and talented players of the 1940s and '50s. He famously cross-field-kicked a ball enabling Ken Jones to gather it and touch down the winning try against the All Blacks in 1953 – a supberb, iconic piece of play, typical of the man. The following stories of Clem Thomas are told by fellow Swansea player of the 1950s, Colin Johnson.

All for the Want of a 'Johnnie'
'On the 1955 tour, the British Lions played Tests at Cape Town and Durban,' recalled Colin. 'At the time there was a large and famous chemist chain in South Africa with a branch in each of these cities run by a pair of brothers as proprietors, one in each outlet. They were very successful and sponsored the Boks and attended the function after the match.

'The reception dinner dance after the Cape Town game was held in a large room from which the tables were cleared away to make room for dancing after the meal. The teams and chief guests were on a large table set on a stage. Before the dinner, Clem and several other Lions were talking to the brothers, whom they had met at Durban.

'Tom Reid, the big Irish second row, sidled up and whispered to Clem, "You wouldn't have a spare johnnie about your person would you?"

'Clem explained the "scarcity" to the brother from Durban, who spoke to the Cape Town man, who contacted his local manager and a carefully wrapped gross carton of Durex arrived shortly after, some of which were distributed immediately.

'After the meal and between dances when the floor was cleared, the double doors at the far end of the room were pushed opened and Tom, with a blushing young lady in hand, emerged in full view of all on the top table.

'The Cape Town brother exclaimed, "Jesus, that's my daughter!" And his brother responded, "Well, at least we know it was safe sex."'

Speech Impediment
'BBC Radio's Ian Robertson and *The Observer's* Clem, as correspondents to the '74 tour, were driving through the outskirts of Cape Town and Ian

suggested they drop in on Chick Henderson, of the Quaggas. In one of the '55 Tests, Clem had tackled Chick very heavily, who after some time prone on the field was stretchered off. Chick recovered but was left with a tic and a stutter. Ian knew that he had completely recovered from the temporary disorder, but Clem had not seen him since the game and was loath to call, even though 19 years had passed since he inflicted the injury.

'However they did call. When Chick opened door he said, "HHHHHallo CCCClem cccome on iiiin," all with a pronounced tic. Clem's face drained of colour and he was shaken for several minutes after until Chick began to act normally!'

Beer Monitor

'In the 1954–55 season when the Baa Baas came on their Easter tour, Clem, who was captain, decided that we should have an upmarket buffet complete with a barrel of Worthington's set up with the proper wooden tap, instead of the usual sit-down arrangement, so that we could chat with the visitors.

'At that time, selection to the Baa Baa's tour was considered to be the highest honour except for the Lions. Amongst the team, nearly all internationals, were Tony O'Reilly and Syd Millar.

'Swansea played on St Helen's ground, the changing-rooms were under the stand and the social areas were in the Cricket Pavilion at the other side of the ground.

'After the game, some of the visiting players arrived in the pavilion before the Swansea lads and were shown into the dining room. Seeing the barrel set with many pint glasses to hand, Syd turned on the tap, which was "bloody stiff", drew a pint, but could not close the tap, so he put his finger under the outlet, which he removed as required to fill glasses for the rest of us.

'Clem had not realised the copper pin through the tap should have been removed before the tap was turned. Syd insisted it was his fault and therefore his duty to sit there manning the tap, being relieved only occasionally to eat, etc. This task placed him very adjacent to the source, did not impair his ability to drink, afforded him total control of beer distribution and suited him "fine" he was heard to say.'

Cecil Pedlow
South Africa 1955, 2 caps
Ireland 1953–63, 30 caps

When I was a wee boy, Dungannon were awarded senior status and the great teams from Belfast began to grace the 'Park'. I eagerly awaited North, with Jack Kyle and Noel Henderson, and Instonians, with David Hewitt, to collect autographs. I marvelled at Cecil Pedlow of CIYMS, who had the largest, strongest thighs I'd ever seen. Cecil was a gifted all-round sportsman, playing at Junior Wimbledon when he was 17. He won the Irish Junior Championship in 1951. He had six squash caps for Ireland and won the vets championship for the over fifty-fives before he retired.

It was in the genes. His great-grandfather was James Cecil Parke from Co. Monaghan, sportsman extraordinaire, who played rugby for Ireland 1903–09, once kicking five penalties in an international, was a scratch golfer, superb athlete, chess champion of Ireland and the best tennis player Ireland ever produced. He was in the world's first top four for many years and won an Olympic silver medal in 1908 in the men's doubles. He was twice beaten in Wimbledon semi-finals, losing to the eventual winner both times.

Cecil's grandfather also played rugby – a great sporting family.

I am indebted to Cecil, who kindly provided his personal diaries, which he kept throughout the 1955 tour. He wrote daily entries for four months from 4 June 1955 when he flew from Northern Ireland with Jack Siggins and Robin Thompson to join the team in London and travel on to Eastbourne to meet the Welsh players, and recorded the routines and tour highlights alongside commentary of the Lions matches played in South Africa.

The Tourists felt homesick from time to time, bolstered each other's morale if injury or illness incapacitated them and grew in friendship over the duration of the tour and with the opportunity to room with different team-mates. Apart from the camaraderie, choir practice and the high jinks of fellow players, Cecil's account reveals how much travel the team had to do. It seems incredible that players were expected to travel considerable distances, often on overnight trains or lengthy flights, and participate in a match the next day without any downtime or recovery before moving off once again to cover the miles required for the next location.

Prior to the second Test, the team, instead of training or warming up, spent the morning signing 400 autographs as preparation for the match, which they lost 25–9. Days spent travelling were tiresome and those spent as hotel guests, or hosted out, demanded attendance at official functions and meetings, even on match days.

A Young Man's Journey – 1955 Social Animals

During the latest Lions tour to South Africa, I was invited to an official function when the British Lions played Transvaal, now called the 'Golden Lions'. I was privileged to meet three ex-Transvaal presidents and after the initial shock when they learnt I was a '74 Lion (a bit like mentioning Cromwell in Ireland) they were extremely friendly towards me. They were quick to tell me that although Willie John McBride's team were a great side, there would never be a team of 'Tourists' like those of Robin Thompson's 1955 side.

The '55 side met in Eastbourne for distribution of kit, alteration of blazers and medical and dental examinations. They watched films of South Africa, had talks about the political situation from W.H. Clark, Under Secretary for Commonwealth Relations, and the first official function – lunch with the Mayor. The characters of the tour began to emerge immediately. Cecil's diary records: 'Cliff Morgan is as full of energy off the field as on it – you just can't tell what's coming next.'

They began serious training in the form of strenuous PT, ably led by Jeff Butterfield. On the way to the ground, they ran over the words of 'Sarie Marais', the Afrikaans national anthem. On finding them a little difficult to manage, Tom Elliot remarked that there were more words than tune. Cliff Morgan conducted the first choir practice with great success and afterwards Tony O'Reilly, on the piano, played jazz.

On the eve of the departure on 9 June, there were two more official functions – a reception at South Africa House and a farewell dinner at the Mayfair Hotel.

The 1955 Lions were the first team to fly. Our journey in 1974 was 13 hours with one fuel stop at Rome. The '55 side were on a marathon. They left at 4 p.m. on Friday, 10 June after a four-hour delay. They landed at Rome at about 8 p.m. and had a magnificent aerial view of the beautiful city. Next stop – Cairo at 2.30 a.m. in stifling heat. After light refreshments they resumed travel and set off for Khartoum, where they landed at 8.30 a.m. From Cecil Pedlow's diary again:

Here we all got a tremendous shock as we stepped out of the plane and into a temperature of 100 degrees Fahrenheit. I have never felt heat like it and at breakfast time too. After an hour we staggered aboard again, stripped to the waist and flopped back in our seats for another four-hour flight to Nairobi. It was decided to miss out our planned stop at Livingstone and fly direct to Johannesburg, a seven-hour journey.

We were met at Jan Smuts Airport by a barrage of cameras as we disembarked and we sang 'Sarie Marais' to the waiting crowd who clapped, cheered and carried some of us on their shoulders.

The Lions spent the next ten days in Vereeniging and apart from training, enjoyed golf, tennis and relaxing in the sun while having photograph sessions, signing autographs and widening their repertoire of songs.

Sunday, 12 June

After dinner we went to the main lounge and Tony (O'Reilly) started on the piano. I got hold of a drum, stick and brushes and we had a great evening as everyone gathered round and joined in. Ernie Michie even let go on his bagpipes.

Every day the team fulfilled their social obligations.

13 June

Lunch, Vereeniging Rotary Club.

15 June

After watching Western Province v N Transvaal, cocktail party under the stand.

16 June

Lunch with the Mayor and Commander of South Africa Police (Mr Stander).

17 June

Dinner at Carlton Hotel Johannesburg with the Administrator of Transvaal. The dining room was lit with arc lights, trees and flowers all round a miniature rugby pitch with the Springbok and Lions colours in the middle. After the speeches, our choir sang 'Sospan Fach' and 'Ging Gang Gooley', which went down very well.

And so it continued until 22 June when the first game was played against Western Transvaal. After a 9–6 defeat in the first game of the tour, the party wasted very little time in hitting the road – or rather the railway. They listened to speeches, danced at the function and then boarded the overnight train to Kimberley via Christiana. The last 70 miles of the journey had to be completed by road as there had been a derailment.

In the next three months they were to visit the sights mentioned in George Cromey's 1938 diary, plus Kenya, Rhodesia (Zimbabwe) and South West Africa (Namibia) as well as criss-cross the length and breadth of South Africa.

They enthralled South Africans with their style of open rugby and were great rugby ambassadors with their good humour and singing. They attended another 43 official functions, the last being the Rotary Club luncheon in Nairobi on 20 September. They met every mayor of every town and city, governor generals, attended police passing-out parades, mixed with locals and folk from home alike.

Demand on their time and company was immense.

The first Test was played on 6 August 1955 and the game is still regarded as one of the finest in Lions Test history.

Before the Second World War, the Springboks had taken on the mantle of world champions. In 1937, P.J. Nel's team had gone to Australia and New Zealand and won both Test series, defeating Australia 9–5 and 26–12. In New Zealand they lost 7–13 but went on to win 13–6 and 17–6 against the All Blacks.

The next season, Sammy Walker's 1938 Lions were defeated 12–26 and 3–19, until the famous last Test when the British Isles won 21–16.

After the war, the Springboks continued with a vengeance. The All Blacks toured South Africa in 1949 and were whitewashed 15–11, 12–6, 9–3 and 11–8. Then it was the turn for the four Home Countries to be put under the cosh by Basil Kenyon's side: Scotland 0 South Africa 44; Ireland 5 South Africa 17; Wales 3 South Africa 6; England 3 South Africa 8; and France 3 South Africa 25.

So, by 6 August 1955 South Africa had won nine Test matches on the trot. All of South Africa wanted to see this game. The official attendance figure was 95,000, although another 10,000 tickets were being sold on the black market for £100. (In 1955, a pint of beer cost 9d – 27 pints of beer per £1.)

Despite their initial defeat by Western Transvaal, the Lions were now also on a run and were playing superb attacking rugby. The only blot on the record was Eastern Province, but the Lions had been decimated by injury. Bryn Meredith, the Test hooker, was injured but so was Robin Roe, who bravely played with cracked ribs. The scrum with the stricken hooker was destroyed and the game was lost 20–0. However, three big scalps had been claimed on the run-up to the Test.

Before such a match in the modern era, the Test side would be living in a cocoon, unavailable to anyone except the vast army of coaches, doctors, masseurs, shrinks, PR men and women, dieticians, chefs, etc. that surround and protect them.

In contrast, Cecil Pedlow's diary records a busy match-day morning:

> Awoke at 7.30 a.m. Tony O'Reilly off to 8 a.m. Mass. David Gamble phoned 7.40 a.m. (tickets). Breakfast 9.30. Wrote some letters home. Many callers at the room, including a most alluring female, all looking for tickets. Located Tony Chase at 11.30 for the key of his Wolseley car for next day. After I got the key I had some lunch. Autograph-signing session. Left for ground at 2 p.m. for 3.15 kick-off.

The keeper of the diary scored the first try after a Jeff Butterfield break. The Springboks replied with two Van der Schyff penalties and he converted a try by Theunis Briers. Butterfield himself then scored and it was 11–8 at half-time. Although they were down to seven forwards when Reg Higgins had to go off, Cliff Morgan scored a wonderful try with an outside break and O'Reilly and Jim Greenwood scored two more from kicks ahead. All three were converted by Angus Cameron. In the last quarter, Chris Koch, one of the Springboks' greatest-ever prop forwards, scored and Van der Schyff converted. Late into injury time, Briers scored a try. With the Lions ahead by one point (23–22) Van der Schyff prepared to take, what was for him, a reasonably easy kick. This was the man who had beaten the Lions in the opening game with two massive boots. But the conversion veered past the post and the Lions had won a fantastic Test match against form. Afterwards, when asked what he was thinking when Van der Schyff was preparing for that last vital kick, Tony O'Reilly said he was in direct contact with the Vatican, so perhaps his visit to Mass, nine hours earlier, had paid off.

Following huge celebrations and three hours' sleep, the team were off again the next afternoon on a sixteen-hour journey by train to Durban.

Pedlow's diary brought back many great memories for me from 1974. We too treasured our weekly allowance of golden Lions badges that were so hugely prized by South African supporters and schoolkids. Any items to be autographed were left in the team room to be signed, but certainly not immediately before a game in 1974!

Pedlow writes, Saturday 20 August (before second Test, Cape Town): 'We had an autograph session at 12.30 and it was the worst ever, with about 400 books and balls.'

The 1955 side drew the series two Tests each and, strangely enough, lost the two games at sea level in Cape Town and Port Elizabeth, while winning at altitude in Pretoria and Johannesburg.

One day in particular epitomises the good clean fun enjoyed by a party of young international sportsmen (no dwarf-throwing in 1955):

Thursday 7 July

I just made it for 9.30 training feeling very sleepy. It was a horrible, wet morning as the bus took us to the Newlands ground. I hadn't intended to go out, but my conscience pricked me and I borrowed a pair of boots from Doug (Baker) and went out to find the foot was quite OK to run on, but a knock on it was still very sore. It poured during training and we were all soaked.

After a hot shower I felt great and we came back to the hotel for lunch. My clean laundry had come in, so I got a few things organised and then at 2.15 off in bus to a farm – as we thought. However, it had apparently been changed, and we arrived at Van der Stel rugby club in Stellenbosch. From here we went in cars for a drive to the coast and had tea in the Da Gama Hotel at False Bay – a very nice place. We returned then to the Van der Stel rugby club and had an excellent buffet dinner and sing song there. We left by bus and were getting along nicely until the driver tried some short cut and the bus got bogged into a couple of feet of mud and we had to abandon ship. Chaos followed with Masser Dan (liaison officer) telling us not to panic. We then decided to take matters into our own hands and set off on our own. Reg (Higgins) got us lined up in threes, telling us to 'take your time from the clubhouse clock'. Jan, Feb, quick – March! And away we went, singing, 'We're marching on Pretoria' in the rain. Things weren't looking too good when a double decker bus appeared, which we managed to stop. It was going to Cape Town, which was 12 miles away, so we piled aboard. The craic was great here – Cliff (Morgan) gave an interview to Phil (Davies) on our terrible experience, to which Phil said, 'Well, chaps, frankly it was hell!' All the boys were in great form and it was wonderful to see the way they all took it. It reminded me of the time we broke down during our American tour (Queen's University) on our way to the airport in LA. When we reached town we got some taxis and arrived at the hotel about 11.15. Tony and I had a hot bath and went to bed.

John Williams
South Africa 1955
England 1954–65, 9 caps

The Lion with the Over-strong Pass

Four John Williamses were British Lions – 1908's John Williams (Cardiff and Wales), J.P.R. and J.J. from 1974 and John Edward Williams from the 1955 tour. The last died on 5 October 2009 after a long battle with Alzheimer's disease and his obituary said: 'And so departed one of the most talented men ever to grace a rugby pitch. His speed and length of service were exceptional, his break from the base of the scrum explosive and his dummy and sidestep quite devastating. There were many who believed he was the greatest British player since the war.'

So why didn't John Williams get the Test spot in front of the uncapped Dickie Jeeps? Cliff Morgan was very influential on and off the pitch in 1955, and rightly so. Josh Lapsley (my old college coach, who is a living encyclopaedia on scrum-halfs) quizzed Cliff on the choice between Jeeps and Williams. Evidently, John Williams had such a powerful pass that it was difficult to take except in the style of a soccer goalkeeper, and the shorter less powerful pass of Jeeps gave him more time to scan the field to control the game. Cecil Pedlow verified this, telling me in one game he played fly-half to John and he had to move back to wing as he too found the pass too powerful.

Mind you, John Williams was based in London and was able to show the team a little of the nightlife before departure. Cecil's diary: 'After dinner at the Mayfair Hotel we visited the "Blue Angel" [Johnny's natural habitat].'

A Tale of Two Sermons

Extra Time

Robin Roe, hooker on the '55 tour, was an army padre. His colonel gave him an awful ticking-off for preaching too long and stressed that on no account was he ever to exceed 15 minutes proselytising from the pulpit.

Next Sunday, Robin looked down to the exasperated colonel's pew as he reached the allotted quarter of an hour. 'Sir,' he announced, 'the game has gone into extra time.'

Intimidation

A new priest was appointed to Tom Clifford's (1959 Tourist) parish in Limerick. His first sermon lasted half an hour, so Tom went to see him in the vestry.

'Father,' he said, 'your sermon was very good but the limit is 15 minutes ... and next Sunday, I'm coming to Mass with an alarm clock.'

Next Sunday, the priest began his sermon and caught sight of Tom, who pulled back his overcoat to reveal an alarm clock strung around his neck.

1959 Tour Itinerary/Personal Expenses

I include the following 'CONFIDENTIAL' excerpt from the Four Home Unions' Tours Committee British Isles Rugby Football Team Tour of Australia & New Zealand 1959 (courtesy of Syd Millar) ... I'm sure it's past its date of secrecy. Back in 1959, cash made up people's wages in small brown envelopes, received weekly. Some salaried folk might have had bank accounts, but most people only had them for savings. In 1959, the penultimate year of National Service, the average male manual worker's wage was £13 2s 11d (about £13.15) a week and an annual salary averaged £190. One in three UK families owned a car. Old wallets didn't have room for credit cards – they were anathema – and electronic banking was unheard of. James Bond didn't hit the screen for another three years.

Personal Expenses

In Memorandum No. 2 sent out by the committee it was suggested that players should provide themselves with a sum of money to cover their normal expenses. This sum most conveniently to be taken in the form of travellers' cheques which may be obtained from a local bank.

Travellers are not allowed to leave the United Kingdom with more than £20 in Bank of England notes, or silver in excess of £1. Foreign currency notes (including those of Sterling area countries) up to, but not exceeding, £100 may be taken out of the country.

Upon departure from New Zealand members of the Team will be entitled to a refund of an amount up to 14/- in Sterling for personal disbursements (under the Terms and Conditions of the Tour Agreement), and in addition to this members will be entitled to a refund of up to 70/- in Canadian Dollars, as far as can be foreseen at this stage. Members will also be able to exchange up to £10 in Sterling for Canadian Dollars with the Hon. Manager (£1 Sterling = Canadian $2.73).

If members estimate that their requirements of dollar currency is likely to exceed the total of the aforementioned amounts, they will need to make arrangements to provide themselves with the necessary sum out of their personal Foreign Currency Basic Allowance of £100 per annum, and should consult their Bank Managers in this connection. Banks are obliged to endorse individual's passports with a note of foreign currency issued against the Basic Allowance whether this be in the form of currency or travellers' cheques. Those members who wish to obtain dollars from their Basic Allowance are asked to let me [G.H. Geddes, Secretary of the Four Home Unions] know as soon as possible in order that I may forward their passports for this purpose. Upon the necessary entry being made members must return their passports so as to reach me well before the Team assembles at Eastbourne.

It is essential that members should give their careful attention to the foregoing and in particular they should consult their Bank Managers immediately.

So what did they spend money on? What were personal expenses for? Film for cameras (listed in the memo with comparative prices for the UK, Australia, New Zealand and USA), stamps, stationery, a coffee or a soft drink when relaxing on a beach, admission fees to the cinema (one of the few forms of entertainment), toiletries, and souvenirs from the exotic locations they visited over four months.

Itinerary for British Isles Tour 1959

This totalled 123 hours of travel just for to and from match destinations.

The following are the Travel and Hotel arrangements for the Tour. Travel times may be subject to some small alterations and if Rongotai Aerodrome is opened in time then arrival and departure times for Wellington will be altered.

Sunday, 14 June: Arrive Auckland from Australia by Air. 10.00 p.m. Stay at Royal Hotel.

Monday, 15 June: Auckland – Napier. Plane; 2 Special D.C.3s. Reporting time 9.00 a.m. Take-off time 10.00 a.m. Arrive airport 11.35 a.m. Arrive Hotel 11.55 a.m. Stay at Masonic Hotel.

Monday, 22 June: Napier – Gisborne. Rail-Car (ordinary service) Leave 8.20 a.m. Arrive 12.57 p.m. Stay at Masonic Hotel.

Thursday, 25 June: Gisborne – Auckland. Plane; 2 Special D.C.3s. Reporting time 9.00 a.m. Take-off time 9.35 a.m. Arrive airport 11.10 a.m. Arrive Hotel Noon. Stay at Royal Hotel.

Sunday, 28 June: Auckland – Christchurch. Plane; Viscount (ordinary service). Reporting time 1.00 p.m. Take-off time 2.00 p.m. Arrive airport 3.55 p.m. Arrive Hotel 4.30 p.m. Stay at United Service Hotel.

Thursday, 2 July: Christchurch – Dunedin. Plane; 2 Special D.C.3s. Reporting time 9.00 a.m. Take-off time 9.40 a.m. Arrive Airport 11.10 a.m. Arrive Hotel 11.45 a.m. Stay at City Hotel.

Sunday, 5 July: Dunedin – Timaru. Special Rail-Car. Depart 9.00 a.m. Arrive 12.45 p.m. Stay at Grosvenor Hotel.

Thursday, 9 July: Timaru – Invercargill. Special Rail-Car. Depart 9.00 a.m. Arrive 5.05 p.m. Lunch at City Hotel, Dunedin. Stay at Grand Hotel.

Sunday, 12 July: Invercargill – Queenstown. Special Motor Coaches. Depart 9.00 a.m. Arrive 5.00 p.m. Stay at O'Connell's Hotel.

Monday, 13 July: Queenstown – Dunedin. Special Motor Coaches. Depart 1.00 p.m. Arrive 6.30 p.m. Stay at City Hotel.

Sunday, 19 July: Dunedin – Christchurch. Plane; 2 Special D.C.3s. Reporting time 1.45 p.m. Take-off time 2.30 p.m. Arrive Airport 4.00 p.m. Arrive Hotel 4.35 p.m. Stay at United Service Hotel.

Monday, 20 July: Christchurch – Greymouth. Special Motor

Coaches. Depart 9.00 a.m. Arrive 4.30 p.m. Stay at Albion Hotel.

Thursday, 23 July: Greymouth – Christchurch. Rail-Car (ordinary service). Depart 10.30 a.m. Arrive 3.40 p.m. Stay at United Service Hotel.

Sunday, 26 July: Christchurch – Blenheim. Plane; 2 Special D.C.3s. Reporting time 1.45 p.m. Take-off time 2.25 p.m. Arrive Airport 3.45 p.m. Arrive Hotel 4.05 p.m.

Thursday, 30 July: Blenheim – Wellington. Plane; 2 Special D.C.3s. Reporting time 9.00 a.m. Take-off time 9.35 a.m. Arrive Airport 10.15 a.m. Arrive Hotel 11.25 p.m. Stay at Hotel St. George.

Sunday, 2 August: Wellington – Wanganui. Special Rail-Car. Depart 8.55 a.m. Arrive 1.30 p.m. Stay at Grand Hotel.

Thursday, 6 August: Wanganui – New Plymouth. Special Rail-Car. Depart 9.00 a.m. Arrive 12.44 p.m. Stay at Imperial Hotel.

Sunday, 9 August: New Plymouth – Palmerston North. Special Rail-Car. Depart 8.30 a.m. Arrive 1.23 p.m. Stay at Commercial Hotel.

Wednesday, 12 August: Palmerston North – Wellington. Special Rail-Car. Depart 9.08 a.m. Arrive 11.18 a.m. Stay at St. George Hotel.

Sunday, 16 August: Wellington – Taumarunui. Special Rail-Car. Depart 8.55 a.m. Arrive 4.55 p.m. Lunch at Taihape. Stay at Taumarunui Hotel.

Thursday, 20 August: Taumarunui – Hamilton. Special Motor Coaches. Depart 9.00 a.m. Arrive 3.30 p.m. Lunch at Waitomo Caves. Stay at Commercial Hotel.

Sunday, 23 August: Hamilton – Palmerston North. Plane; 2 Special D.C.3s. Reporting time 10.00 a.m. Take-off time 10.35 a.m. Arrive Airport 11.55 a.m. Arrive Hotel 12.20 p.m. Lunch at Commercial Hotel. Palmerston North – Masterton. Special Motor Coaches. Depart 1.30 p.m. Arrive 3.15 p.m. Stay at Empire Hotel.

Wednesday, 26 August: Masterton – Paraparaumu Airport. Special Motor Coaches. Depart 8.30 a.m. Arrive 11.00 a.m. Paraparaumu Airport – Christchurch. Plane; 2 Special D.C.3s. Take-off time 11.30 a.m. Arrive Airport 1.05 p.m. Arrive Hotel 1.40 p.m. Stay at United Service Hotel.

Sunday, 30 August: Christchurch – Wellington. Plane; 2 Special D.C.3s. Reporting time 2.00 p.m. Take-off time 2.40 p.m. Arrive Airport 4.15.p.m. Arrive Hotel 5.25 p.m. Stay at Hotel St. George.

Thursday, 3 September: Wellington – Auckland. Plane; 2 Special

D.C.3s. Reporting time 9.00 a.m. Take-off time 10.25 a.m. Arrive Airport 12.20 p.m. Arrive Hotel 1.25 p.m. Stay at Royal Hotel.

Sunday, 6 September: Auckland – Rotorua. Special Rail-Car. Depart 8.30 a.m. Arrive 1.00 p.m. Stay at Grand Hotel.

Thursday, 10 September: Rotorua –Whangarei. Special Rail-Car. Depart 8.30 a.m. Arrive 5.50 p.m. Lunch at Royal Hotel, Auckland. Stay at Whangarei Hotel.

Monday, 14 September: Whangarei – Auckland. Special Rail-Car. Depart 9.00 a.m. Arrive 1.00 p.m. Stay at Royal Hotel.

Tuesday, 22 September: Depart Auckland for Canada 4.50 p.m. by air.

Bill Mulcahy
New Zealand and Australia 1959, 2 caps; South Africa 1962, 4 caps
Ireland 1958–65, 35 caps

The Lions have had many 'battles' – the Battle of Potchefstroom 1962, the Battle of Auckland 1966, the Battle of Canterbury 1971 and the two Battles of Port Elizabeth 1974.

In 1962, the Lions played South Africa Combined Services – a fixture never to be repeated. The Combined team – army, police and air force – had been locked up in a prison for two weeks and indoctrinated with tales of the Boer War. Syd Millar was up against Chris Bezuidenhout, who was pulling the scrum down. Syd whacked him and was warned by the referee. Bezuidenhout continued to scrum illegally and as Syd couldn't sort it out himself he asked Bill Mulcahy for a little assistance.

As Bill explains it, 'I misjudged it a little,' as he swung through from the second row. Syd's nose was badly broken. Bill reckons it was worth it because Syd destroyed the whole scrum on his own.

Standing Up to the Opposition
Bill Mulcahy said: 'Data from the Metropolitan Life Insurance Company, 1959, only shows male height up to 6 ft 2 in. including information on army personnel. David Marques, our tallest forward, stood 6 ft 6 in., towering above most players in those days. Running, or stretched out in a tackle, the huge gentleman's presence could not be missed on the pitch. Marques further extended his immense stature throughout the tour by wearing a black bowler hat befitting his position in the City of London.

Ray Prosser sabotaged the hat on many Saturday nights – the method shall remain unmentioned – but the hat was always sent to the cleaners and remained intact to the end of the tour.

'I spent the afternoon of 27 June 1959 sat in the stand beside renowned Welsh rugby writer J.B.G. Thomas when the Lions played Auckland. The Maori, Albert (Albie) Pryor, was playing for Auckland in the second row. He was a delightful personality off the pitch but notably over-vigorous on it. In one particular ruck, he danced on David Marques' head. Following the encounter, Marques required medical attention. After he'd been patched up and was ready to continue play, Marques stood up and shook Pryor's hand. I turned to J.B.G. Thomas and said, "Jesus, I've seen it all now."

'After the game, I sought Marques out and asked him about the Albie Pryor incident. "You wouldn't understand, you're Irish," he replied. "I shook his hand and called him a cad to make him feel small."

'"With an attitude like that, no wonder you lost the British Empire!" I said.'

Phil Horrocks-Taylor
New Zealand and Australia 1959, 1 cap
England 1958–64, 9 caps

Phil Horrocks-Taylor flew out to New Zealand in 1959 to replace the injured Mick English. Such were the injury problems in the side, he was not given much time to settle in, playing against Wairapara Bush as soon as he arrived and the third Test at Christchurch on the Saturday when the Lions lost 22–8.

He had also caused the Twickenham crowd to boo for the first time in history – not at him but at the late, heavy tackle made upon him by the Australian Jim Lenehan during the game against the Tourists in 1958. Phil was unable to continue and every time Lenehan touched the ball for the remainder of the game, he was loudly booed.

Tony O'Reilly tells a humorous story about an Ireland v England match when in the dying minutes of the game Horrocks-Taylor made a wonderful break and scored the winning try. His opposite number, Mick English, normally a great crash tackler, had missed his man. Behind the posts, the Irish team awaited the conversion. Mick was receiving a bollocking: 'Jesus, Mick, how the hell did you miss him?'

'Well,' replied Mick, 'Horrocks went one way, Taylor went the other and I ended up tackling the bloody hyphen.'

(It's a great story, but the two Lions out-halves never actually faced each other at international level.)

Benefiting from Injury

'In my mid-70s, it gives me great pleasure to reminisce about rugby, which was of course when I was in my prime of life,' said Horrocks-Taylor. 'I was lucky enough to be a player during the late '50s and early '60s, so it is no surprise that a story involving Tony O'Reilly is brought to mind.

'At Tony's 50th birthday celebrations, I spotted Mick English across the room and went over to him, only to be momentarily taken aback by his refusal to shake hands. It had been many years since we had met each other on the playing field and I didn't think there was any grudge held over from our playing days. His face fell and, sad and despondent, he said, "I can't shake hands with you – O'Reilly ruined both our lives." I knew exactly what he meant – the hyphen story amused many a dinner party on the rugby circuit even if it wasn't true.

'The story in fact does a disservice to Mick, because he was one of the best fly-halfs I ever faced. God bless him, 2010 is growing further away. Playing on a Wolfhounds tour, I noticed my then unknown opposite number eying me with obvious evil intent – clearly thinking that this double-barrelled Englishman was a descendant of the absentee landlords of the unhappy past (totally untrue incidentally). He was thwarted, however, by my open-side who was doing such a splendid job in blocking Mick's intrusions that I heard this exasperated shout, "Hey, boy, out the right so I can have a cut at the feller."

'Mick's injury on the 1959 Lions tour, and later Bev Risman's, led to my call-up as replacement, for which I shall be ever grateful to them both.'

Syd Millar CBE
New Zealand and Australia 1959, 3 caps; South Africa 1962,
   4 caps; South Africa 1968, 2 caps
Ireland 1958–70, 37 caps

Dr Syd Millar is the greatest rugby person I have ever met. His international career spanned three decades. He immediately became active when coaching was in its infancy in the British Isles, coaching Ireland from 1973 to '75 and the Lions in 1974. Syd managed Billy

Beaumont's 1980 Lions side in South Africa, and Ireland at the first World Cup in 1987. He was President of the Ulster Branch in 1985, the IRFU in 1995 and Chairman of the International Board from 2003 to 2007. He was inducted into the International Hall of Fame in 2003. In 1992, Syd received an honorary doctorate in science from the University of Ulster and the Freedom of Ballymena, his home town, in 2004. In 2007, he received the *Légion d'honneur*.

In 1974, he was a hard but fair taskmaster and astute in his choice of referees. The big danger to our lineout was John Williams, easily the best jumper in South Africa. Syd spread the rumour (knowing that the source would report back to the South African selectors) that we regarded John Williams as soft. Williams was dropped, Gordon Brown breathed a sigh of relief and ruled the lineout in the vital third Test.

One of Syd's proudest moments was when at a ripe old age in the early 1980s he turned out for a winning Ballymena 5th XV in the McCambley Cup Final at Ravenhill with his two sons, Jonathan and Peter.

Truth and Lies

'The Irish team travelled to Wales in the late '60s for a Five Nations match in Cardiff,' recalled Syd. 'While sat in the lounge at Dublin Airport after a team training session in the morning we sipped at a few soft drinks when some half a dozen supporters, obviously golfers from their conversation, arrived looking forward to playing Royal Porthcawl. (The Irish team in those days was based in Porthcawl for the Welsh game.)

'The gentlemen proceeded to have a few large gin and tonics before we boarded and continued with the gin and tonics during the flight.

'We disembarked, got to Porthcawl and the next sighting of the gentlemen was in the bar adjoining the dining room where they were all in very high spirits and very noisy. I noticed one of them had worn a white glove on his right hand at Dublin Airport and on the flight to Cardiff and still wore it in the hotel bar. Curiosity got the better of me and I took the opportunity to ask one of his friends. "Oh, he promised his wife not to touch a drop of alcohol over the weekend," he said.

'The next sighting of the party was in the dining room where, as well as their food, they consumed a large amount of wine, followed by port. Suddenly, one of them rushed to the door of the dining room towards the toilets. He never made it. His dinner reappeared on the floor – not a pretty sight for the rest of the diners. The group made a hasty exit, hugely embarrassed, as the staff cleared up the revolting mess.

'Next evening, they appeared in the bar again but very subdued and quiet. The head waiter approached them. "Had a good day's golf, gentlemen?" They nodded. "Well then," he said, "I will leave the menu with you and I'll be back in ten minutes when perhaps you might let me know what you want to throw up tonight."'

'On another Welsh trip, Cambridge University, who in those days had a very strong fixture list, made their way by coach to play Cardiff. With a South African in the squad, the team wag had arranged that when they neared the Welsh border he would ask if everyone had their passports. Everyone other than the South African player answered affirmatively. The poor man was distraught. Other than the Colours match, this was the biggest game of the season.

'He had talked for weeks about playing against Barry John, Gareth Edwards et al. and was virtually in tears. After discussion, a solution arose – hide him in the luggage compartment. The bus stopped and he was suitably concealed surrounded by kit bags.

'Further up the road, the bus stopped for a few minutes as if to have the passports examined at border control. Half an hour later they let him out, very relieved and delighted he could play. Going back, they repeated the experience. The bus stopped at the English border and moved off, but due to the pints consumed in Cardiff and the cans consumed on the bus, the poor fella was forgotten about and not discovered until the coach arrived back at Cambridge hours later.'

Stan Coughtrie
New Zealand and Australia 1959
Scotland 1959–63, 11 caps

Stan Coughtrie was unique in his era as he was a tall scrum-half, 6 ft 2 in. He was unfortunate to sustain a serious back injury on his Lions tour and returned home. He missed two seasons but came back in 1962 to gain another seven caps for Scotland.

Follow My Leader

Stan commented: 'In the '50s and '60s, the Edinburgh Football Club – Edinburgh Accies – had an annual London tour, playing Wasps on Saturday and St Thomas' Hospital on Monday. The usual routine involved leaving Edinburgh by train late on Friday afternoon to arrive at King's Cross, after which we made our way to the Regent Palace Hotel just off

Piccadilly Circus. At the time, the Regent Palace had a slightly risqué reputation, but I can assure you this in no way influenced the club secretariat or players in the choice.

'Saturday's match against Wasps was taken very seriously and on arrival at the hotel it was straight to bed. After a lazy morning it was out to Sudbury by Tube for the match.

'Our club secretary at the time, Jim Stevenson, had played for the Accies and had also played cricket for Scotland. Also with us was the great Edinburgh Accie and Scotland flanker W.I.D. (Douglas) Elliot. Jim, who was a fine piper, proudly piped us onto the pitch – our team walking behind him to a warm welcome and applause from a large Wasps crowd.

'Victorious, we enjoyed wonderful Wasps hospitality throughout the evening and reluctantly had to return to Piccadilly. Jim Stevenson by this time was in fine form and played his pipes non-stop on the Tube all the way back to central London. The other night passengers seemed as delighted as him.

'We reached our stop and filed out of the train and onto the escalator. Jim led the way, still playing his pipes, followed by Douglas Elliot, an impressive figure with huge straight shoulders accentuated by a fawn coat that made him look like the side of a house, and the rest of the team behind, like a lobster migration caravan.

'I'm not precisely sure what happened, as I was quite far down the file, but . . . as Jim and Douglas approached the top of the escalator, Douglas staggered backwards. Everyone fell like ninepins – bodies, kit bags and grips. Luckily no other passengers were on our bit of the escalator and no injuries were sustained, probably due to the relaxing effect of the odd beer or wee dram taken at Wasps.

'Behind Jim, we tried to regroup. Leading the front, he had no idea what had happened so continued marching on playing his pipes. As we waited to see if everyone was all right, Jim marched out of the station, strode across Piccadilly Circus ignoring all traffic, still piping, and advanced straight through the swing doors into the Regent Palace Hotel. Regulated breathing and concentration on the great skirl kept him oblivious. His impassioned piping remained unbroken as he made his way directly to the bar and was astonished to find he was completely on his own, until we caught up with him and were able to reveal the details to him about his solitary march.'

4

THE SWINGING SIXTIES

Ray Hunter
South Africa 1962
Ireland 1962–6, 10 caps

Ray Hunter's first love was not rugby but cricket. Indeed, he was capped at cricket five years before his rugby debut against England in 1962. He was a right-handed batsman and medium-pace bowler, and he scored 74 not out against the Free Foresters in his first Irish game in 1957. I had an auntie who lived in Lisburn and in the summer I often went to Wallace Park to see Ray show off his talents for Lisburn. He was a big, strong-running, hard-tackling winger and centre for CIYMS, Ulster and Ireland, and brother of Lawrence who played for Ireland in 1968.

A Name to Remember

'I was selected on the wing to play against Northern Transvaal on the 1962 Lions tour,' said Ray. 'The game was regarded as the fifth Test. Northern Transvaal fielded an extremely strong pack with five Springboks, including the huge Mof Myburgh at prop and the brilliant Frik du Preez at flanker. Piet Uys, the Springbok scrum-half, played his international position and Mannetjies Roux, who had caused mayhem on the 1960–61 Springbok tour with his attitude, especially against Cardiff, played in the centre.

'The Lions had shown great respect to Northern Transvaal by picking 11 players who were to feature later in the first drawn Test (3–3) in Johannesburg. The Lions side that day was:

15 Tom Kiernan
14 Arthur Smith (captain)
13 Ken Jones
12 Mick Weston
11 Ray Hunter
10 Richard Sharp

9 Dickie Jeeps
1 Syd Millar
2 Bryn Meredith
3 Kingsley Jones
4 Keith Rowlands
5 Bill Mulcahy
6 John Douglas
7 Alun Pask
8 Budge Rogers

'Richard Sharp, the exceptional English fly-half, was regarded as a certainty for the first Test but this was not to be due to a contentious incident that is still talked about. From a scrum, Sharp had taken a position on the left but moved right from Jeeps' pass. Roux tackled him high, with his head breaking Sharp's cheekbone. Roux, although knocked out, was able to continue. As no substitutes were allowed, Mike Weston moved to fly-half and I moved to the centre to mark – guess who – Mannetjies Roux. For the rest of the game I was subjected to late tackles, early tackles and obstruction. The loss of Richard Sharp was too much for us, we lost 14–6 and as I trooped off I indignantly asked Mr Roux what the hell he was at.

'"That was for what you did to Jannie Engelbrecht at Lansdowne Road last year when we played Ireland."

'"I wasn't even playing," I protested. "Who the hell do you think I am?"

'"Niall Brophy," he replied.

'"No – meet Ray Hunter."

'At least I was ready for Mannetjies when I next met him at the Battle of Potchefstroom.'

W.J. McBride MBE
South Africa 1962, 2 caps; New Zealand, Australia and Canada 1966, 3 caps; South Africa 1968, 4 caps; New Zealand and Australia 1971, 4 caps; South Africa 1974, 4 caps
Ireland 1962–75, 63 caps

Willie John had a large area of land behind his house. He had cleared away the rough scrub and his vegetable garden, bantam hens and lawn were his pride and joy. However, he had a big problem when he went off on one of his many tours – his goat.

The goat was tethered and each evening, when Willie shifted the rope and pole so that it had new pasture to graze, he would talk to the animal. When he was away, the goat pined for him and would break the tether and eat the vegetables.

Shifting It

McBride said: 'Top-level rugby, now a professional game, is played in superb modern stadia around the world that reek of money. Corporate followers watch the action and excitement from luxurious facilities. Hospitality is a huge industry, now part of the game.

'When I stop to think of the long road the game has travelled, it evokes memories. It's not quite the smell of success but . . .

'I can go back 50 years and reminisce fondly on how I joined a little junior club, close to my home in Moneyglass, the year I left school. Randalstown was a young club without money or resources. Lord O'Neill of Shane's Castle had kindly allowed the club to play on a fairly flat piece of land within the castle grounds.

'The club literally had a set of posts and a hut to change in. I played on the second team – I think you had to own a motor car to qualify for the first XV. I would ride my bicycle to the game on Saturdays, a distance of five or six miles, and after, wearily pedal home.

'We had a rota system and every four weeks our duty was to report an hour early to the ground for our responsibility as dung duty shit-shifters. With a wheelbarrow and shovels we collected and removed sheep droppings and cow pats from the pitch. However, if we were playing a team of city slickers from Belfast, we didn't bother. Being country boys we found it gave us a great psychological advantage. We didn't mind the occasional clump of crud and the texture and smell of it could gross out some opposition players.

'Since those raw beginnings, I played rugby all over the world, including five Lions tours, but I remember fondly those wonderful days at Randalstown RFC.'

David Rollo
South Africa 1962
Scotland 1959–68, 40 caps

David Rollo had his nose broken in his first international game against England in 1959 – no substitutes in those days! After running repairs he returned and was ever present on the Scottish team for two seasons. He could prop on either side of the scrum. The first international I saw was Ireland v Scotland, and David Rollo, from schoolboy to Fife club, was the first player I ever saw with his socks rolled down. His legs looked like pillars of granite, but our PE teacher, Ken Armstrong, warned us not to emulate him, as rolled-down socks were regarded as being improperly dressed.

For the Love of Rugby . . .
Braids Hills Hotel – lunchtime (Murrayfield, 4 January 1964, Scotland v France)

'I relaxed as forward reserve, able for the first time to enjoy my lunch. Normally I only had a plain omelette, so that day I had the full three courses. Then, after the meal was finished, Charlie Drummond (convenor of selection) said, "Come on, Dave; come over to the Buckstone and have a pint of beer" – then a second one. I finished that and halfway through the third, John Raw (secretary) came in and started speaking to Charlie. They called me to come over and I wondered what was up. Charlie told me I was playing! I could have fallen through the floor. Play – on a full lunch and two and a half pints of beer?

'Cameron Boyle, who should have been playing that day, had called off with flu. It was my good fortune, as I kept the prop position for the rest of the season.

'After that incident, all players were banned from taking a drink before a game. I learnt after that I could eat a good meal before playing – in fact, "stoke the boiler".'

From the Driver's Seat
County Ground, Gosforth, November 1962, Baa Baas v Canada

'We came back from the game to the hotel in North Shields with a quick change on the bus for dinner at Gosforth. Everyone on board – but no driver! A shout went up from the captain, Ron Jacobs, "Come on, Dave; you know what to do." I had already driven one in Cardiff and also in South Africa on the Lions tour.

'We started off for Gosforth and halfway up the motorway the blue flashing lights appeared. I stopped, jumped out of the seat and went back to sit with the rest of the players. The police appeared – no driver to be seen. They asked, "Where is he?" No answer. "Right then, the whole team will have to come to the police station." Time for me to own up. So with a bit of negotiating the players continued to the dinner with another driver and I left with the cops.

'The understanding was that if I made a personal appearance at the court the following Monday, there would be a good chance I would not be charged. So, 7 a.m. Monday: leave Cupar Station. 9.30 a.m. arrive Newcastle. 10 a.m. appear at North Shields Court to meet up with the lawyer pleading my case.

'I sit in the waiting room with weekend drunks and prostitutes. I am charged with taking away the bus, no PSV licence, and as my own driving licence was just out of date, am charged on that count also. I am fined £60 and disqualified for six months.

'I have to face my wife, who was not amused. The "I was just helping out the lads" defence fell on deaf ears, both in court and at home.'

Peter Wright
South Africa 1962
England 1960–2, 13 caps

Points Mean Prizes

Peter Wright, who featured in a player profile by Basil Werdan in *Rugby World*'s 1962 April issue, was unfortunate not to play any Test matches on the Lions tour that year to South Africa. However, despite an injured back, he turned out for nine provincial matches. The wing forward, although wrecked by his injury as far as international representation was concerned, continued to play in his old position for Devizes A XV, a far cry from the play he experienced in Blackheath, his former club.

Forwards are regarded as hard men both on and off the field and especially in the clubrooms, where many a drinking session with opposition makes up for any insult or assault that occurred on the field of play. Peter, at this time, happened to be a trade manager of Wadworth Brewery, based in Devizes, a marvellous happenstance which he exploited when he decided that a motivational 'carrot', and a jest against the opposition, would be that he provide a jug of beer for every ten points they scored.

With such a hospitable arrangement, the opposition teams endeavoured to make sure they played an open game with plenty of point-scoring opportunities and equally for his own side to defend against such an assault.

Legend has it that Devizes once beat the opposition by 70 points and Peter honoured the wager and set up seven jugs – probably four pints per pitcher – so twenty-eight pints were furnished for the team's excellent play. Three and a half gallons is a fair amount on anyone's tab regardless of their connections. Undoubtedly they were shared, as there were no reports of hospital admissions for alcoholic poisoning.

Mike Weston
South Africa 1962, 6 caps
England 1960–8, 29 caps

Mike Weston, like C.D. Aarvold, was both a classical centre and a product of Durham School – an Old Dunelmian. He captained England on five occasions. He continued to work as an administrator after retirement and was the manager of England at the first World Cup in 1987.

Media Secrecy
'When Durham played Cheshire in the 1968 County Championship,' recalled Mike, 'it was imperative we negate the threat of the giant Scottish second row Peter Stagg, who at 6 ft 10 in. was the tallest second row in first-class rugby. We exceeded our ambitions and even scored a try from a planned lineout move.

'I was captain of England that season and on the way to Edinburgh to play Scotland we trained at Peebles and discussed the same Peter Stagg and the nuisance his stature could be. We also decided to execute the exact same lineout move that led to a try when Durham had played Cheshire.

'The forwards moved to a secluded part of the ground and, in the middle of their clandestine lineout session, noticed a gentleman with binoculars behind a shrub who was following the practice and every move. A Scottish spy! This was totally foreign to the ethos of amateur rugby. The entire pack sprinted to the bush intending to shake the miscreant out of the branches and perhaps ruck him in the fashion of the day (I haven't seen a proper ruck for years) when the culprit explained in a wonderful Borders accent, "Dinnae worry, dinnae worry. Ma name's Bill McLaren, I'm covering the match frae the BBC and I promise I willnae say a word about your moves or codes."

'Satisfied by the honest demeanour of the interloper, the practice continued. Next day at Murrayfield the planned lineout move worked a treat and Mike Coulman, the great Moseley and Lions prop, scored a try to win the match.

'At the tea room after the game, the BBC "spy" smiled as he offered me a Hawick ball [famous boiled sweets that Bill was renowned for offering people] and whispered in my ear, "I didnae tell." What a wonderful man.'

Tom Kiernan
South Africa 1962, 1 cap; South Africa 1968, 4 caps
Ireland 1960–73, 54 caps

Tom Kiernan was my first Irish captain and I thought he was a superb leader. However, I was not expecting the silent treatment! After lunch at the Marine Hotel in Dun Laoghaire, Tom would make us sit for an hour, instructing us to turn over and over and over the simple things that were the responsibilities of our position. If we all did the simple things well, then the bigger things would happen, he said.

Have you ever tried to sit in total silence for an hour with 14 other players? It is bloody difficult. Mickey Quinn fell asleep during his baptism in 1973, as Willie John had continued the practice, and got an awful dig in the ribs from Ray McLoughlin for his irreverence.

I felt sorry for Tommy as he had every chance to captain a Triple Crown and Grand Slam team in 1972 when after leading us to victory in Paris and Twickenham we were let down by Scotland and Wales as they refused to play in Dublin.

Defends the Queen's English

Tom recalled: 'During a provincial game on the 1968 Lions tour to South Africa, a young Gareth Edwards was becoming increasingly agitated with the decisions of the local referee. At one point, he called him a "cheating fucker".

'The referee told Gareth he was sending him off for bad language. Before Gareth took his marching orders, as captain I sauntered up to the referee and asked him what the problem was.

'"Your scrum-half called me a fucker and I'm sending him off," he retorted, somewhat aggrieved.

'"He certainly wasn't," I protested. "He was talking Welsh to his out-half partner."'

'"That's all right, then," he replied. Gareth was spared and the game continued.

'Gareth's out-half partner that day was the genius Mike Gibson from Ulster, who only spoke the Queen's English.'

Delme Thomas
New Zealand, Australia and Canada 1966, 2 caps; South Africa 1968, 2 caps; New Zealand and Australia 1971, 3 caps
Wales 1966–74, 25 caps

Delme Thomas had one of the greatest sergeant jumps ever measured in rugby. At 6 ft 3 in. he was not particularly tall by modern standards, but he could leap like a salmon and also tap (not slap) with total control to Gareth Edwards, who would service the best Welsh back line in rugby (my opinion), with the best lineout ball – fast ball.

Delme played in the Battle of Auckland in 1966 and at one lineout Willie John noticed the prostrate body of Syd Millar, an opposition forward, back down the pitch.

'What happened to him?' asked Willie.

'He got a tap with a size 13,' replied Delme.

An Alarming Room-mate
'Contrary to popular belief about those of us who are a certain age now, I can recall the '60s,' claimed Delme. 'Touring with the British Lions was a great experience for me, especially when my room-mate was Willie John McBride, whom I met on my first tour in 1966.

'The 24-hour flight to Auckland seemed longer than a day. On the first night, after arriving at 3 a.m., the fire alarm blared. Startled and concerned for my room-mate, I looked across to the other bed – already empty. Hmm . . . the entire hotel had been evacuated and staff were unable to find out why the alarm had gone off. Not knowing the man as I do now it did not occur to me that it could be – him? Now I know beyond doubt who caused the mass exodus.

'On the second day in Auckland he suggested that we go to the cinema and in those days the national anthem played before the film started. It started, I stood up and as I did so he said, "Bloody behave yourself and sit down."

'As the tour progressed we became very close friends. I discovered if

Willie forgot our room keys, he did not bother to go down to reception but just put his shoulder to the door. This happened at most of the hotels where we stayed. Being the paymaster on tour, every Sunday morning he issued our allowance of ten shillings a day, i.e. £3.10s per week. He had the payment register on one side of the desk in front of him and the hotel damages book on the other side. Not one week went by without us having to pay towards some damage or other as no one would own up, but usually there was only one culprit (the great Irishman).

'Weekly mock court sessions went through the events of the previous seven days and the judge was of course W.J.M. On one occasion a question arose regarding the damages fund. "Why should we all be made to pay for damages we have not caused?" Straight-faced and upholding the ethos of team spirit for which he is renowned, McBride answered sternly, "WE ARE ALL IN THIS TOGETHER, BOYS!"

'I suggested to the management at the end of the tour that in future instead of 32, perhaps 31 players and a 'carpenter' should be taken on tour.

'It was a great experience to have travelled with the British Lions on the three tours.'

Roger Young
New Zealand, Australia and Canada 1966, 3 caps; South Africa 1968, 1 cap
Ireland 1965–71, 26 caps

Roger Young attended Methodist college in Belfast where Josh Lapsley then taught PE. Josh noticed Roger was a great mover in the gym and immediately considered him potentially good rugby material. However, when it came to rugby practices, he was a reluctant participant. It was then that Josh discovered Roger was on the books of Distillery, an Irish League First Division soccer club, and was turning out for their third XI. With much cajoling and help from family, Josh managed to persuade Roger Young to switch codes. He was soon playing for Methodist College first XV and Ulster Schools. The rest is history and Roger remains one of the nicest people in rugby.

Beating the Spies
Roger said: 'I missed the chance to join with the Ulster Lions who gathered in Belfast City Hall on 3 February 2012, as I was scheduled for

a knee operation and my surgeon wouldn't sanction the flight from South Africa back to Northern Ireland. I'm sorry I missed the affair; I'm sure plenty of tales were told. It would have been wonderful to have met up with players I looked up to before my time and with youngsters who have come through since. Had I made the occasion I would have taken great pleasure relating this tale.

'On a very rare occasion, Willie John was entrusted with giving the lineout signals on the Irish team. I was quite new in the "park" and enthusiastically followed the mighty man to the letter! Playing Wales one time, a certain spy informed us before the kick-off that the Welsh were aware of our lineout code. This demanded a change in plan, so W.J. decided to shout out a code to me so that I could inform the wing three-quarter (in those days it was the wing who threw the ball in!).

'Well, he decided a well-known car name (e.g. Ford, Austin, MG, etc.) would go to number 3 in the lineout and an insect's name for the number 5 position. It was beyond anyone's comprehension to think of a code for the back of the lineout, so that was left clear.

'Everything was working very well and the Welsh were flummoxed – *until* the great Willie John shouts out to me "Volkswagen Beetle".

'Well, what can you do, except have a titter and hope for the best? Great days and great times, and, despite the cock-up, I think we won that particular game.'

Ken Kennedy
New Zealand, Australia and Canada 1966, 4 caps; South Africa 1974
Ireland 1965–75, 45 caps

The dodo is now extinct, so is the striking hooker. Ken Kennedy was the best striker of a ball I ever played with; he was like a cobra. He was also meticulous in his preparations – he practised yoga so he could get into the most contortionist-like positions in the scrum. He hung from the wall bars for half an hour at a time (so it was rumoured around Belfast) so he could hang from his prop's attempt to retrieve a ball from the opposition number 8's feet. He is certainly comparable to the great Lions hookers like Bryn Meredith, Ronnie Dawson and Bunner Travers. He has also kept my body together for the last 30 years.

The Man with the Iron Chest

'My father was a GP in Holywood, Co. Down,' said Ken. 'As a student at Queen's University he had boxed and played rugby with Blair Mayne and so knew well the escapades of this Ulster hero. When the Second World War came, Blair Mayne joined the army and my father joined the navy, and it was only after the war that their paths crossed again.

'Paddy (as Blair Mayne had become known) lived in Newtownards and one day, on his way home, he stopped at our house for a drink with my father. I was a raw 12-year-old schoolboy and was summoned to meet the man with the "iron chest". My father introduced me and told me to hit Paddy's chest as hard as I could. As he was a giant of a man, with hands like shovels, I was apprehensive. Later in my rugby career I came across the likes of Walter Spanghero and Moss Keane, men with huge hands, but none to compare to Blair Mayne, who I also learnt wore size 13 gloves. When I hit him there was a feeling like hitting a stone wall and an echo banging like a steel drum. I was totally taken in, believing this giant man did have an iron chest. At my age in Ireland we knew all about giants like Finn McCool. Now I had met one!

'It was only later that my father told me Paddy had been put in a plaster of Paris corset to treat his long-standing spinal problems. However, the memory of that meeting of the man with the iron chest still remains vivid in my mind.'

Ray McLoughlin
New Zealand, Australia and Canada 1966, 3 caps; New Zealand and Australia 1971
Ireland 1962–75, 40 caps

Some people reckon that the Irish aren't that bright. I would challenge any of them to sit on the back of the bus when Ray McLoughlin, Tom Grace and Moss Keane were setting each other, and solving themselves, problems of logic.

We all had the same Adidas bags in those days and after training one day I took the wrong bag. Once I opened it, I realised whose it was – Ray McLoughlin's. The solution to every possible problem was in that bag – studs of every length and diameter, toilet roll, plasters, a cosh (God help anyone trying to mug him on the way to the game). Ray McLoughlin left nothing to chance and was one of the great thinkers of the game as well as having immense strength.

Ray McLoughlin's Thoughts on Lions Touring

'Perhaps the most defining landmark of rugby in the old days was the Lions tour. It was an experience money just could not buy. So many things about it are different from a modern Lions tour and we will never see the old style, full of true adventure, again.

'The New Zealand/Australia 1966 tour took also took in Hawaii, San Francisco, Vancouver, Toronto and New York. It was a much bigger world then with a greater sense of wonder for the young man travelling 13,000 miles to the other end of the globe.

'Still coffee-aroma fresh, I remember my first breakfast in Perth and I can recall the excitement as I looked forward to playing for the Lions for five months in Australia, New Zealand and Canada. What more could a young man ask for? The fact that you had no money, you could not buy an air ticket home and you faced almost half a year of rugby increased the sense of transportation into a different world. I also remember, as if it were yesterday, arriving in Christchurch, New Zealand, for the first time, late at night, to be welcomed by a choir of Maori girls singing welcome songs and at that moment I fell in love with New Zealand. For me, New Zealand holds a special magic – the romanticism of the names as they roll off the tongue . . . Rotorua, Whangarei, the Bay of Islands, Milford Sound.

'Only 18 supporters made it out to the 1966 tour in New Zealand, which increased the sense of expedition and adventure. Brian O'Driscoll will never have the experience of playing in front of a 60,000 crowd with 59,982 shouting for the other side. Surreal! But this lack of crowd support created a stronger bond within the team.

'We had an excellent relationship with the press; they stayed in the same hotels, they mixed with us in the dining rooms, they travelled on our buses and never did an indiscretion leak into the papers.

'Of course in 1966 and 1971 we were very much in the amateur era. We had no money, except 50p pocket money a day; we travelled economy but did we complain? Of course not, why would we? For us it was a privilege to be there. We got everything we needed.

'The rugby challenge was a deadly serious business. Most days we trained morning and afternoon to prepare for the gladiatorial dimension inherent in the Test matches, but there was also a great social dimension on those tours. In a modern tour, it is all about the Test matches. The various provincial matches hardly count. In our day, many of the provincial matches were virtually Test matches in their own right: New South Wales, Queensland, Taranaki, Auckland, Wellington, Canterbury and Otago. The sense of achievement from playing at the highest level and the pride that follows from that were important at the time, but it is the legacy of these tours that is so important in later years.

'There is no doubt membership of the Lions can be a powerful calling card in subsequent years, but the bonds made on these tours are more important. Not only with fellow Lions but also with fellow travellers from Australia, New Zealand and South Africa that we keep bumping into over the years. These bonds are no more enduring than those made at school or in a club like Blackrock or Lansdowne. They are just different. They are a further piece added to the tapestry of life.

'I suppose there is a bit of the pioneer in all of us which makes us want to look over the ditch and talk to the guy on the other side. Cliff Morgan, who is more poetic than I am, refers to it as "breaking bread with the rest of the world". Most important of all are the comradeships. Comradeships are the heartbeat of our lives. Syd Millar is fond of a quote from William Butler Yeats which says, "Think where man's glory first begins and ends. Our glory was we had such friends."

'The modern Lions tour is an equally important landmark on the rugby landscape. Whispers circulate about Lions tours being disbanded, but I think it would be a tragedy and I hope that it does not happen. Having said that, the modern Lions tour is as different from the old tour as fudge is from water. The Lions tour to Australia in 2001 was a five-and-a-half-week trip of eleven matches. With 20,000 visitors from Ireland and the UK, you could hardly turn a corner without meeting somebody you knew; it was a fantastic atmosphere. Test matches retained their combative dimension as ever, but the other matches in a present-day Lions tour are very secondary.

'Hourly press coverage of every stirring within the tour party informed us about players' aches and pains, and every squad member's utterance with the multi-media coverage that's the norm these days. That tour's party included 13 staff, forward coaches, defensive coaches, psychologists, medical people, graphologists – the lot. In the 2005 tour of New Zealand, there were 26 or 27 members of staff, with all of them wanting/needing to get a piece of time with every player. Surely the players did not have a minute to themselves. I remember Willie John once saying that he could not handle 27 guys telling him what to do. That came as no surprise to me because, as his former captain, I can tell you that Willie John had difficulties when there was only one guy telling him what to do!

'The old Lions tour, in my view, was a better experience for a player

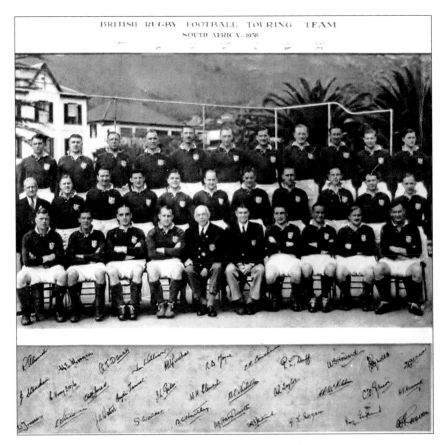

BRITISH RUGBY FOOTBALL TOURING TEAM
SOUTH AFRICA—1938

1938 Lions team with signatures.

1938: L-R: B. Mayne, G. Morgan, B. Graves, G. Cromey,
S. Walker, C.V. Boyle, H. McKibbin, B. Alexander.

Queen's University Team, 1937: Blair Mayne
middle row, third from the left.

Darvel, Ayrshire, 1944 training for Army Championship,
scrummaging session with Blair Mayne.

R.B.Mayne playing for the Army against the Empire

Cigarette card: 'R.B. Mayne playing for the Army against the Empire'.

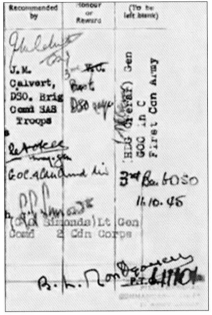

Blair Mayne's VC recommendation crossed out.

Blair Mayne's medals: L-R: DSO & 3 Bars, 1939–45 Star, Africa Star, Italy Star, France and Germany Star, Defence Medal 1939–45, War Medal 1939–45, *Légion d'honneur* and *Croix de guerre*.

Norma Ann Sykes aka 'Sabrina' (the British Jayne
Mansfield) with 1959 team members in SA.

Syd Millar with
Danie Craven, 1980.

H. McLeod, R. Dawson,
S. Millar, 1959.

Members of the 1962 Lions Team in Rhodesia.

Willie John catching a ball.

1968 team in South Africa.

Barry Bresnihan's Graduation in South Africa, 1968.

1974 mafia – both sides.

Left: Willie John gives Chris Ralston a piggyback.

1974 team visit Kimberley.

Willie John and Mike Burton.

G. Brown scores try, B. Windsor and F. Cotton look on.

1974 Reunion.

Murphy, Millar and Beaumont, 1980.

than the modern Lions tour, but the modern Lions tour is a better experience for supporters and followers than years ago.

'People talk a lot these days about the changes that are taking place in the game and institutions of rugby. Major changes are hardly a surprise. There are radical changes in every aspect of life. Of course players are bigger, stronger and fitter than they were, the game is definitely more attractive to watch and there are many more games to see. But sometimes the extent of change is exaggerated. Listening to some people you would think that in our day we never trained at all. There is also the view that there is none of the fun in the game these days that we had in our time. I think the truth is somewhere in between. We took it more seriously than legend would have it and I have no doubt that the players of today really enjoy what they are doing.

'Some people say that players and coaches take the game too seriously today. I don't agree with that. Professional is professional. After all, the game for today's professional players is their job whereas for us it was a recreation. A very serious recreation, but a recreation nonetheless.

'Some of my fellow players from the past are inclined to complain that "things" are not like they used to be. But I think we had the best of all possible worlds. It was great to play in our time. We broke bread with people we admired in our own sport and we were lucky enough to get up there and to test our mettle with standard-bearers like the Wallabies, the Springboks and the All Blacks. And today in our autumn years we are spectators and the spectating is better than ever before. Better rugby and more of it. Today also, there are many dinners, reunions, celebrations, etc., which provide old guys with continuing opportunities to reconnect with fellow travellers from the past and also players from younger generations.'

1966: Ken Jones

Ray said: 'I recall one occasion when the Welsh centre, Ken Jones, left the tour to go up the mountains shooting deer with some locals that he fell in with. He got no formal permission, nor did he mention it to the coach. Ken had bothered to ask one of his colleagues to mention it to the management, but nobody had done so. Perhaps he thought, why bother Des O'Brien, the manager, about it as Des was such a nice man and he should not be troubled by things of that kind?

'Ken's presence went unmissed for a day, but eventually his absence was noticed. Des, a very laid-back manager who never panicked, did not ring the police. His attitude was "Don't worry boys, he will be back."

And sure enough he did come back. He walked into the hotel restaurant on a Friday night while we were having dinner, cheeky as you like, and Des, who epitomised the ultimate in unfazed calm, said to him, "Oh, nice to see you, Ken. Will you be at the match tomorrow?"

'How could you not enjoy a tour like that?'

1966: Piggy Powell

'Although training was taken very seriously, there was always room for the bizarre. During training in Christchurch before the Canterbury game, a serious pre-match session, the coach, John Robbins, sent the second team (the "Wednesday team" as they were then called) down to a second pitch to practise while he went through some drills with the team picked for Saturday's match.

'After three-quarters of an hour or so, he sent one of us down to call up the Wednesday team. The rest of us stood waiting and there was no sound for a while, when eventually we heard a low rumbling of an engine. The rumbling got louder and louder until the source of the noise became clear. A tractor appeared through a gap in the hedge separating our pitch from the second pitch. The tractor was driven by Piggy Powell, a farmer from Northampton, who obviously knew how to start tractors left unattended in a farmer's field, and all the rest of the team were hanging out of the tractor. Piggy drove it right into the middle of our training pitch and switched the engine off, turned to John Robbins and said, "Right, John, we are here."

'John responded with a tolerant smile. What else could he do?'

1966: Curfew

'Management imposed a curfew on the team at one point, which meant we could not leave the hotel after 10 p.m. We were in North Auckland at the time.

'Willie John and myself did not do curfews, so we sneaked out and went to a pub we knew and had a few beers. We returned about 11, an hour after the curfew deadline. We anticipated getting back late and had left a fire escape slightly ajar on the third floor, through jamming a piece of paper between the door and the frame.

'When we arrived back, we sneaked up on the fire escape, removed the piece of paper and opened the door ever so slowly in order to avoid any creaks. It must have taken an entire minute or two to fully open the door. What we did not know was that Vivian Jenkins, Bryn Thomas and

Terry O'Connor were inside the door having a chat before heading to their rooms. They spotted the opening door and stood looking at it transfixed. By the time we opened it enough to see them, their three mouths gawped so wide each of them could have swallowed a 6 lb trout.

'The three press men knew all about the curfew and knew that we had broken it, but did they say anything about it? Absolutely not. In those days, *omertà* was the name of the game.'

1971: Barry John

'Barry John regarded all forwards as "donkeys" and kept asking people to explain what they were in rugby teams for. At least two or three times a week he would come up to me in the restaurant, put his hands on my shoulders and say, "Tell me again, Ray, are you a loose-head donkey or a tight-head donkey?"

'I played a role in training/coaching the forwards in the earlier part of that tour and at one point I pressed for a set of signals by which the backs would tell the forwards what they intended to do with the ball if we gave it to them. This created a rebellion on the part of Barry and Gareth Edwards, whose response was along the lines, "There's no way we'll tell you donkeys what we're going to do with the ball, you'll only get in our way."

'But the coach, Carwyn James, sided with me on this matter. We got our signals and Gareth and Barry have never forgiven me.'

1971: Gareth Edwards

'A great thing about participation in sport is the high level of mutual respect and indeed affection that is generated, not only among those who take the field alongside team members but also among those that play against each other. Lions rugby provides a unique opportunity whereby you can face comrades in opposition colours when you return to Home Championship matches and you know their playing strengths, their personalities and their attitudes. The Ireland v Wales game at Lansdowne Road in 1974 finished in a 9–9 draw – not particularly memorable for the scoreline but memorable to me for an outburst by Gareth, frustrated by an interruption to the passage of play.

'While the doctor attended to one of the Welsh forwards who had experienced an "accident", Willie John and I stood next to each other on the Welsh 25 waiting for play to resume when Gareth Edwards turned around with a glower and said, "I know it was one of you two fuckers who did that and you're going to pay for it before the match is out." Gareth had been very much a junior to us on the previous tours, so it was a surprise to say the least that he would talk to us in those terms. Following a pause for a second or two, Willie John looked down at him menacingly and said in a quiet voice, "Gareth, are you speaking to us?" The angry look stayed on Gareth's face only a second or so before he began to laugh and we did too.'

1971: Sydney

'Back in 1969, I played with Athlone Rugby Club. The coach was Paddy Creagh and when I arrived, he wanted me to take over as coach. I did not want to do that and instead I wrote out a 26-page document called "How to Coach and Develop a Rugby Team".

'We all met in the Shamrock Lodge Hotel one night and I handed over the document and said, "Paddy, it's all yours." I'm not sure if Paddy ever read it, but one of the people present sent a copy to his brother, who was a priest teaching in a rugby school in Sydney.

'Two years later, when the Lions visited Sydney, this priest was invited to the press reception and, as I subsequently discovered, he did a lot of talking about my document.

'Now roll back a few days before that press reception when the Lions played Queensland in Brisbane and lost. This led to panic stations in the Lions camp because we thought we had a team good enough to challenge the All Blacks and we lost the first match! I was leader of the pack for the match against New South Wales and I sat with Carwyn James and John Dawes on the plane from Brisbane to Sydney and we talked about how to handle New South Wales.

'I had a pad out, drawing diagrams about defensive positions and attacking positions and this, that and the other, and every time we finished discussing a topic, I folded up the relevant page and stuffed it in the basket at the back of the seat in front.

'The travelling press on the plane (they used to travel with the Lions in those days) saw all this and when we landed they went straight off to the aforementioned reception. And they obviously talked about the discussion John Dawes, Carwyn James and I had on the plane.

'Somehow or other the two stories got mixed up and emerging from that mix-up was the myth that I wrote a 26-page document for the Lions on how to beat the All Blacks on the flight from Brisbane to Sydney, a journey of one and a half hours! And of course this myth gathered legs when the Lions eventually did beat the All Blacks.

'No matter how often I have denied this, people just won't believe the denial. It has even been written about in a book!'

Mythology

'One of the aspects of sport is that followers, fans, particularly younger people, are always looking for heroes. As a result mythology and legend can grow very quickly (and without sufficient foundation). I have heard stories about myself which are completely untrue and I have heard feats of strength attributed to me which even superman could not do.

'I remember going into Egan's pub in Ballinasloe about ten years ago and a local man, well known to me, who went to Garbally with my brother, came up and said, "Ray McLoughlin, you used to run up and down the fields of Garbally with a hundredweight block of concrete under each arm." Which of course I never did. I said, "No, I did not" and he said, "Yes, you did." This went on for some time and eventually he said "Indeed you did, it is well known." And that was the end of that. There was no way he was going to let that piece of mythology die.

'But most of these myths are positive in nature so no harm is done and of course it is nice to be the subject of folklore even if that is what it is.'

Rodger Arneil
South Africa 1968, 4 caps
Scotland 1968–72, 22 caps

Rodger Arneil was an all-action open side wing forward who was a terror to out-halves everywhere he played. Sandy Carmichael tells me that no one ever wanted to room with him, not because he was untidy or bad company, but because of his nocturnal movements on the eve of a game. He would bash the opposition pack up in his sleep, often smashing up the furniture in the process. Rodger kindly came to Dungannon to play in our centenary game.

Yes, I Remember it Well

'When I stopped playing rugby, I was in textiles,' recalled Rodger, 'then marketing, then independent television. Then I founded the Head and Browning sports goods companies in the UK, then started and sold a number of companies in the disaster-recovery business, which all in all covers the last 40-odd years.

'The thought of retirement is not on my mind and I work as a consultant for various organisations, helping them to grow and prosper. Playing tennis and golf, going to the gym and having the occasional glass of French wine, are all pastimes which I very much enjoy.

'I am very lucky to have an old farmhouse in France where I go in the summer and where we can invite family and friends. It is smack in the middle of rugby country and I have made some great friends there through the rugby connection. I am not the only rugby Francophile in the area and we have great reminiscences of rugby days sitting in the sun, by the pool with a glass in hand. Sad, isn't it – all old farts talking rubbish! It is fun, though!

'Rugby is all a bit of a blur, as it happened such a long time ago and it's difficult to remember what happened. I treasure meeting old rugby pals who are able to relate great "do you remember" stories – "no, but go on tell me" and the memories come flooding back. Some things however stand out:

'I was selected for the Barbarian Easter Tour in 1967 as a new boy from Scotland and picked to play against Cardiff.

'I know Gareth Edwards will remember his wonderful try against Scotland, which happened to be played week after week in the opening clip for *Rugby Special*, the only rugby programme on TV and just introduced the year before so it had a monopoly on viewers. You can catch a glimpse (only a glimpse) of me trying to tackle him. It was wet and Mervyn Davies was holding my jersey (my story and I'm sticking to it) which, had he seen it, the referee would have blown immediately for an instant penalty. History has shown this was not to be and the injustice of it lives on.

'Anyway, on my first visit to Cardiff Arms Park playing for the Baa Baas I scored no fewer than three tries – guess who was scrum-half? Yes, Gareth Edwards. I remind him every time I see him; his eyes seem to glaze over, can't understand why. Three tries, this was my passport to rugby heaven – selected for Scotland to play against Ireland and then for the Lions to South Africa.

'On the tour I met some great guys, one of whom was Barry Bresnihan. Where else except through rugby would this acquaintance have been made? I doubt our paths would have crossed otherwise. The prof, sadly missed, stood as my best man and became a lifelong friend until his death last year [2010].

'Rugby was an experience not to be missed and it was a privilege to be able to play it for the memories and the friends made. It is a great game and

I miss the selection card dropping through the letterbox to tell me the committee has decided to select me again – so I can live another week!'

Peter Larter
South Africa 1968, 1 cap
England 1967–73, 24 caps

Chris Ralston reckons that Peter Larter of the RAF and Northampton turned him from a club player to an international player. I'm sure his advice wasn't to smoke 50 cigars a day. There is controversy over the end of Peter's career. As he was in the RAF he chose not to come to Dublin with the English team in 1973. His place was taken by Roger Uttley and he wasn't selected for England again.

Dressed for the Occasion

'It's not all glamour in rugby,' said Peter, 'or it wasn't back in the '60s when I was selected to play for the Combined Services XV against the All Blacks at Twickenham on Boxing Day 1967. I spent Christmas Day in Dartmouth with my parents and sisters, and travelled to Twickenham on Boxing Day morning. I'd met up with my second row partner Mike Davis (Royal Navy and England) in Torquay, and was then chauffeured by Mike's dad.

'We had had a warm-up match earlier in December but no other preparation for playing against some of the best rugby players in the world! Lunch at the Winning Post was followed by the match, which we lost but played quite well, then on to the dinner at the Royal Air Force Club in Piccadilly. The dinner was a dinner-jacket do and, as most of the team were young servicemen, we didn't possess our own DJs, so the Combined Services Secretary, a lovely army colonel called Jack Dalrymple, hired some DJs from Moss Bros and positioned them in a small room in the RAF Club.

'I was one of the last to arrive at this room and found a jacket that fitted me, but the only trousers left were a very tight fit and about six inches too short. So I wedged myself into them and went down to the pre-dinner reception. There, just inside the entrance, I spotted the Royal Navy and London Irish flanker Kevin Lavelle (Kevin was a great drop-goal expert, and from the back row that took some doing!) wearing very baggy trousers with 6 in. turn-ups! It took me quite a while to convince Kevin that he was wearing the wrong trousers, but he eventually succumbed. We managed to do a quick swap in a dark corner just before going in to dinner and both spent the remainder of the evening in reasonable comfort!'

Keith Jarrett
South Africa 1968
Wales 1967–9, 10 caps

On 15 April 1967, Keith Jarrett, still only 18, made his debut for Wales against England. He kicked two penalty goals, five conversions and scored a try that was voted number seven in a list of all-time great Welsh tries. The precocious youngster burst away with the ball on his own 22 and ran the length of the pitch to score in the corner. Keith was also an extremely talented cricketer playing for Glamorgan and later went to Barrow to play rugby league.

Milk – No Cookies

'Food is important,' said Keith. 'Rugby players expend immense bouts of energy and need regular sustenance to keep them in top shape. In 1968, after playing Rhodesia in Salisbury in my first game on tour, there was a reception dinner. Around 11 or 12 o'clock, we'd returned to the Meikles Hotel for a last drink before we retired for the evening. I was in good spirits – we'd won comfortably and I'd scored my first try – but I had also sprung a shoulder and didn't realise the significance of this until later.

'Late that night, Willie John, captain Tommy Kiernan, Tess O'Shea, myself and maybe John Taylor were talking about the day when hunger struck, despite the match banquet where the food was plentiful and thoroughly enjoyed at the time. One of us rang the kitchen on the off chance someone might still be there at midnight who would be willing to cook us a hearty breakfast or something similar – no luck.

'I got up, resigned to going to bed, and began to plod towards my room. A couple of the group must have been a touch disgruntled and suddenly one of the armchairs we'd been sitting on in the hotel foyer flew across the space and hit the milk dispenser, standing at the reception counter. About 50, maybe 100, litres of milk cascaded on the floor. What a mess!

'Suitably ashamed, we made our way upstairs to the captain's room (I think he was sharing with Willie John). After ten or fifteen minutes, there was a loud knock at the door. Two huge, nasty-looking policemen and the largest Alsatian I can remember stood in the doorway. The officers removed their hats, drew themselves to their full height and glared in. All three looked rabid and seemed to froth at the mouth, clearly unhappy about the incident. The atmosphere grew thick with tension. Conversation was not forthcoming and the dog grew nastier by the minute.

'Suddenly, Tommy Kiernan, who had gone missing, returned – holding one of the policeman's hats full of milk, which he placed in front of the dog. The dog began lapping it up, the policemen started talking and the atmosphere had changed in a second. So, with a mild rebuke, the two officers and the dog bid us goodnight and left the hotel. I was beginning to learn the many qualities of a Lions captain and luckily we had one with us that night.'

Tony Horton
South Africa 1968, 3 caps
England 1965–8, 7 caps

Robin Challis was an extremely strong scrummager for London Scottish, London Counties and the Barbarians. Year after year he was a Scottish trialist who tested the up-and-coming contenders. If they played well against him, they were picked for Scotland, and if they played badly, they were never heard of again. He regards Tony Horton as one of the most difficult props he ever played against by the very nature of his physical make-up. As Robin puts it 'he'd a stumpy neck', which meant he could never get to work on him. High praise from a hard, hard man.

Lion Returns
'When selected for the 1968 Lions I was delighted and honoured to be touring with such a wonderful group of players,' recalled Tony. 'For me, this was going to be a very emotional and exciting return to South Africa. In 1964, my father sold his wine business and through family connections I was offered a job at Stellenbosch Farmers Winery. This I accepted and spent a wonderful 12 months making wines and playing rugby for the town side Van der Stel. Van Der Stel were the poor relation to Stellenbosch University, who at the time fielded eight Springboks and were coached by the renowned Dr Danie Craven. I was the only English-speaking person in the first XV and you had to prove your worth, but after a few games they accepted me with open arms and that season Van der Stel beat Stellenbosch University. On asking Dr Danie

Craven for a comment he said, "Miracles do happen". He did not like losing!

'The 1968 Lions accepted an invitation to visit Van der Stel the week before the third Test in Cape Town and to this day Van der Stel still have a photo of the 1968 Lions team in the club room. After the visit, Stellenbosch Farmers Winery invited us back for a tasting that went on well into the afternoon and then up into the hills for a sauna and swim. It was my 30th birthday on 13 July 1968, the day of the third Test in Cape Town.

'What wonderful lasting memories and rugby friendships through which I earned my nickname, "Pinky". Perhaps I ought to explain . . .

'With my neck size of 21 inches, I had great difficulty getting shirts to fit. The only shirts close to fitting me ballooned over the rest of my body. So I had a friend visiting Hong Kong who managed to have some made, but they were all in pink cotton. Arriving at the hotel before the tour to have our measurements taken for our Lions blazers and trousers, I found no shirts were available in my size. So I took all my pink shirts with me on tour – thus the nickname. After the Boland match, there was a purge on shirts by the Lions "Wreckers". Shirts were torn off any other Lions who came into their radar and burnt in the garden. I could hear them shouting: "Let's get Pinky." I managed to avoid their clutches by hiding in the garden for an hour.'

John O'Shea
South Africa 1968, 1 cap
Wales 1967–8, 5 caps

In 1968 against Eastern Transvaal, John O'Shea was the first Lion to be sent off, unjustly so, as he was only protecting his scrum-half who had been attacked by a total thug. On the way off the pitch he was pelted with 'narejes'(small oranges) and assaulted by a spectator who was flattened by Willie John, who had vaulted the fence to go to the aid of his team-mate. John O'Shea received the full support of the management, David Brooks, Ronnie Dawson, Tom Kiernan and the rest of the team, and actually played the next game against Northern Transvaal. The sending off had its repercussions however, as six years later in 1974 it was decided amongst ourselves that if anyone was attacked we would all go to battle, the theory being that we couldn't all be sent off. So John O'Shea was the cause of the infamous '99' call.

Colours

John said: 'It came to me whilst watching Wales against Victoria at Melbourne Olympic Park in the heart of Australian Rules territory during their 1978 tour of Australia. I had come down from Sydney to see the game that evening and it was raining slightly as Victoria and Wales ran onto the field, the boys in blue from Victoria and the boys in red from Wales. As I looked at the scene, I reflected on the fact that I had played for each of these sides at some point in my rugby career. I had been retired for over two years when I made a very modest comeback for Victoria in the 1972 season.

'The boys in blue would play their matches in front of friends, relatives and only those that loved them, a small crowd indeed. The results of any games might be found in the local Melbourne newspapers in the Stop Press if we were lucky. Nobody wrote about us and nobody sang about the boys in blue.

'I had in earlier days been fortunate enough to play for Wales in front of 60,000 fans at what was then the cathedral of rugby – Cardiff Arms Park. Local papers wrote numerous pages about us before and after the game. Sixty thousand fans sang in praise of the boys in red. The boys in red were heroes of the nation.

'As I looked at the scene, I realised the boys in blue and the boys in red had given their all whenever I played with them. There was no difference in attitude or commitment; I was lucky with my opportunity to play the game of rugby with them.

'The rain came down that evening and the colours on the pitch ran the blue of Victoria and the red of Wales. The red ran into the blue, the blue ran into the red and together they made the one wonderful colour – the Colour of Rugby Football.'

5

FROM GLORY TO DESPAIR

Sean Lynch
New Zealand and Australia 1971, 4 caps
Ireland 1971–4, 17 caps

Sean Lynch went to New Zealand in 1971 as second-string tight-head prop to Sandy Carmichael but covered himself in glory, playing in all four Tests after Sandy was punched out of the tour against Canterbury.

In the first Test, after 15 minutes, he turned to Willie John and said, 'Could you count the opposition, because, bejaysus, I've tackled 30 already.'

I always loved Dungannon's fixtures against St Mary's, especially when he and J.B. Sweeney got together after a few scoops.

A Major Gaffe

'The 1970 Irish tour to Argentina was brutal,' remembered Sean. 'We weren't even awarded caps, as Argentina weren't recognised as an International Board country. Disgracefully, the likes of Frank O'Driscoll (Brian's father) and John Birch were never recognised as Irish internationals.

'The Argentine referees, as well as being biased, were totally ignorant of the rules, which gave the home players licence to play filthy rugby. Apart from a trip upcountry to play Rosario, we were based for the whole tour in one hotel in Buenos Aires and because of the military rule and political unrest, sightseeing was minimal. Even the names of the teams were unimaginative – Argentina, Argentina A, Argentina B and Argentina C.

'We did, however, receive tickets for the final of the World Club soccer competition between Estudiantes and Feyenoord. Even then there was a disaster as we'd had a few drinks and one of the players (who shall remain nameless) was singing an Irish song on the way to the stadium. He was arrested as the Argentine President was passing in his limousine at the time and his rendition was regarded as disrespectful. He spent a night in the cells and diplomatic pressure had to be applied for his release.

'Then to cap everything, Air Braig overbooked our flight home, excusing their mistake on a trumped-up charge that we were all drunk and possibly under the influence of drugs. What? Did they think the pipe smokers had filled their bowls with something illegal?

'On our arrival in Argentina, the Irish Ambassador, Mr Michael Leo Skentelbery, met us at Buenos Aires Airport. Now, I'm not the best with remembering names, especially after a 16-hour flight and a few in-flight beers with the lads. However, I did notice that the Ambassador had quite a shake and someone said he had Parkinson's disease.

'In between all the mayhem of this tour, I made the biggest faux pas of my life. Two weeks after we had met the Ambassador we were invited to his flat for drinks and I had completely forgotten his name. While in conversation with him, making small talk I became befuddled and tongue-tied when I had to address him. I asked, "How have you been, Mr . . . Parkinson?"

'All the boys like Terry Moore and Phil O'Callaghan doubled up with laughter. He tried to ignore me but to make matters worse, delighted that I thought I had remembered his name, I pulled him by the sleeve and said, "I'm talking to you, Mr Parkinson. Would you listen?"

'One of the lads advised me to abandon my line of conversation. When I discovered my gaffe, I was never more embarrassed in my life.'

Mike Roberts
New Zealand and Australia 1971
Wales 1971–9, 8 caps

The first time I played against Wales was at Cardiff Arms Park in 1973. I stood for the Welsh national anthem. A wave of emotion came over me and tears ran down my face as I listened to the greatest choir in the world. Facing me across the halfway line was a bearded giant of a man – Mike Roberts. I looked at him and I could read his lips as he mouthed at me 'I'm going to kill you, I'm going to kill you!'

Welcome to Wales.

In 1988, Mike organised the first tour to the Golden Oldies Festival in Bermuda, where I needed running repairs in hospital. I had to do a runner as I didn't have the money to pay the bill. Serves him right for threatening to kill me.

Golfer Extraordinaire

Mike recalled a golfing anecdote from the 1971 tour to New Zealand. 'We were on the west coast and had a Saturday match – David Duckham scored six tries and the tour was going well. It was time for a little R&R on the Sunday before the Monday match.

'Choices offered were a visit to the Franz Josef Glacier or for two or three players to attend the opening of a new golf clubhouse at Greymouth – to add a little sporting glamour to the occasion. The glacier held little appeal, so I volunteered along with J.P.R. Williams and Derek Quinnell to attend the clubhouse opening event. In those days, none of us were golf players – certainly not of any significant standard – and we thought we would be shouldering our Lions blazers with the jackets of golf club members schmoozing in a bit of a reception. If not, it was closer to home than the glacier. We could always slip away if it became heavy or boring.

'New Zealand people appreciate sport – all sports – and they expect standards from their international representatives. The Lions, apparently walking on water to have succeeded against the New Zealand teams, were expected to have a transfer of skills for a credible performance on the golf course. Whoops! This was apparent when we arrived directly at the first tee to find the golf course lined with 5,000 spectators. Teamed with the club captain, Derek Quinnell acted as caddy for us – acted barely describes it, but he carried the clubs anyway.

'The clubhouse was a splendid new building with huge picture windows so members could have a view over the course. I teed up ready to drive the ball down the spectacular fairway and took the three iron handed to me by Derek. Stance, shoulders, wrists – all correct as far as I imagined from watching other golfers. Swipe. Miss. I suspect I somewhat disillusioned the spectators, but anyone can suffer nerves and miss the first stroke. Derek sniggered in the background. Pretending it was a practice stroke, I loosened myself up and addressed the ball again. I steadied myself, checked where I wanted the flight of the ball to go, looked earnestly at the small white sphere and whacked the golf club at it – and missed again. My caddy's sniggers had become guffaws and he creased up with laughter.

'I'm not a quitter. Third time lucky. I went through the routine again, completely focused on the tiny white beast and this time I connected with a wonderful strike or so it sounded, but it hooked left . . . towards the new clubhouse and the picture windows. The bugger I whacked rose majestically over the clubhouse roof, across the road and scattered a field of sheep. To cover the ignominy I turned to the captain and said, "Difficult course you've got here, skipper." Neither amused nor sympathetic, he just looked dreadfully disappointed. This really wasn't a display to impress the 5,000.

'The captain looked embarrassed as I struggled on. Things didn't improve. By the fourth hole my giggling caddy suggested he play and I carry. We never said we could play even mini-golf, never mind competition standard.'

David Duckham OBE
New Zealand and Australia 1971, 3 caps
England 1969–76, 36 caps

David Duckham was a classical English back, flowing blond hair, wonderful sidestep and dummy, change of pace, and speed. He was part of the excellent 1971 back line and star of the great Baa Baas game against the All Blacks in 1973.

However, Irish rugby should always be grateful to David Duckham as he used his influence to persuade his team-mates to come to Dublin in 1973 after the let-downs of Scotland and Wales the previous season.

There's Always One
David recalled: 'Sometimes when you tour, pranks are played when you aren't permitted to follow wine, women or other distractions that might usually occupy your leisure time – especially when you are young and foolish. You have to keep the grey cells occupied as part of being able to react to game situations. Usually they are quite innocent and are only meant to alleviate the boredom that accompanies the tedium of long-haul travel. At 25 years of age, the Lions tour to Australia and New Zealand in 1971 was nothing less than an adventure for naive young international players like me. It was also very memorable, for a number of reasons, not least for an incident when we first landed in Brisbane, very jet-lagged, for the two provincial matches in Australia before hopping across to New Zealand . . .

'Australia, clearly paranoid about foreign invaders, demanded that visitors fill in a rather complex immigration form. As we passed through the border control point, the queue came to a standstill when a stern and humourless customs officer on duty seemed to spend rather a long time studying Bob Hiller's entry form. He scrutinised the document, looked up from it and glared at Bob. Like something from a 1960s movie about the Cold War and the Eastern Bloc countries, the official picked up a phone and suddenly two burly officials appeared, to frog-march Bob away.

'Two hours later in our hotel, Hiller appeared, fortunately none the worse for wear with no bruises or evidence of having been tortured by overzealous defenders of the state, but he did look embarrassed. We soon found out why. In answer to one of the bizarre questions on the immigration form – "Is it your intention to bring down the Elected Government of Australia?" – Bob had written, "Sole purpose of visit!" Whoops.'

J.P.R. Williams
New Zealand and Australia 1971, 4 caps; South Africa 1974, 4 caps
Wales 1969–81, 55 caps

J.P.R. Williams was so competitive. He was also a perfectionist. I never saw him drop a ball in three months either in a game situation or at practice. I never saw him fail to find touch or miss a tackle.

Then . . . it was find a squash court or a tennis court to beat someone at racquets. He also never denied his desire to win. He took Mike Gibson out of the game at Lansdowne Road in 1978 when Gibson looked certain to score. After the game, he admitted he had meant it. J.P.R. – a winner every time.

Thumbs Up
'I made a little piece of history in 1971,' remembered J.P.R., 'and though I'm delighted people recall it, the story has become legend and the legend has fallen into myth.

'Over 40 years ago in New Zealand I helped Bob Hiller, our full-back, and Barry John, our out-half, with their kicking practice. After training, the boys would spend some extra time getting the ball between the posts from a variety of angles and distances. I acted as gopher and I'd field the ball for them, making drop kicks back to them. They were very encouraging to me and suggested I have a go myself, so I would take the ball to the halfway line, aim its flight and give a good straight kick. Now and again I would get the ball through the posts and I would practise more to get better. Only the three of us knew of this.

'By the time we faced the last Test we were 2–1 up in the series. The team was very nervous, tired after three and a half months being on tour and wanting to go home. I tried to lift their spirits and joked, "Today I'm going to drop a goal." It seemed to amuse the lads. They didn't know I'd been practising.

'Towards the end of the game, my opportunity came. We were going backwards and I had the ball in my hands. Full of confidence from the practice sessions with Bob and Barry, I dropped a goal from near the halfway line. I turned to the stand and gave thumbs up. "Told you that would happen," I said.

'Now for the eerie part of this legend. At the start of the tour, our manager, Doug Smith, predicted the result would be two wins, one loss and one draw. My dropped goal drew the last Test match and fulfilled the prediction made. It was my one and only drop kick attempt in international rugby and I'm proud of my 100 per cent record.'

Derek Quinnell
New Zealand and Australia 1971, 1 cap; New Zealand 1977, 2 caps; South Africa 1980, 2 caps
Wales 1971–80, 20 caps

Derek Quinnell was uncapped by Wales when he was selected for the victorious 1971 Lions. He had the ability to play anywhere in the back five of the scrum. He was selected for the third Test with the specific job of marking Sid Going, who had controlled the second Test. Derek Quinnell followed Carwyn James' instructions to a T and Going never got going.

Derek got his first Welsh cap in February 1972, coming on in the dying seconds for the injured Mervyn Davies. It was a dramatic entrance as he tore off his tracksuit and knocked over a policeman in his haste to represent his country.

Missed Opportunity
'The Barbarians teams are always fortified by players fit and ready to face the fray and in 1973 they were scheduled to play against the mighty All Blacks,' said Derek. 'The British public regarded the team as their own Lions with a few interesting newcomers in the mix, ones to watch for the future. Our team that day featured twelve of the 1971 Lions Tourists who had faced the All Blacks on their own patch two years earlier and

beaten them in the Test series: 9–3, 12–22, 12–9 and 14–14. Though the results were close and the battles hard fought, the thrill of that victory still ran through our blood. We imagined they still stung from the unexpected defeat, were determined to settle old scores and that this would be a difficult match. The All Blacks were riding on a high after they had beaten the Scots, English and Welsh, and drawn with the Irish.

'Cardiff Arms Park was the venue – no better ground for a Welshman – and we met only a couple of days before the fixture to prepare ourselves under the genius 1971 Lions coach Carwyn James – a flash of brilliance from our captain, John Dawes, who came out of retirement to play in the game.

'Assembled in Penarth, with no sign of Carwyn James, we went through the motions of some light training on the Thursday and Friday, rekindled friendships and got acquainted with the new boys. There was no great intensity in anything we did despite the public expectation that this was virtually a fifth Test and an opportunity to show the southern hemisphere what the northern hemisphere could really do.

'On the Saturday morning at the hotel in Cardiff we met for breakfast, but there was bad news: Merv the Swerve [Mervyn Davies] was out of the side. He had developed a chest and throat infection and was deemed unfit to play. Feeling sorry for him, I went up to Merv's room to see how he was – no player likes to miss a match. Lying in his bed, coughing and hacking between puffs on his cigarette, he spluttered his view on the situation. "To be honest, I think this'd be a good game to miss. I'll be happy to watch from the stand."

'Gerald Davies was also out through injury, so the replacements were David Duckham and Tommy David, who both had a terrific game. Weren't they happy boys to have had the opportunity to play in one of the greatest rugby matches of all time?

'Carwyn James did appear and over morning coffee he gave a fabulous motivational peptalk that finished with his remarkably inspiring send-off initially addressed to Phil Bennett. "We all know what you can do," and then included us all. "Now go out there and show the world."

'Just as Carwyn's words were prophetic, Merv's were miserably inadequate when he spectated from the stand with his fellow Welshman Gerald Davies. His earlier words haunted him and he said, "I think we've made a bit of a mistake."'

Sandy Carmichael
New Zealand and Australia 1971; South Africa 1974
Scotland 1967–78, 50 caps

David Rollo and Sandy played for one season together and David gave Sandy advice on how to impress selectors. 'Always be first to a lineout and yell at the rest of the forwards to come on; be first to every scrum, hold up your hand and beckon the rest to hurry up. That is the system to keep you on a side.'

When Glasgow played North and Midlands (Rollo's team) in a Scottish Districts game, Sandy tried to put this advice to good use, but no matter how quickly he got to lineouts or scrums, Rollo was always there telling people to hurry up.

Mistaken Identity

'The small press party on the Lions tour to South Africa in 1974 contained internationally renowned rugby writers acclaimed for their journalistic skills,' said Sandy. 'Reporting for *The Times*, Vivian Jenkins, vice-captain of the 1938 Lions, was the senior writer. Chris Lander of the *Daily Mirror* ably supported him, as did Edmund Van Esbeck of the *Irish Times*, Terry O'Connor of the *Daily Mail*, Pat Marshall of the *Daily Express*, Bryn Thomas of the *Western Mail* and David Frost of *The Guardian*. However, my favourite was Colm Smith, a lovely Irish reporter, from the *Irish Independent*.

'One evening he and Chris Lander took me to a wonderful restaurant in Pretoria. It wasn't long before one of the diners approached and asked politely, "May I have your autograph, Ian?" Now, Ian McLauchlan is a totally different shape from me and even speaks a different type of Scots, and although I wasn't best pleased I signed "Ian McLauchlan" anyway.

'Following 38 further requests for Ian McLauchlan's autograph, I became totally pissed off. Colm Smith smirked behind his beer, amused by my predicament. After much drink we left the restaurant and the reporter from the *Irish Independent* held open the door of the first cab. "After you, Ian," he said. It was too much to take. I gave my favourite journalist a light punch, just the sort of thing McLauchlan would have done had he been signing "Sandy Carmichael" all evening.

'However, I had a laugh at his expense two days later when the said Colm Smith was again in our company and Bobby Windsor lit a fire in the hotel lounge. As the Pretoria Constabulary were not renowned for their humour, we thought it would be prudent to scatter before they arrived and Colm Smith took shelter in my room.

'After an hour or so, I assured Colm that it would be safe to leave the room, but before he got ten paces down the corridor he was taken captive by the local gendarmerie who wanted to make an example of a British Lion. After a night in the cells, he managed to convince the Pretoria police that he was not a British Lion but an Irish rugby writer.'

Fergus Slattery
New Zealand and Australia 1971; South Africa 1974, 4 caps
Ireland 1970–84, 61 caps

Fergus Slattery had the constitution of a horse. He played sometimes 60 to 70 games a season – club games, provincial games, games for Ireland, tours with the Lions, tours with Public School Wanderers, the Barbarians, opening of grounds, exhibition games – Slats was always available.

I've roomed with him – quite an experience as it was like living with a whirlwind, everything everywhere. He didn't need much sleep, and the next day he'd be out in front, sprinting against international athletes like J.J. Williams – we donkeys weren't a big enough challenge.

His energy came from food. I remember, nervous before my first cap, at Twickenham ordering a little bit of fish in the restaurant of the Mitre Hotel in Hampton Court while he munched his way through the menu – starters, main course, pudding, cheese and coffee. What would modern dieticians have done with him?

Anglo-Irish Relationships

'Jason Leonard is a lovely man,' said Fergus. 'I journeyed together with him one day and after a couple of hours travelling he mentioned how he loved the Ireland v England games in Dublin, as he was able to meet his cousins. Most people love it when they can get the chance to catch up with family. So, it turns out, Jason Leonard is one quarter Irish . . .

'My mind drifted as I thought of that and I began to wonder about a story for this book. Irishness, English players that may have held dual qualification – wouldn't it be something if certain players had chosen to wear the green shirt rather than the white? I thought on those players who had claimed Irish heritage and how they were talented fellas that enjoyed a bit of craic. Definitely, there's something in the genes if you're Irish. Hmm . . . Lawrence Dallaglio was half Irish and Kieran Bracken was one hundred per cent Irish.

'A couple of months after travelling with Jason, I attended a rugby dinner and was speaking to Austin Healey, who showed little interest in my conversation until I questioned him about his Irishness.

'Indifference and ennui left him. He instantly became animated. His eyes burned, he glowered and bellowed, "I'm half Irish, but I will never, ever play for you."

'To which I replied, "Thank God for that."'

Ian McLauchlan
New Zealand and Australia 1971, 4 caps; South Africa 1974, 4 caps
Scotland 1969–79, 43 caps

Ian McLauchlan is one of my favourite people, on or off the pitch. He had an astute rugby brain and preached the principles of Bill Dickinson, the Jordanhill and Scotland coach. He also was one of the most ruthless players I ever saw on a rugby pitch – he took no prisoners.

Before we did up to 50 scrums each morning, we completed the sets of conditioning and strength exercises that he had us do. Modern fitness advisors would probably scorn the programme, but they were geared to aiding our invincibility in the scrum.

Music to His Ears
'Bobby Windsor is a legend,' said Ian, 'and thinking about the things he has said always brings a smile to my face. On the 1974 Lions tour we played Transvaal. The province had a reputation for playing hard rugby and among their players that day was Johan Hendrik Potgieter Strauss. The tight-head prop, who went on to play for the Springboks, was a monster and known as the hardest scrummager in South Africa.

'On this occasion, to add to the intimidation, we exited the tunnel in the ground together, gladiator style, facing each other. Psyching out the opposition is nothing new and always a good ploy for international rugby. Bobby would be the first to tell you he's not much good at spelling and hasn't had a classical education, but any tongue-in-cheek one-liner he delivers is as good as a fist in the face. So, Bobby walks out beside Johan and asks, "Are you Johan Strauss?"

'Strauss, a gruff character who wasn't keen on speaking English, grunted, "*Ja.*"

'Bobby sneered at him and said, "Well, the Mouse will tune your piano for you this afternoon."'

Piggyback

'Doug Smith of London Scottish, a manager with the experience of having played for the Lions on the 1950 side that toured New Zealand and Australia, took charge of the 1971 Lions team. He had faced Australia in Brisbane in the side that won 19–6. By 1971, the good doctor was rather heavier than the flying winger of 21 years previous.

'Chico Hopkins, our Maesteg scrum-half was having an argument with Doug and coming off the worse in the exchange. In exasperation he called Doug "a fat fucking bagpipe" and added that as a manager he should be training every day.

'The next day Doug turned out for training, track-suited, with fag in hand and beckoned Chico towards him. Once Chico was near, he jumped on his back and ordered him to do a lap of the pitch for his cheek. Thanks to Chico's outburst, the rest of us were subjected to the same punishment if Doug decided we weren't pulling our weight and forced us to carry the hefty manager round the ground on our backs.'

Melrose 7s

'Simon Scott, the best centre never to be capped by Scotland, is a proud recipient of a Melrose 7s medal – something Jim Renwick never achieved. The Borders event is the most famous of the Scottish 7s tournaments at the end of the season. Although Kelso and Hawick would claim parity, Melrose has a special place in the hearts of rugby followers.

'Such is his pride, it wouldn't surprise me if Simon kept the thing in a sporran just to take out and show at functions. When he bragged about his Melrose 7s medal in front of Jim and asked how he felt about the award, Jim's dry riposte was probably lost on him: "I'm proud of my 52 caps."'

Sunday School Teacher

'Travelling by train from Glasgow to Edinburgh gave our coach, Bill Dickinson, an opportunity for a peptalk with players before the match. Ali McHarg, Gordon Strachan, Gordon Brown, Sandy Carmichael and I, all forwards, sat together for the journey. Bill called every one of the group, except Sandy, to join him as he wanted to speak with them. Sandy looked aggrieved and checked in case Bill had overlooked him.

'"No, not you," said Bill.

'The rest of us huddled with Bill and talked tittle-tattle, nothing of any consequence, but spent a fair quarter of an hour or so away from Sandy. Bill demanded we say nothing to Sandy when we returned to our seats. "And I mean, say nothing. D'ye hear me?"

'We agreed to stay schtum as requested by Bill. Sandy of course wanted to know why he hadn't been included and asked as much. "I don't need Sunday school teachers in the scrum. I need real men up front to beat Edinburgh today," Bill said dismissively.

'Sandy fumed for the rest of the journey. By the time we entered the dressing-rooms, his fury had festered until blood vessels throbbed at his temples. When we took to the field, Sandy vented his anger with such ferocity he almost beat Edinburgh single-handed.

'I can just see Bill drumming his fingers and smiling as Sandy's temperature rose to boiling point – job done. Nice one.'

Tommy David
South Africa 1974
Wales 1963–76, 4 caps

It is always wonderful to meet team-mates from past tours as the bonds formed are there for life. Tommy David moved back to Pontypridd from Llanelli in 1976 and when I travelled there with London Irish in 1981, we were both captains of our respective clubs. Both sides were advocates of 15-man rugby and Pontypridd narrowly won a fantastic game. After knocking lumps out of each other all afternoon, we talked of former glories in South Africa and sank a lot of pints.

Tommy changed codes to play rugby league for Cardiff and Wales and now is a golf fanatic.

Sometimes You Get Lucky

'My rugby-playing days started in school at Hawthorn Secondary Modern,' recalled Tommy, 'though when I left, I played soccer at centre-forward for my local team. The soccer coach said to me, "When you play number 9, you're supposed to go around players – not through them," and suggested I switch back to rugby. The rest is history ...

'I played 404 games for Pontypridd, scoring 171 tries, and made the 1974 British Lions tour to South Africa.

'The making of my reputation happened on 27 January 1973 when the Barbarians played New Zealand, a game that went down in history as the greatest rugby game of all time.

'Weeks earlier I'd played for Llanelli at Stradey Park, beating New Zealand 9–3. On the Thursday before the Barbarians v New Zealand game, I received a phone call from my coach at Llanelli, Carwyn James, coaching for the Barbarian side as a one-off. Carwyn was the most talented coach for whom I have ever played. Andy Ripley, the great England number 8, had dropped out through injury and Carwyn asked me if I would replace Andy on the subs bench for the team. I accepted straight away.

'On the morning of the game, Wales number 8 Mervyn Davies dropped out with flu. Replacing him, I entered in the biggest game of my life at 24 years old, playing alongside my rugby idols – an uncapped player facing the mighty All Blacks.

'Two things happened in this game which made my name. The first, I late tackled the New Zealand wing Grant Batty. He kicked the ball ahead, I tackled him – late. He was annoyed. We rolled on the floor and when we got up from the ground, his name "Batty" summed up how he reacted. Now I wish I could say he was a giant of a wing man, but he was very small in stature compared with myself. Rather than punch an opponent smaller than me it seemed more appropriate to have a word with the man to make things clear if he was considering any further entanglement during the match. "Come back when you're this bastard big," I said whilst patting him on the head.

'The second, receiving the ball from John Dawes, I was involved in the defining move of the game, which went down in history as one of the greatest tries ever and has been shown all over the world many times. Bryan Williams, the New Zealand wing, kicked a high ball from the halfway line. Phil Bennett caught the ball under his posts and jinked past three players with typically magical sidesteps. The ball went through seven pairs of hands, going the length of the field, which ended with Gareth Edwards scoring the great try.

'Without a doubt, the chain of events and those couple of incidents in a game that I wasn't supposed to have played in created my reputation in rugby and allowed me to enjoy a playing career that took me around the world.

'The try is shown on TV so often people still think I am still playing

and many ask me about it. I cannot understand why they get so excited
... we practised that move in training the previous day (honest!).'

Roy Bergiers
South Africa 1974
Wales 1972–5, 11 caps

On 31 October 1972, Roy Bergiers scored a try that will be forever part
of Llanelli folklore because it was against the mighty touring All Blacks.
Phil Bennett will probably say it was a planned move, as his penalty
attempt had rebounded off the crossbar into the arms of Lyn Collings,
the scrum-half. Bergiers was chasing Benny's kick like an express train
and as Collings attempted to clear to touch, Roy charged it down and
snatched up the loose ball to score. Roy Bergiers was a great Tourist in
1974. Sometimes he poured more beer over his head than down his
throat in the games of 'Thumper' and he remains a close friend of mine
to this day.

Impressing the Tánaiste

Roy said: 'As guest speaker for the pre-match banquet (Llanelli RFC v
South Africa, November 1996), Dick Spring (Tánaiste), Deputy Prime
Minister of Eire and former Irish rugby international, travelled to Stradey
Park for the evening function on the eve of the big match as a favour to
Ray Gravell. He flew into Cardiff on a private jet and it was our job
(Llanelli RFC Club President Elect, Ray Gravell, 1980 Lions and
Chairman, Roy Bergiers, 1974 Lions) to meet him off the plane and
travel with him to the banquet at Llanelli.

'In order to impress Dick and do justice to his position as a top
politician, Ray insisted on borrowing his friend's brand-new top-of-the-
range, state-of-the-art, with all modern accessories and gadgets, Jaguar.
Ray normally drove a mid-range Renault Laguna. He picked me up in
Carmarthen to travel along the M4 and confessed he was still getting
used to the automatic gearbox and the indicators on the opposite side.
We attracted some attention dressed in our dinner suits and bow ties, as
well as the fact that we were travelling relatively slowly, cautiously
allowing Ray to get used to the car.

'By the time we met Dick on the tarmac of Rhoose (Cardiff) Airport
we felt extremely important, being allowed through security as expected
personnel on a secret mission – 0012 and 0013. This feeling was enhanced

as we travelled back down the M4 with Dick and his PA in the back taking phone calls and discussing the Iraq situation. Approaching dusk, the Margam steelworks and BP Llandarcy industrial complexes all lit up made an eerie backdrop for this international project.

'The sky darkened and heavy clouds loosed a downpour. Ray – cool, blasé and sophisticated – pressed a switch for the wipers. The wipers did not come on, but the roof opened instead letting rain lash down on the Tánaiste and his PA! Still thinking the secret-agent dream could be retrieved, Ray, nonplussed, pressed another switch. Once again, it did not have the required result. The windscreen washers started bouncing jets of water off the screen and in through the roof of the car. Ray's sangfroid attitude disappeared to be replaced with panic and anxiety – the more switches he pressed the bigger hole we were digging!

'Thank God, the hard shoulder came to our rescue. Ray got things under control, eventually, and we got going again. I swear, he never touched another button.

'Dick must have wondered how these two idiots beat the All Blacks with Llanelli in '72 and later became Lions. He was too much of a gentleman to say anything even after Ray kept teasing him that he played for Wales when Dick dropped a high ball resulting in a try allowing Wales to beat Ireland 24–21 in 1979.

'Later, at the banquet, I did not improve his impression of us when I introduced him and asked him – the Deputy Prime Minister of Eire – to propose the Loyal Toast. Luckily, I was quick enough to follow that with the words – Rugby Football – although it did raise quite a few chuckles and a broad smile from Dick.'

Geoff Evans
South Africa 1974
England 1972–4, 9 caps

Towards the end of the tour in '74, Geoff Evans knew, like ten or so others, he wasn't going to break into the Test side. We didn't go off the rails, continued to train as hard, as we still had our 100 per cent midweek record to defend and above all we were proud to support the Test players. That was the strength of '74 – we were all in it together. Still, the likes of Mike Burton, Chris Ralston (who did play in the last Test), Roy Bergiers, Sandy Carmichael and Geoff Evans did enjoy each other's company and when there are reunions, invariably the group reforms to catch up on news and to reminisce about those wonderful times.

Rugby Ramblings from Days Long Gone

Geoff said: 'So what was the main difference when you played? It's a question all old ex-international players must be asked frequently – I certainly am. Well, we weren't professional, we held down full-time jobs and played for the fun of it – sorry, that should be Fun with a capital F.

'Even on the all-conquering Lions tour to South Africa in 1974 we weren't told what to eat and when. The term "rugby nutritionist" hadn't actually been coined. We used to wear extra-thick, strong, reinforced cotton jerseys and when they got wet they weighed a ton; the opposition could easily grab hold of them and it gave us all the same shape!

'When we were injured on the pitch, a wet sponge on the back of the neck fixed the problem – whatever it was. A swig of water from the single bottle . . . gargle and spit it out . . . don't drink the water – 85 degrees of heat, but still don't drink the water! Stay on the pitch in a huddle at half-time, suck on a small segment of orange . . . and above all don't drink the water! Though we weren't told not to drink alcohol after the game . . . and here lies the major difference. Today the professional players are just not allowed to drink pints and pints of beer, whereas in our day it was compulsory.

'On tour we used the word "professional" to describe what attitude we should have towards our preparations, our tactics and our training. Naturally we were also encouraged to show a mature and articulate persona in any contact with the media and with officials of our hosts in South Africa. Whilst we may have complained bitterly about the ineptitude of some of the scribes in interpreting the game, we were very fortunate that they didn't report half of the fun and frolics as we let our hair down off the pitch – and of course Lloyd's Law dictates that a lot of it can't be repeated even now.

'Moreover, to a man we mixed with our fellow team-mates, English or Welsh, Scots or Irish – it didn't matter – rich or poor, university educated or no education – it was just not relevant to us . . . although some of the differences led to some amusing incidents.

'Like the time the fellow who had been to school at Rugby – you know, the public school where the game was invented by William Webb Ellis – was overheard chatting with the guy from a Birmingham comprehensive.

"'So weer did yo goo to skool?" asked the Brummie.

"'I went to Rugby, actually," came the plum-in-the-mouth reply.

"'Oo ar," said the Brummie, "weerabouts in Rugby?"

'Priceless!'

Mike Burton
South Africa 1974
England 1972–8, 17 caps

Mike Burton's grandson, George, was visiting him recently and was browsing through some old *Rugby World* magazines when he came upon the issue covering the tour party of 1974.

'Grandpa,' George said, 'I've found your Lions team in this magazine, but there's some pages missing.'

Mike looked at it and said that there wasn't.

'But there must be,' George protested, 'there is only the captain and 29 other players.'

George then counted the forwards and said, 'There are only 16 forwards. Where are the missing forwards?'

Mike again explained that there were only 16 forwards.

'You were away for three months. How many replacement forwards were sent for?'

'None.'

'Amazing!' said the grandson.

It was amazing too.

Serve You Right!

'I first met Stewart McKinney, the meanest man to come out of Dungannon, when we travelled to South Africa with the 1974 British Lions,' recalled Mike. 'As always on those tours you pal up with the most unlikely people. McKinney was a schoolmaster, which indicated that he would be half smart and at the same time – with the right measure of cool South African beer – be articulate and intelligent; a back row forward would mean that he had pace, flair, physical fitness and above all vision. I am not sure any of this is true, but what I can confirm is that he enjoyed every minute of his tour and we have remained good friends since.

'Teaching is behind him and he is now an author. His calls now demand – "Can you do me 500 words for my latest book?" Or, "What is your recollection of the fight we had in the match against Eastern Province?"

'Well, Stewart, let me take you back to the mid-'70s and the England v Ireland match at Twickenham in the then Five Nations. Having been such good friends on the '74 tour just a couple of years before, I expected a little more charity from you when you had occasion to tackle me near the halfway line on the west side of the field and right in front of the Royal Box. You may recall, I had already completed the relatively simple task of passing the ball to a team-mate (so I never actually had the ball at the time) who could run faster than me (which meant any one of fourteen). You generously left your knee for me to fall on and quite accidentally fractured two ribs.

'Anyone who has ever had that type of injury will know how difficult it is to cough, never mind anything more adventurous. But Gloucester props play on and I did – only to have you fall on the very same ribs ten minutes later. At least this time you helped me up by one arm and enquired in that lilting Ulster accent, "You alright, Mike?" I think you smiled. Anyway, spectators close to the field of play applauded, probably the action of helping me up because they would not have been able to hear. *What a good sport he is, that McKinney.* Only you and I know different . . .

'Still, there was no question of complaint. In those days, you took your medicine and made a mental note to see the miscreant later – sometimes it was years later. But I only ever met you in a pub after that and we never played against each other again. So I console myself with the memory of the Lions v Western Province, the sixth match of the '74 tour played at Newlands in front of 45,000 spectators, which the Lions won 17–8. However, seated as I was in the dugout and just a few yards from the touchline alongside the other members of the Lions squad not playing that day, I had a first-hand view of a perfectly fair head-on dive-tackle by Springbok captain, Morne Du Plessis, who played his provincial rugby for Western Province. His shoulder caught you directly in the "married quarters" – in boxing it would have been called "below the belt" and the referee would have had good cause to intervene. Those of us watching were not sure whether to wince or laugh.

'Significantly, Du Plessis was unaware of the discomfort he had caused and all the players sitting beside me in the dugout burst into a round of applause of their own when you played the ball to Andy Ripley before hitting the mud on that wet day in Cape Town. But, Irishmen get up too and that is just what you did, although at the after-match function the pitch of your voice was just a little higher than normal.'

Andy Irvine
South Africa 1974, 2 caps; New Zealand 1977, 4 caps; South Africa 1980, 3 caps
Scotland 1972–82, 51 caps

In 1974, the first time I shared a room with Andy Irvine was in Cape Town. He had a wonderful zest for life and wanted to cram as much into each day as he could. And then disaster struck the two of us. The worst thing that can happen to a Tourist is to lose a blazer. We got back from training at Hamilton Green Point and our room had been ransacked. Our number one blazers were missing. Still, we had replacements sent out within a week.

Broon frae Troon

Andy said: 'One of my all-time favourite characters was Broon frae Troon [Gordon Brown], who sadly passed away in 2001 at the relatively young age of 53. Big Broonie was a giant of a man in every respect, both on and off the field.

'On the field of play, he was an incredibly hard, uncompromising second row forward who excelled not only for his country but more particularly for the British Lions on their successful tours to New Zealand in 1971 and South Africa in 1974. Off the field Broonie was also a great character and I fondly remember my first ever game for the Lions in 1974 against one of their provincial sides, South West Africa (Namibia).

'In the dressing-room before the match, Willie John McBride, our captain, told me in no uncertain terms, "The first 20 minutes we have to play a conservative game, not take any risks and if in our own half make sure we thump the ball down the park, so that we're out of our danger zone." This tactic was alien to me. I was always keen to run the ball, but if Willie John said "play safe" then that was what I intended to do.

'About two minutes into the game, Namibia won a lineout inside their own half and their fly-half kicked a huge, long diagonal down into our left-hand corner. I retrieved the ball just before it bounced into touch and was about to thump it down the field when I noticed their right-winger flying up at such a speed I had a slight chance of my kick being charged down, so I gave a little sidestep and he flew past. I then steadied to kick the ball. His inside centre dashed up in the exact same way and, a bit worried about being charged down, again I sidestepped. The exact same thing happened with the following centre. I had beaten three men and all of a sudden a huge gap opened up. Adrenalin surged. Synapses snapped, processing information. A decision had to be taken. "I've got to have a go here." I started to run across the field under my own posts. Unfortunately, I didn't appreciate Jan Ellis was slightly quicker than I expected and just under my posts the famed Springbok flanker tapped my ankles. I fell to the ground, dropped the ball and one of the opposing backs picked up the loose ball, dived over the posts and we were a try down within two minutes.

'Whilst I was on my knees, all my Lions colleagues trudged behind the goal line for the conversion. I picked myself up, stood on the goal line waiting for the kick to be taken, looking around and not one fellow player was prepared to even catch my eye. I have to say I felt pretty down and isolated. Even Willie John, when he looked over at me, shrugged and shook his head. At that point I saw a huge shadow emerging behind me and a giant hand tapped my shoulder. I looked up and there was Broonie. He gave me a big reassuring hug. "Andy, I don't think any of the boys really want to speak to you at this moment. I just want you to know, no matter what they think of you, I think you're an asshole!"'

John Moloney
South Africa 1974
Ireland 1972–80, 27 caps

An amazing fact is that 15 of the 32 players who made up the '74 Lions were either past, present or future captains of their respective nations. One of them was John Moloney, who made his debut, like me, in Paris in 1972 and captained Ireland in the 1978 season. John was like a greyhound, but in 1974 he was only occasionally able to show his blistering pace as he had dreadful hamstring problems, which was a terrible pity as his athletic prowess would have been fully shown off on the hard grounds of the Highveld.

Playboy
'In 1974 a young, cocky kid arrived on the Irish international rugby scene,' remembered John Moloney. 'When the team gathered in the

Shelbourne Hotel, within five minutes he dominated everything and you would think he had a hundred international caps. He made more noise than the rest of us combined. It was like being on the top deck of a bus listening to 20 Spanish students blabbering away. I am talking about – Mickey Quinn. Who else?

'When we played against England, the lads determined to take Mickey down a peg or two. After arriving at Heathrow, a mad dash to the nearest newsagent's shop secured a copy of *Playboy*. (No such enticements were available in the Republic of Ireland then.) On the bus on the way into the Kensington Close Hotel one of the lads read out the ads on the back. "Luscious Linda, will travel. Will satisfy all your needs."

'As a group, we decided when we got to the hotel that we would ring up Luscious Linda and book her for Mickey. I roomed with him and was duly instructed by some of the more knowledgeable players, who shall remain nameless, that she would probably ring back and confirm the booking, so I was to answer any calls to the room.

'Mickey and I were relaxing when a call came through at about 5.30 to confirm the appointment for 7 p.m. and verify that I was Mickey Quinn, which I duly did. At about 6.45, I told Mickey I wanted to see Joe Doran, our physio, for about 10 to 15 minutes and would he wait until I came back so we would go down to dinner together.

'I slipped out of room 241 and left Mickey on his own. At 7 p.m. on the dot, this tall, attractive, blonde, leggy girl, suitably attired for her occupation, glided down the corridor with her vanity case. She knocked. The rest of the team had their heads sticking out of their bedroom doors along the same corridor to see the outcome.

'Mickey opened his door. Luscious Linda duly entered and nothing happened for about 30 seconds until Mickey bounced out of the room and roared, to 25 heads peeping out of their doors in total hysterics, "You bastards, you set me up." Mickey had to pay Luscious Linda £25, which we of course did not reimburse.

'He was quiet for half an hour, but he soon got us back, reverting to his normal rowdy self.'

Bobby Windsor
South Africa 1974, 4 caps; New Zealand 1977, 1 cap
Wales 1973–9, 28 caps

Anytime I feel a bit down, I ring Bobby, as he cheers me up and always has a funny story to tell. However, many a Saturday night I didn't find him so amusing. I'd go down to Wales to watch Pontypool play in a cup final or attend a dinner with him. Always, with me being three sheets to the wind, he'd put me on a train at Cardiff assuring me it was the last one to London. I got as far as Reading once, but Newport was the usual stop for the night.

He also has a lot to answer for regarding my eldest son, Samuel. A hard man on the pitch, Bobby is a softie with kids. He had Sam on his knee, feeding him jam and bread after we had watched Saracens play Pontypool at Southgate. He then stuck his finger into the froth on the top of my stout and put it in the child's mouth. Sam liked it so much he dived nose first into the pint and almost drowned. Duke – you have a lot to answer for!

The Unbiased Touch Judge

Bobby said: 'Max Boyce, in 1974, wrote a piece about the sunshine home in Ireland for blind Irish referees, but he could have penned another, called "blind Pontypool touch judges".

'Ray Prosser was a true man of the valleys, a great coach and an even better touch judge. Our games with Neath were bastard hard. At the time, Neath's manager was Brian Thomas, a very hard man who had played second row for Wales. When he played for Neath they used to have BBT (Bitten by Thomas) banners waving.

'The Gnoll in Neath was also a cricket ground and the crowd were only on one side. Prosser ran the line on the cricket square side and, looking back, that was lucky for him. There were two minutes left. It had been brutal and Pontypool were losing 12–7 when Dave Hussey, our left-winger, received the ball. He ran off the pitch behind Prosser and back in again to score in the corner. It was many years before video refs or TMOs came into operation and, as the official was unsighted, he came over to consult with Prosser. "Was your winger in touch?"

'He replied, "Our left winger's so bad I cover my eyes each time he has the ball. I can't say."

'Amazingly the try was allowed. Brian Thomas went berserk and to make matters worse for him we converted the try and won 13–12.

'We beat them again that season 13–12. Needless to say Ray Prosser was not running the line.'

Phil Bennett
South Africa 1974, 4 caps; New Zealand 1977, 4 caps
Wales 1969–78, 29 caps

I phoned Phil Bennett a couple of years ago and he was recovering from an ankle injury. 'You can't blame me, Phil,' I said. 'I never got close enough to do you any harm.' Not many did get near him. He reckoned he developed the sidestep through fear of being tackled, but I shall never forget his display in the second Test in Pretoria in 1974. On his way to the line for his score he so unbalanced the Springbok full-back Ian McCallum with a beautiful sidestep that all McCallum could do was stick out a foot and try to trip him. The stud caused a dreadful gash, but Phil courageously stayed on to orchestrate the rout of the Boks.

I think Phil has shares in the brewery from his native town of Felinfoel, judging by the number of crates of the stuff that were sent to South Africa for his own personal consumption!

Making it in Neath
'Neath, in the early 1970s, were an immense side boasting international forwards like prop Glyn Shaw, the terrific wing forward Dai 'The Shadow' Morris and the giant Brian Thomas,' said Phil. 'The smallest scrum-half in Welsh rugby, Dai Parker from Briton Ferry, was invited to play for the great club side. Built like a jockey, he was only 5 ft 5 in. with size 5 feet.

'Now in those days you couldn't call yourself a Neath player until you played five games for the club and the man from Briton Ferry's big day arrived when Neath travelled to play Cardiff, arguably the best club side in world rugby. Gareth Edwards, Barry John, P.L. Jones, Mike Knill, Lynn Baxter, Ian Robinson and Carl Smith all played for them. Dai Parker was so proud. He was even prouder after the game as Neath had beaten mighty Cardiff. He packed his little boots into this little bag and headed for the Cardiff clubhouse. He was finally a Neath player.

'A large official at the clubhouse door stopped him and asked what he wanted. "I'm the Neath scrum-half and I'm here for my tea," replied Dai. The official told him in no uncertain terms not to be so ridiculous and to clear off. Dai stood distraught, not knowing what to do. Two minutes later help arrived in the form of Brian (the Giant) Thomas – 19 stone of hard man. Nobody would dare to stop him now as he was in the company of the enforcer.

'"Brian, Brian," said Dai, "they won't let me in for my tea."

'"Bugger off, you little shit," replied Brian. He turned to the bouncer. "All afternoon this kid has been pestering us for autographs – throw him out."

'Despite the Giant's denial of Dai's entitlement that day, Dai Parker went on to play for Neath for the next ten years.'

Chris Ralston
South Africa 1974, 1 cap
England 1972–5, 22 caps

I roomed with Chris Ralston in London before we left for South Africa. Through the haze of Villiger cigar smoke he complained that being picked for the Lions was damned inconvenient, as he was moving flat. What I didn't find out until later was that he had sent his wife back to France for three months, cancelled his leasing agreement and put the contents of his flat into storage (charged up to the Home Unions). I enjoyed his complaints for the duration of the tour, as he was brilliant company.

Social Culture

Chris recalled: 'Years ago, when I joined Richmond, most players were ex-public school from establishments favoured by the President, Frank Menim, such as Radley or Marlborough – names in the academic world that also suggested a particular rank and connections in the social milieu. I had attended a public school, but King William's College, on the Isle of Man, despite being a fine institution, didn't hold the same cachet as those with more history behind them.

'I slipped in mid-season, under the radar, and after two years earned a position on the first XV – the only non-Oxbridge player, and was awarded an honorary Blue. Richmond was a splendid club playing first-class rugby, but it also had an immense social aspect that revolved around the consumption of alcohol. No matter, the heavy-drinking culture often added to the bonding within the club and no more so than when on tour.

'Such was the camaraderie and the social life, when Easter came round Richmond never had a problem providing a full-strength team for their tour. A regular fixture for the Easter tour took place in the south-west of France. The journey to Terrasson in the Dordogne by necessity took us via Bordeaux. At a wine-tasting en route in Bergerac, one of our star players, England winger Peter Cook, had consumed a goodly amount of the local produce. Richmond's visits were popular with the local community and we arrived in Terrasson to a mayoral reception. Bunting flapped in the breeze, a brass band played to welcome the team. To reciprocate the greeting, we put forward our star player to shake hands and say thank you. Amidst all the pomp and ceremony, he promptly threw up over the Mayor.

'Though he, we, were forgiven for this solecism, and the social gaffe was accepted as the result of over-indulgence and not a direct insult to the town, things went from bad to worse. However, on the rugby pitch, Richmond ventured out against prestige teams and gave a good display and held their own against lesser sides delighted to have the opportunity to face the mighty English club.

'I returned five times to the Easter tour to France, even rejecting the invitation to play for the Barbarians. France was great. Why would anyone choose to get their head kicked in at Cardiff in the cold and rain? Other destinations further afield in Hawaii and San Francisco also offered magnificent rugby and social opportunity, but the best tours and my fondest memories are of those to France.

'Richmond is a fantastic club and since relegation forced them down nine divisions, the club spirit and the quality of players has seen them claw their way back nine years later to Division Two. There is a strong fraternity still, and the social scene is as vibrant as ever. Although most of my exertions nowadays might be on the golf course or on a bike, my heart remains with the club and I feel blessed to have been part of it. Friendships made through shared goals and hard work, along with an inimitable team ethos, may not be exclusive to rugby or Richmond, but they are exceptional and long-standing. Cheers!'

Andy Ripley OBE
South Africa 1974
England 1972–6, 24 caps

Andy has passed away (2010) since the last book was written, but I still hear him singing Wings' 1974 hit 'Band on the Run'.

Ripley's Bar
Andy's children, Marcus, Claudia and Stephanie, reminisced in early 2011: 'Next week, on 16 February 2011, we will be heading over to

Rosslyn Park Rugby Club, to have a drink at Ripley's Bar and to collect the Obolensky Award that has been bestowed on Dad, posthumously.

'Our dad passed away eight months ago, but the love and appreciation of his spirit has continued with full force. Going to these events is not easy; we cannot expect it to be. No longer having Dad with us in his world is strange and seems out of context, but we must go because it is a privilege: a privilege to recognise that outside of our close family unit our dad was truly loved. And with good reason! We have received so many kind and heartfelt letters of condolence since our dad passed away, with some sharing fun stories of good memories with him and others simply expressing their thoughts on him as a person, "A splash of colour in a world of grey."

'It is a joy to read our dad's book, *Ripley's World,* and others such as Stewart McKinney's *Voices from the Back of the Bus,* that retell stories of our dad on the 1974 British Lions tour. It is a rare treat to get an insight into your parents' life before they were even aware that one day they would become your parents – but we love those stories from the tour!

'Our dad reminisced that in May 1974, when staying at the Union Hotel in Pretoria, he had reorganised the letters on the noticeboard outside the hotel, which had originally read "Union Hotel", to now read "Le Onion Hut", and commenting, "Not very big or clever, but it made me laugh – every time."

'Our dad never lost his sense of fun and his love of life. And so next week when we go to Rosslyn Park Rugby Club to collect his award, we will raise a glass to our dad at Ripley's Bar, think of "Le Onion Hut", and smile!'

Then I was one of Willie John's Invincible Lions
Now I am just trying to be a sun-tanned hero of life with my own towel
Then I was a young man full of expectation and all his own teeth
Now I'm happily married with three kids, lots of dental work, and a
    mortgage
Then I had to get over being in the Wednesday side . . . the dirt trackers
    (players not playing or on the bench for the next match) . . . the racs
    and the B XV
Now I have to get over getting older and walking with a limp
Then I thought I had experienced troughs and crests
Now I know that sharing a room with Gordon Brown wasn't that bad and

    listening to Tommy David sing wasn't that great
Now it's Sanatogen, fast forward and fading
Then I thought it all ended at Heathrow after a 747 flight home
Now I know different
Then I was one of 31 players on a rugby tour
But now . . . whatever . . . I am one of Willie John's Invincible Lions . . .
    forever.

Poem written by Andy for the team's reunion in 1994

J.J. Williams
South Africa 1974, 4 caps; New Zealand 1977, 3 caps
Wales 1974–7, 30 caps

J.J. Williams did not like Fergus Slattery during sprint-training in South Africa in 1974. Slats thought that the rest of us donkeys did not pose a big enough test for his sprinting ability. So, he would join the backs and always position himself beside J.J., who was a Commonwealth Games sprinter. J.J. wasn't allowed to relax for a split second or Slattery would have him. Still, J.J. Williams must have benefited from Slattery's close attention as he scored a record four tries in the Test series.

Support from Strange Quarters

'Scoring the winning tries in the third Test in Port Elizabeth during the 1974 tour to South Africa was the highlight of my rugby career,' said J.J. 'Having won the first two Tests, we knew we had to win the third Test to win the series and that whatever happened in the fourth Test we could not be caught.

'The tension leading up to the match was unbelievable. The Springboks were under enormous pressure from their own people, and this showed in the fact that they had not decided on the scrum-half until the morning of the game. The first half was as brutal as you could get, and it seemed that the Boks were coming and coming but didn't breach our defence at all. Just into the second half the biggest punch-up of the tour started – it resulted in Gordon Brown being decked three times – but the "99" call came to our rescue once again.

'Amazingly, the referee gave us a lineout and the same Gordon Brown leapt up to win a superb lineout. He palmed the ball perfectly to Gareth, who threw out a beautiful pass to Benny, who in turn gave it to McGeechan and on to Dick Milliken in fingertip fashion. Milliken then missed out J.P.R. and passed a long ball to me – and I was away sprinting for the corner. I could see that I was going to be cut off by the corner flagging Springbok back row, so I passed it back into the hands of J.P.R., who immediately passed it back to me on the switch, and there I was with the line at my mercy. I managed to sprint around under the posts, and ironically it was the beleaguered Springbok captain, Hannes Marais, who was there trying to ankle-tap me. I touched the ball down under the posts – and the Test series was won.

'I have a photograph at home which illustrates the whole occasion. The photograph shows me touching down under the posts and the whole of the area behind the posts jumping for joy – it was the area where the "coloureds" were allowed to stand, and they together with the "coloured" policemen were saying – "Thank you, Lions!!"'

Graham Price
New Zealand 1977, 4 caps; South Africa 1980, 4 caps; New Zealand 1983, 4 caps
Wales 1975–83, 41 caps

Whenever the Pontypool front row were together, I never got much of a chance to talk to Pricey, as Bobby Windsor and Charlie Faulkner talked so much he couldn't get a word in. Recently, I've seen him on his own more often and I realise the man is a total masochist. He loves running up hills and mountains – and hates the flat!

No wonder he was so superbly conditioned. No one worked harder in the scrums than Graham Price, but an example of his outstanding stamina came on his debut against France in 1975 when he ran in a try from 70 yards. Astonishing.

Getting Bobby Right
'International fame and success has at times affected the personality of the players,' said Graham. 'Take Bobby Windsor for example: he went on the '74 Lions tour to South Africa when they won the Test series and played in all four Test matches. He subsequently became accepted as the best hooker in the world.

'This produced a marked change in his personality. From being a relatively modest person before the tour he became, to put it bluntly, rather conceited! His next international tour was to Japan with Wales in 1975. We got on the Tokyo plane at Heathrow Airport and took our allocated seats in economy class at the rear. That is, everyone apart from Bobby, who sat in the first-class cabin!

'The stewardess asked him to leave and join the rest of us in economy class, but he refused saying, "I'm Bobby Windsor. I played in the British Lions Test team and I'm not sitting in economy class. I deserve to have a seat in first class." The chief steward tried to influence him to move but met the same reply. The Captain was called and he explained, unsuccessfully, to Bobby that unless he moved to his allocated seat at the back of the plane he would not take off.

'The chief steward spoke to the team manager, explaining the predicament. Overhearing this, the team captain, Mervyn Davies, assured them he could fix the problem. "I know Bobby very well from touring with the Lions. I'll speak to him."

Mervyn shuffled down the aisle to the first-class cabin and had a quiet word with Bobby. Without protest, Bobby stood up and walked to the rear of the plane to take his allocated seat in economy.

'The chief steward said to Mervyn, "That was amazing. What did you say that so easily persuaded him to change his mind?"

'Mervyn replied, "I know Bobby's not the most intelligent of people. He's a bit like one of those lava lamps; you know what I mean – fun to look at, but not very bright. I simply told him the first-class section wasn't going to Tokyo!"'

Moss Keane
New Zealand 1977, 1 cap
Ireland 1974–84, 51 caps

Headstone

Sadly Mossie's no longer with us, having passed away in 2010. His wife, Ann, actually didn't know him when he went on his Lions tour to New Zealand in '77, so the only thing she can recall is the answer Moss gave when he was asked what the highlight of that tour had been. If you remember, it was a long, very wet and ultimately disappointing tour.

He said that the highlight of the tour had been when he heard that Kerry had beaten Cork in the Munster final!

His funeral was a truly amazing affair with an astonishing turnout. The tributes and respect paid to Moss were appreciated by Ann even though the circumstances were unfortunate. She managed to get the headstone finished the day before his first anniversary as was her aim for the previous year. For fun, on the headstone, she has Moss's date of birth and date of death in Roman numerals. If people can work out his age, she will be happy enough, but all the better if they can't!

She thought Moss would enjoy that!

Golden Oldie High Jinks

The First Golden Oldies Festival was held in November 1988 in Bermuda. We all enjoyed ourselves to the extreme, reliving past glories and drinking and drinking. The moped was the mode of transport. Robin Challis lost his the first evening and never found it again. Peter Bell was arrested for being drunk in charge of his and if he'd only mentioned that he was staying in the Governor of Bermuda's annexe he might have avoided a court appearance next morning. Charlie Faulkner too was apprehended, as he was trying to ride with his helmet on back to front and Ian McCrea ended up in hospital after falling off.

Sometime during the week, Ann Keane lost Moss and asked Willie Duncan if he'd give her a lift on the back of his machine to find him. As Willie took off from the Elbow Beach Hotel he spun the back wheel and Ann shouted, 'Jesus, Willie, go easy or you'll kill us, and me the mother of two children in Ireland and the minder of one here.'

Breakfast Beer

A tired, jet-lagged Peter Wheeler was woken on the first morning of the 1977 Tour by his room-mate, Moss Keane, turning on his bedside lamp. Moss promptly lit a cigarette and ripped open a can of beer.

'Moss!' Peter protested. 'It's five o'clock in the morning and we're on a Lions tour to New Zealand.'

'Ah,' said Moss, 'it's five o'clock in the evening in Dublin and I always have a pint at this time.'

Terry Cobner
New Zealand 1977, 3 caps
Wales 1974–8, 19 caps

The name of Terry Cobner will always be synonymous with Pontypool. He, along with Ray Prosser and a fearsome pack of forwards, turned them into the most feared club side in Britain. I was honoured to be asked to play my last serious rugby for the men of Gwent. Terry took over the pack leadership on the 1977 tour to New Zealand and such was their superiority that the All Blacks were forced to play three-man scrums in the last Test. Unfortunately the back play was not of the same quality of 1971 or 1974 and the series was lost, but it certainly was nothing to do with the efforts of the great man from Blaenavon.

Bless His Socks

Terry recalled: 'As captain of the Wales tour party to Australia in 1978, I stood proud, tried to ensure the boys in red gave their best and encouraged the team to battle out the matches. Australia still smarted from their defeat in Wales in 1975 and were determined to avenge the disgrace. We were on their home turf now – a different landscape from that of Wales where we had enjoyed terrific fan loyalty and rugby supremacy – and we were without Gareth Edwards and Phil Bennett. Graham Price's jaw was broken in a hotly contested second Test match, and Australia's Andy Slack has since claimed that the winning drop goal in the first Test actually went to the right of the posts. It was not a cheery tour as far as results were concerned, especially with the bad feeling that followed those incidents, and it signalled the beginning of the end of a hugely successful period in the history of the game in Wales.

'The Queensland game on 11 June, a week before the second Test match, was a tough one with no quarter given on either side. It is in those no-nonsense affairs that you need a referee with a firm hand and an unbiased whistle. No such luck here!

The referee was a legend in those parts for his total support of the home side. We were warned beforehand that we might be up against it but thought the game to be too high profile to be refereed anything other than fairly and without bias. How wrong can you get?

'As I went for the toss, I noticed the referee wore Queensland socks. Almost immediately after the start of the game we had the first scrum of the match. I asked, "Whose ball, ref?" Failing to hear his reply I then asked our hooker Bobby Windsor what he said.

'Bobby replied, "He said 'ours'."

'"What do you mean – it's ours?"

'"No, fucking theirs!"

'Needless to say, we lost the game.'

Wales Tour to Australia 1996

'As manager of the 1996 tour to Australia I was able to observe the players from more of a distance than I was able to as captain in 1978.

'Some fine wits were on the trip, the most notable being Kingsley Jones, son of Kingsley Jones Snr, manager of the great Jonah Lomu and himself a great humorist. Throughout the tour Kingsley competed with Gwyn Jones for the number 7 jersey.

'The game against NSW Country was played in the outback at Dubbo. The little town of Dubbo (sorry, regional city!) had a small airstrip that could only accommodate small propeller-driven planes and consequently we travelled in two parties. I travelled on the first plane, as did Kingsley. While waiting at the airstrip, Kingsley wandered outside only to come back and say, "I've got good news and bad news. Which do you want first?"

'"Give us the bad news."

'"The other plane has gone down."

'"Good god! What's the good news?"

'"Gwyn Jones was on it!"'

Allan Martin
New Zealand 1977, 1 cap
Wales 1973–81, 34 caps

Allan Martin – the Panther – followed two other Aberavon second rows, Max Wiltshire and Billy Mainwaring, into the Welsh side.

When one mentions the great Welsh teams of the '70s, it is usually the backs who are admired – Phil Bennett, Gareth Edwards, Gerald Davies, Barry John, for example – and I never think that the front five donkeys receive enough accolades.

The Pontypool front row, Windsor, Faulkner and Price, and the second row pairing of Wheel and Martin were a powerful engine house. Allan Martin excelled as a number 4 jumper. He was also the last player I can remember to kick goals by the toe-pointing method and he was a fine long-range exponent of the art.

Hats Off to You

'Way back, nearly a quarter of a century ago,' recalled Allan, 'the Bermuda Classic featured teams that played under their nation's colours. November in Bermuda, when the weather is right, makes for a luxury holiday. But, who cares about that? We were there for the rugby, for Welsh pride and perhaps a taste of the culture and entertainment so kindly offered by the organisers.

'To make sure we could give our best performance, Charlie Faulkner,

Spike Watkins, Mike Roberts and I regularly met in the Elbow Beach Hotel, where we could concentrate on team moves, soothed by the ocean lapping against the pink, coral beach and sipping a cold drink or two. It was hard work. Sometimes we had to sit there all afternoon discussing tactics. One dark 'n' stormy afternoon, after a prolonged strategy session, we were expected at an evening reception. Charlie had been thinking really hard, so he staggered out of the bar to stride his moped and go back to get ready. I could see he was a mite unsteady, so I watched him. Fortunately, in Bermuda, the speed limit and the limited engine power of the mopeds used to travel around the island cause little more than road rash for anyone who topples off them. Coming off a rugby pitch you could be in much worse shape.

'The police in Bermuda had their own rugby club that played against touring sides visiting the island. They appreciated how things played out on and off the pitch – fortunately. Two police stopped Charlie on South Shore Road not long after he had mounted his machine. I hung around in the background in case my intervention or assistance might be required, possibly even to provide translation services. I wasn't needed. Charlie became animated and gestured to the police he was quite capable of removing his helmet and putting it back on to face the correct way. How he managed to wear it back to front in the first place is one of life's mysteries; he couldn't tell you how he did it – then or now.'

The Beast

'Taking care of mates is essential to rugby. On the pitch there were all sorts of individuals keen to make life unbearable for you. Referees do a good job, but much of the skulduggery is done out of sight of the whistled official.

'Playing against France during the 1970s, opposition teams had to face the Beast of Beziers, Alain Esteve, a 6 ft 9 in., 19-stone, bearded monster of the French second row. Our hooker, Bobby Windsor, frequently came up against him and often mentions how when we packed down, he'd hear him say, "Bob-bee, Bob-bee" and then this big fist would come through and smack him in the chops. To get his own back, Bobby booted him in the mush as hard as he could. He got up and gave Bobby a wink.

'Esteve – evil, enormous and equipped to do damage – tested the mettle of Graham Price on his debut at Parc des Princes in 1975. Geoff Wheel and I gave him a nod and said, "We'll get him."

'We had an opportunity to redress the wrong, and stood behind the gigantic troll. Unseen by the referee, Ken Pattinson, Geoff and I hit him with our best blows. The creature remained unmoved. Esteve turned his head, glared at us and growled, something that probably translated as "You are dead." Perhaps the threat spurred us on and gave us a greater turn of speed; we were leading the French by ten points at half-time (17–7) and beat them 25–10.'

Phillip Orr
New Zealand 1977, 1 cap
Ireland 1976–87, 58 caps

One of rugby's iconic photographs is of Moss Keane, Fran Cotton and Phil Orr absolutely covered in mud at a lineout in New Zealand in 1977. Phil Orr had risen to the fore very quickly, as a year before he had made his debut in Paris against France. He had devastating speed over short distances and was the cornerstone of the Irish scrum for 11 years.

Why I Became a Prop Forward
Phil said: 'I thought I'd share with the readers how it was actually decided that I should play prop forward. September 1961, when I first went to secondary school, I turned up at a rugby training session. I played soccer and had never even seen a rugby match let alone played in one. The pitch seemed the same except the goalposts were "H" shaped.

'I vividly remember the scene at the High School, Rathgar, in Dublin that afternoon when a teacher was confronted with around thirty ten-year-old boys (it was the under 11's) who had varying knowledge of the rudiments of rugby football.

'Obviously the teacher had confronted this situation before, as he lined us up on the goal line and asked us to race to the end of the pitch and back in order to sort out the forwards from the backs. Now I was fairly nippy when I was young, even though I say it myself, so I was fairly confident of finishing in the top ten.

'The teacher called "go" and off we went. Well placed in the front group, I managed to be one of the front-runners as we reached the far end of the pitch. I then saw (for the first time ever) the dead ball line after the goal line and made for it full belt. Wind in my face, eyes screwed shut in determination, legs and arms pumping hard, I realised I'd held first place and made a quick turnaround at the dead ball line.

'I was suddenly at the back of the field and realised I had made a dreadful mistake. All the other lads had turned around to run back on the goal line and I had to yet to reach it again before I could start to claw back some of the distance I had kindly given to my future team-mates. I finally finished about two-thirds back from the leaders and was immediately informed that I would be a forward, more precisely, a prop forward as I had the proper shape, whatever that meant.

'I played prop forward all through my school career except for one season at hooker, obviously because no one else would play there that season. Little did that teacher know at the time how correct and how perceptive he was all those years ago.'

6

SINCE I RETIRED

Colin Patterson
South Africa 1980, 3 caps
Ireland 1978–80, 11 caps

Colin Patterson's first year in representative rugby was in 1976 when he appeared on the Ulster scene. I immediately knew he would make it because, apart from his passing ability and searing pace, he was a cocky little bastard. We came to an arrangement in club games: I wouldn't trouble him if he didn't make breaks from set pieces. So, at the first scrum in a Dungannon/Instonians game, I would show him my studs as he put the ball into a scrum and he would wink at me.

It was a tragedy that injuries he sustained on the 1980 Lions tour cut his playing career short – he would have developed into a formidable scrum-half.

Recently Colin told me if he had a problem with his game he would consult my old mentor, Josh Lapsley, who he regarded as the best scrum-half coach he had ever encountered.

Terry Kennedy and the First Night on Tour

'Imagine if you will two young Irish lads, well 24 and 25, only recently capped for their country and who, in 1979, find themselves in Australia on a six-week tour,' said Colin. 'Both are full of excitement, curiosity and energy. Well, that was Terry Kennedy, the Rat as he was affectionately known, and me. We were both capped in November 1978 against the All Blacks and the team very nearly pulled off an unlikely victory. Added to that were very good showings in the Five Nations with draws against Scotland and France, a narrow loss to Wales in Cardiff and a win over England. The two lads were in confident mood.

'It was the night before the tour opener. Jet lag left the two of us finding it hard to get to sleep and we decided a stroll around Perth, Western Australia, would be a good thing to calm us down. With this in mind, we headed out to investigate our surroundings, intending to return to the hotel well before midnight and certainly sober.

'Rat informs me as we leave the hotel that Noel Murphy, "Noisy", will most certainly be doing the rounds of the pubs that night, not because he likes a drink – Noisy is teetotal – but to make sure all his lads are safely wrapped up in bed preparing for battle the next day. Together we hatch a plan to foil him and this takes us a little further afield from the hotel than we believe he would venture . . .

'We enter a bar and embrace the atmosphere therein. Wonderful! We buy a couple of light refreshments, non-alcoholic, and just to be safe we head to the very back of the bar where we take a table. Now, as luck would have it, a couple of the local girls heard our accents and joined us at the table. We were all having a very pleasant evening when Rat exclaims loudly, "Oh Jaysus! Noisy's here!" I immediately stopped talking and glanced towards the door but saw no sign of him. I turned around to tell the Rat he must be seeing things only to find myself alone with the girls.

'My thoughts were less than agreeable at the realisation he had disappeared so quickly without further help or assistance to me. I thought he must have disappeared out the rear door. I was just about to call him to come back when a familiar voice said, "Cahlin! What are ye doing here? Don't ye know ye have a big game tomorrow?"

'"Yes" I replied. "But it's only orange juice and I'll be back in the hotel well before midnight."

'"Ye need to be getting to your bed now, not gallivanting out here!" commanded Noel.

'I was really seething now because of the perceived injustice of having to take the flak for both the Rat and me on this most innocent of trips and because it wasn't really my idea in the first place. I could merrily have choked him as I took the full blast from Noisy. Eventually I said, "OK I'll go back to the hotel right away!"

'I excused myself from our most gracious Australian hostesses and was just about to head for the door when Noisy said in a loud voice, "And YE can come out from under the table, Terry!" I spun around and looked in amazement as the table cloth peeled over the top of Terry's head and the Rat slowly crawled out. I burst into howls of laughter at the sight of the Rat on his hands and knees making his way out to join us, mumbling something about it not being anything serious, just a bit of fun.

'Despite the ignominy and humiliation we felt, we still laugh about it to this day.'

Tony Ward
South Africa 1980, 1 cap
Ireland 1978–87, 19 caps

Tony Ward was hailed as the new star of Irish rugby in my last season with Ireland – his first. Next season, '79, he scored 33 points out of Ireland's total of 53. But when the team left for Australia in 1979, Ollie Campbell got the nod and the controversy is raging still. Personally, I would have converted Tony Ward to full-back and have accommodated the two great players into the side.

Beat the Bok
'Throughout our lives there are certain events and happenings that change the shape of our thinking at that point in time and in some cases ever after,' said Tony. 'For me, South Africa 1980 made for one such life-changing experience.

'When the call came to jump on board Billy's [Beaumont] bus, I couldn't get to the terminus quickly enough. To be a British and Irish Lion was, and I should imagine still is, the ultimate aim for every self-respecting wannabe in this part of the rugby-playing world.

'The call to colours came on Sunday, 18 May as I was making my way back from participating in a charity walk organised by a former student colleague of mine – Denis O'Boyle – for his local GAA club in Castlebar, Co. Mayo. Ronnie Dawson, Syd Millar and Noel Murphy were in touch from Dublin and South Africa respectively to see if and when I could make the earliest flight out, as both Gareth Davies and Ollie Campbell had been struck down by injury.

'By Thursday I was on my way and on Friday touched down in Jan Smuts Airport after a brilliant kip courtesy of Jan Pickard who was on the flight and had organised a row of seats for me to put my head down. Different times, different standards. Jan has since passed on, but boy was his gesture appreciated at the time.

'Within a couple of hours I was on a connecting flight to Bloemfontein and no sooner had I arrived than I was included on the bench to face Orange Free State the following day. The greatest rugby experience of my life was under way. I wouldn't have changed it for the world . . . and yet.

'Rugby-wise I loved every nerve-testing minute whether in training or on big match day, be it Saturday or midweek. As we were part of only the second ever "dirties" [dirt trackers] to go through a Lions tour unbeaten, the buzz in the shadow XV was pretty neat. To room with donkeys of the calibre of Allan Martin, Johnnie Beattie, Gareth Williams, Ian Stephens, Alan Tomes et al. was, well, different. If donkeys are from Venus, then pretty boys are from Mars for sure!

'The treatment we received from the rugby authorities throughout the tour was five-star. The South African Rugby Board and individual host unions left no stone unturned in looking after our every need. And yet at no stage did I feel comfortable. Along with Colin Patterson we scratched beneath the surface. We went to places we weren't meant to go. We met with the Watson brothers – Cheeky, Valence and Ronnie – and a different, more sobering picture emerged. We visited townships outside Bloemfontein and Port Elizabeth. Seeing what we weren't meant to see hurt.

'It also went someway to explaining why the ordinary man in the street was urging us to "beat the bok". It was something that had bewildered me as much as the first lavatory sign in Johannesburg Airport indicating "whites only" had taken my breath away. Being addressed as "Masta" (master) by indigenous people touched a nerve. I loved South Africa and loathed it. I loved being a Lion yet hated what I was doing to these lovely but so clearly oppressed people.

'Long before this tour of a lifetime ended I had made up my mind not to return with Ireland 12 months on. It reflected no arrogance on my part. Not for a minute did I ever think that by me not making myself available for rugby selection would the course of South African history and the curse that was apartheid change one iota. Put simply, my conscience wouldn't let me return while the apartheid system prevailed. Errol Tobias was breaking the mould, but it was much too little taking far too long.

'The building-bridges – i.e. keeping up communication – argument I had listened to (from rugby people) in favour of ongoing contact no longer rang true, as the harsh and brutal reality hit home. Conversely I felt that by denying them the pursuit at which they excelled it might, just might, lead to those in charge taking a long hard look at themselves. Rightly or wrongly, it is a course of action I do not regret to this day.

'It may have cost me a couple more caps and another Ireland tour, but so what? I have been back several times since in a journalistic capacity and while change is pitifully slow, the Rainbow Nation is gradually taking shape.

'Selfishly speaking, I loved my eight-week stint with the Beaumont Lions. We may have lost the Test series, but we were a happy, hugely united group under an exceptional captain and an immensely popular leader in William B.

'Personal memories are too many to recall now, but playing with a torn thigh in the opening Test at Newlands yet managing reasonably well with the boot represented a self-satisfying high. Almost drowning in Umhlanga (saved by John O'Driscoll's alert reaction when summoning a lifeguard to my rescue) was at the other end of the scale. There was so much in between, not least sharing so much time in a common cause with people of the calibre of Bruce Hay, John Carleton, Peter Morgan, Ray Gravell, Jim Renwick, Clive Woodward, Elgan Rees, Andy Irvine, Paul Dodge, Steve Smith . . . the list is endless. Sadly Boofer and Grav are no longer with us. Smithy arrived on the penultimate day for the last Test in Loftus. He may as well have been there for the entire tour such was his impact. He was that type of player. It was that type of tour, a special time in all our lives and a privilege to have been part of it.'

Colm Tucker
South Africa 1980, 2 caps
Ireland 1979–80, 3 caps

Colm Tucker has sadly passed away (January 2012) since he kindly contributed to this book. I was finishing my career when Colm was coming to the fore and we only crossed swords once in an Ulster/ Munster game. He was probably brought too late into the Test side on Billy Beaumont's 1980 team, but played well in the last two Tests at open-side flanker with John O'Driscoll at blind side. His great power and speed were evident in both these games and especially the fourth Test at Pretoria.

I was delighted recently to meet his son Colm Jnr at Ballymena, where he coached Limerick Bohemians to a win, proudly carrying on the traditions of his great, late father.

Turned Out Well
'Describing a Lions tour as the equivalent of a university education is particularly apt,' commented Colm. 'The wonderful mix of camaraderie, cultural integration and the beginnings of enduring friendships is an experience which for me has remained unsurpassed.

'In 1980, an official touring party consisted of 30 players, along with one manager, one coach and a medical officer. We did not have any spin doctors then. Much of the organisation was done by the players themselves. There were always two "duty boys" amongst us. Our responsibilities included organising room sharing, team activities and assisting with the kit.

'I loved every minute of it, even from the not-so-promising start. Elated, excited and keen to meet up with my team-mates, I arrived at Heathrow Airport, where a hostile, ill-humoured taxi driver almost became apoplectic at my request to take me to the Holiday Inn, which happened to be quite near the airport but much too near for his liking. He ranted all through the short trip and finally induced (browbeat) me into paying him £7, about twice the normal fare. In hindsight, I think he was the meanest person I met on the entire tour. It was an indication to me that I needed to toughen up, as £7 was far more than I could afford to spend on my first day on tour.

'Attired in my Lions number one dress, carrying two full suitcases along with my kitbag, I arrived at the hotel after saying a pleasant farewell to the surly driver. I suddenly felt overdressed and a bit of tube [idiot] when I noticed almost everyone else turned up in their casuals. Superstar and veteran Tourist Fran Cotton arrived with only the clothes on his back. I heard later he bought a pair of shoes on the way to the hotel. Fran was a tough man.

'Ray Gravell, who sadly passed away in 2007, was one of my greatest friends on tour. I will forever remember our "two pints of draught", as he called them, each Wednesday night after the midweek game. It was Ray who made that classic reply to the referee when penalised for a late tackle, "It wasn't late, ref; I got there as fast as I could." Ray was a great man and a great friend, and I am proud to have shared many great experiences with him. "*Ar dheis De go raibh a anam uasal*" (May his noble soul stand at the right hand of God).

'I have vivid memories also of Jim Renwick's rendition of "Flower of Scotland" on the way to each game, and me being asked to sing my own club's beloved Shannon anthem, "There is an Isle", on the return trip. That was the pinnacle of my singing career.

'Odd little memories jump into your mind when you think back. Hymie, our kit man, chain-smoked. On one occasion our bus driver kindly decided to bring all the kit to the dressing-room without telling Hymie. Thinking that it was forgotten, Hymie became so animated he lit a second cigarette and stood there unaware with a cigarette in each hand and puffed at them alternately. His obvious distress made us all fall around laughing. I don't believe we ever saw that bus driver again while on tour.

'My Lions tour to South Africa in 1980 remains a most enduring memory and will always be a special part of my life. I was privileged to have travelled the journey with a party of exceptional men.'

John O'Driscoll
South Africa 1980, 4 caps; New Zealand 1983, 2 caps
Ireland 1978–84, 26 caps

John O'Driscoll played his first game for Ireland against Scotland in 1978, but unfortunately for him and very fortunately for me he was concussed and I replaced him from the bench. Fifty-eight seconds later, Fergus Slattery actually passed me the ball and I scored from the great distance of two yards.

John didn't return to the Irish team until 1980, but when he did, he had obviously done a lot of strength training and became a great blindside in what I consider was one of the finest Irish back rows: Slattery, Duggan and O'Driscoll.

He was outstanding on two Lions tours and continues to make a huge contribution to Irish rugby by his devotion to the Irish Exiles in Britain, and is a committee member on the IRFU. John's brother is Barry, who played full-back for Ireland . . . and sometimes another 'brother' used to appear on a Saturday night, though I haven't seen him recently.

Sunday School with Three Greatly Lamented Friends
'On 29 June 1980 it was "Sunday School" in the lounge of the Holiday Inn in Port Elizabeth,' John remembered. 'Sunday School had become a custom on that Lions tour whereby on the day following a Test match a few of us would while away the afternoon with some quiet post-lunch libation. I sat at one corner of the group with Ray Gravell, the Welsh centre, Maurice Colclough, the English second row and Bruce Hay, the Scottish full-back/wing: three great players who were to become lifelong friends following that trip. Very sadly they are no longer with us.

'The previous day we had lost the third Test match, and thus the series, to South Africa. Our desperate disappointment exaggerated a disconsolate feeling throughout the squad that we should have been ahead in the series at that stage. We now faced the prospect of a whitewash a fortnight later if we lost the fourth Test. This was against a background of no Lions team ever having won the last Test match in South Africa before.

'It had been a very happy trip despite the results in the Test matches. Lions tours are a unique sporting tradition. On selection, I considered the opportunity to travel to compete against one of the great rugby-playing nations an enormous privilege. I hadn't, however, realised just how much fun it would be not only to spend three months training and playing flat out at the highest level but also getting to know and enjoying the craic with 30 players from the different home nations. Only a few weeks earlier, these same players had been knocking the stuffing out of each other.

'It was a united party, attributable to the management team of Syd Millar, "Noisy" Murphy and Bill Beaumont, who understood the requirements to make Lions tours work both on and off the field and the ethos behind this.

'Maurice, Bruce, Ray and myself discussed how tragic it would be should we return home with nothing to show results-wise from the Test series. A few songs later we resolved that no matter what it took, we were going to change that history of final Test match failure.

'Great commitment came from the entire squad at training sessions over the next two weeks in the build-up to the final Test. We also completed our unbeaten run in the provincial matches with victories over South African Barbarians, Western Province and Griqualand West.

'For the final Test played in Pretoria we had had a very stable pack. Throughout the series only nine forwards played in the Tests. The only change up front had been Colm Tucker deservedly coming in for the last two Tests. The back line on the other hand had been severely disrupted by injuries during the tour, but we had perhaps our best combination out for this match.

'That sunny day had the sort of crisp atmosphere only felt on the Highveld. Loftus Versfeld, a magnificent stadium, had a hard playing surface made for the fast-action match that was to follow. A capacity crowd of 68,000 gave the touts a roaring trade, as all of South Africa bayed to see the anticipated Springbok series Grand Slam.

'The first half's pattern of play was similar to the first three Tests – unrelenting pressure from our pack and attacking flurries from the Springboks who, in this series, proved to be devastating on counter-attack. It was once more a very close encounter, but with – I am sure –

the team spirit we had developed over the months playing a major role, we prevailed in the end.

'Celebrations that night were quite something and merged seamlessly into Sunday School the following afternoon. I again sat sandwiched between Ray and Maurice. That session moved into a phase of various games and quizzes with drinking penalties for failure. The key is to avoid drinking too much, as mistakes become increasingly frequent. A self-perpetuating cycle of mistake/penalty-drink/mistake leads to rapid oblivion.

'The gathered crew were drinking cane spirit, greatly diluted with orange juice, from pint glasses. I became aware that when I wasn't looking, Ray, on my left side, was adding volumes of cane to my glass. I considered myself far too wily to fall for this old ruse, so when he was distracted I filled my glass to the brim from the large jug of plain orange juice on my right. Unfortunately what I hadn't noticed was, whilst Ray talked to me, Maurice emptied a bottle of cane into the orange jug. Suffice to say, I felt no pain that afternoon; more than can be said for the following morning!'

Ollie Campbell
South Africa 1980, 3 caps; New Zealand 1983, 4 caps
Ireland 1976–84, 22 caps

I played against Australia for Ireland in 1975. We lost 20–10 and it was also the debut for Ollie Campbell. It wasn't a successful day with the boot for Ollie, but he re-emerged in 1979 in Australia and was outstanding in the historic wins in Sydney and Ballymore. Ollie is one of the most modest, self-effacing, kind and generous individuals, who was a great help with getting Ann Keane's recollections of Moss for this book. He doesn't blow his own trumpet and claims his success was down to the team and the management that surrounded him, leading my researcher to call him 'a fibulous little rodent', which he has accepted as his latest moniker.

Memories of Grav
'The late Ray Gravell of Llanelli, Wales and the Lions was one of the most unique characters I have met in my life,' said Ollie. 'A passionate and proud Welshman who spoke Welsh as his first language amazingly also spoke some Irish. He was the only person in the world who always called me by my first name Seamus – naturally always with an Irish accent too.

In memory of him, by mutual agreement, his wife Mari has continued this tradition since he passed away.

'He was the warmest, most magical and wonderful human being imaginable. It was an honour to have played with him and against him, and a privilege and a blessing to have known him. He epitomised everything that is good in rugby and indeed everything that is good in the human spirit.

'From the outside he looked fearless, intimidating, imposing and indestructible. Being over six feet, weighing well over fourteen stone and having a beard added to this impression. What made him so appealing was the fact that in reality he was so insecure and vulnerable. He had an electric personality, though, and enriched the lives of everyone he came into contact with throughout his life.

'St Ermin's Hotel in London, on the eve of our departure to South Africa with Billy Beaumont's Lions team in 1980, was where I first met Grav. He pulled me aside to say how delighted he was to meet me. I was extremely flattered by this but then somewhat confused. He said he felt we could be soul mates on the tour as he had heard that I was reserved, quiet and even shy – just as he was himself!

'His unusual warm-up before coming on as a substitute in the first Test at Newlands in Cape Town beggared belief. On the side-line, getting geared up to take to the pitch, he repeatedly beat his chest with as much energy and volume as Johnny Weissmuller in his role as Tarzan would have been proud to claim.

'On that tour we played Orange Free State in Bloemfontein. In the very first play of the game, Grav tackled his opposite number so late it was almost posthumous. Asked to explain himself on TV immediately afterwards he explained that since a young boy he had always been told how important it was to get your first tackle in early – even if it's late! (In a similar vein he once made another late tackle when playing for his beloved Llanelli against local rivals Cardiff. In his defence he told the referee, quite seriously, that he had gotten there as soon as he could.)

'Grav's normal pre-match routine in the dressing-room included crying with emotion as he listened to Welsh ballad singer Dafydd Iwan on his Walkman and alternately vomiting with nerves in the toilet. This never varied, but before the so-called "fifth Test" against Northern Transvaal the wailing and retching took on a new dimension when frustration was added to the equation because he couldn't find his gum

SINCE I RETIRED

shield. He refused even to consider playing in the match unless it was found. So while Grav sang his heart out with Dafydd Iwan and wept and vomited, the other 15 members of the team scrabbled on their hands and knees looking for his missing gum shield. Some poor unfortunate did eventually find it.

'Grav passed away on 31 October 2007 exactly 35 years to the day after he had played for Llanelli when they famously beat the All Blacks 9–3 in one of the proudest moments of his life. In an extraordinary outpouring of emotion, over 10,000 people turned up at Stradey Park to pay their last respects. Not a bad turnout for such a reserved, quiet and shy man. He has been sadly missed since that day and Llanelli, Wales and the whole world of rugby is a much lesser place without him in it.'

John Robbie
South Africa 1980, 1 cap
Ireland 1976–81, 9 caps

When John Robbie emigrated to South Africa after losing his job for touring there with Ireland, I sort of lost touch with him. I didn't realise what an illustrious career he had playing for Transvaal, dropping a record 18 goals from the scrum-half position. But for sporting isolation, he would have been capped for his adopted country. I had a very enjoyable lunch with him recently and was delighted to hear him host a very successful radio programme every morning. He is also an extremely articulate and knowledgeable rugby critic who doesn't shrink from controversy. Good to see 'Junior' doing well.

I Played for Poola!
'It's quite sobering to realise one actually played rugby in the good old days,' John recalled. 'The best thing about being a dinosaur is you are actually a part of history and that is kind of nice. I was lucky to play for a short time with a genuinely legendary team, coach and club. Here is how it happened.

'Born and raised in Ireland, I sprang from a Scottish dad and a Welsh mum. My maternal grandfather, Bob Richards, lived with us and was a teacher from the Rhondda. He gave me my love for rugby and my early passion for the Bective Rangers Club in Donnybrook, South Dublin. You see, Cliff Morgan married an Irish girl and played for Bective for a short while. As a result some Welsh clubs – Cardiff, Neath

185

and Ebbw Vale – played annual fixtures and my gramps, with me in tow, used to watch every game. I never played for Bective but remain a fan. Of course, during my career, Welsh club rugby, along with French, was a cut above the rest. Cardiff, Llanelli and Swansea were the giants, but for a decade or so Pontypool, with their magnificent pack, were a club of legend. Songs were written about them and are still sung.

'One night at university in Cambridge I was drunk as a skunk with the varsity number 8 Edward Butler. I remember vaguely reeling off my Welsh heritage and expressing my life's ambition to experience playing club rugby in the Principality. Next morning I got a call from Eddie telling me that on Saturday I was playing for Pontypool against Tredegar in the club trial.

'I played, was amazed at how Tredegar piled into the giants, went off injured, but qualified to play for "Poola". After the Varsity match, I got a call to join the run-up to the Welsh Cup against mighty Cardiff. I stayed with Eddie and his marvellous folks and with much trepidation went for my first training session. We ran the famed grotto run and I finished well up the field. A good start. I trained with the backs under Ivor Taylor and enjoyed it. They were good. Then a summons from the legendary Ray Prosser boomed across the ground. "Robbie, you Irish cunt, leave the boys and come over 'ere with the men!" I did and thus gained my Pontypool nickname, "the Irish cunt".

'From then I was part of the legendary Pontypool pack because Poola included number 9 in the forwards. That's my story and I'm sticking to it. They were not big but quite magnificent. They scrummed with science not muscle and perfected the rolling maul to a degree not seen since. I might have been an Irish international, but I was in awe of them: Charlie, Bobby and Pricey, Steve Sutton and Perkie (John Perkins), Jeff Squire, Eddie and Dick Cobner. Mind you, Mike "Fingers" Gregory who played at flank sometimes never got a cap but was the crowd's favourite. What a pack. What a coach. What a club.

'The great cup day arrived and so did the snow. On the day of the game, hundreds of Pontypool fans arrived early and swept the pitch clean of its white covering. We started. I nearly scored. Dammit, the snow came down and the game was abandoned. That night, full of drink, Eddie and I had a snowball fight with the Pontypool front row outside their unique downtown clubhouse. It was surreal.

'We went close but lost the replay and were out of the cup. Somewhere I still have a faded *Western Mail* photo of the Pontypool team with me and those legends. It remains a proud memory and a cherished memento.

'However, my favourite memory is of training the week before the first game. Because the pitch was frozen we were not allowed to train on it. As an alternative training ground, the club managed to secure the use of the extensive rolling parkland belonging to the local psychiatric hospital. I kid you not. We arrived and club members, obviously road workers, had rigged up a series of lamps used to facilitate night-time maintenance. They held them, we trained and the snow fell and swirled as the wind got up. At one stage we were shuffling around in a blizzard. One of the players tapped my shoulder. He pointed to the old Victorian building that housed the main facility. The lights on the top-floor windows shone and against them, silhouettes of dozens of heads looked out at us. I've always imagined them looking at each other and saying, "And they tell us we are mad!" They would have had a point.

'So many memories, so much rugby history. Ray Prosser, you were a legend and so was that Pontypool team and club. To have worn that jersey in your company, even for a few games, was an honour and a privilege I will take to my grave.'

Michael Kiernan
New Zealand 1983, 3 caps
Ireland 1982–91, 43 caps

Munster's Michael Kiernan is a nephew of Tom and I will never forget his drop goal for Ireland against England in 1985 that secured the Triple Crown – footage of which is probably the most replayed in recent years. He was one of seven along with Hugo MacNeill, Trevor Ringland, Paul Dean, Phil Orr, Ciarán Fitzgerald and Donal Lenihan who had also played in the team of 1982 that secured the first Triple Crown for Ireland since 1949.

Get in First
'In 1981, the Irish rugby team undertook a controversial tour to South Africa,' remembered Michael. 'Many front line players such as the late, great Moss Keane were unable to travel due to work commitments. Donal Lenihan, UCC's second row forward, didn't make the trip either.

'Our captain on that tour was Fergus Slattery. Slatts was a hero of mine as a kid. He'd played on the Irish team with my uncle Tommy so to be on the same tour as him was a huge thrill for me. As it turned out, I wasn't disappointed. He was superb on the pitch during matches; he led every training session: sprints, push-ups you name it – and boy could he party. He was last out of every pub reception, bun fight; whatever was going on Slatts was last out and first to training next morning.

'Donal Lenihan was much the same as Slatts, bar the matches and the training.

'The 1983 Five Nations championship was a good one for Ireland. The final tally showed: played four, won three, joint winners with France, whom we had beaten in Dublin. Our last match was a 25–15 win over England, also in Dublin, on 19 March. There were high hopes of a big Irish contingent on the Lions tour to New Zealand to be announced on 21 March. We were not disappointed – eight Irish, which included one Donal G. Lenihan, now of Cork Constitution.

'As we were the only two Munster players selected based in Cork, Donal suggested we should train together for the six weeks prior to the tour as there was no directive from the Lions at that time. I thought that made sense as Donal was a giant 19-stone, 6 ft 5 in. second row and I was a 200m Irish sprint champion who played in the centre – we could learn from each other (ya, right!)

'Donal and myself reported to the Lions management in St Ermin's Hotel, London, on 3 May in tremendous shape. Our right arms were the strongest of the whole squad and neither of us had gone to boarding school! However, disaster was to strike and Donal was diagnosed with a hernia and had to return home.

'The tour party left Gatwick on Thursday, 5 May and arrived in Wanganui, the venue for the first match, on Saturday, 7 May, some 36 hours later. I had my suspicions about Lenihan's injury. I knew he loved a few pints on Fridays in his local.

'I'm sure the vast majority of players agree that a Lions tour is an unforgettable experience. For me, the people I met, places I visited and the friendships forged within our own squad made it a special time, not to mention the New Zealanders' passion for their national game. Despite the series loss it's something I'm glad to have done.

'In any case, the tour flew by. Before we knew it we only had a few weeks to go. Decimated with injury, it seemed every week we had replacements arriving to join us. Having recovered from his hernia operation, one D.G. Lenihan was summoned to join the tour and I was delighted to see him. He arrived in good shape considering his last training session was a few "shuttle sprints" during a stopover at LA Airport.

'So, for the final part of the tour in Auckland, Donal and I roomed together. We got wind that a few squad members were planning to target some rooms for a "turn over" on the last night, so we staged our own in our room before we went out on the town. I got back sometime before my room-mate and went to sleep only to be woken by him some hours later and greeted with, "Kiernan, wake up. We've been ransacked!"

'It was time to go home.'

Trevor Ringland MBE
New Zealand 1983, 1 cap
Ireland 1981–8, 34 caps

I had been to Dublin to watch Ireland play Wales in 1980. It was the St Patrick's weekend and I returned to Belfast to take part in a College old boys team against the students with a dreadful hangover. Jimmy Davidson was lecturing at Stranmillis and turned out for the students to strengthen their side. He purposely tripped me in the first minute as he had noticed my state. In between seeking revenge on Davidson and the suffering, I noticed a tall, powerful blond kid on the left wing who oozed class. Whoever he was, even in a gather-up game like this, he was very special.

After the game, I was friends with Jimmy again, so I asked him who the kid on the left wing was. 'His name is Trevor Ringland,' he replied. Trevor Ringland became one of Ireland's all-time great wingers.

Taking Care of Friends

Trevor said: 'A highlight of leaving school and beginning to play senior rugby in the amateur days was that you could end up in the same match as some of your schoolboy heroes either as a team-mate or opponent. It was a step up. You weren't just watching the games. You were part of them alongside your idols on and off the pitch.

'As a young Queen's University side we played against the very experienced Ballymena team. Running out onto the pitch was the great Willie John McBride, one of my all-time rugby heroes. That day he provided a lesson in life. I pondered reasons why my schoolboy hero tried to pull my head off in the middle of a maul I was caught in with the ball and yet was so friendly to me after the game and since. Such is rugby.

'In my first cap match for Ireland against Australia in 1981, I played with the likes of Fergus Slattery, Willie Duggan, the late Moss Keane, John O'Driscoll, Ollie Campbell and others. Shortly after that game I received an invitation to play for the Barbarians against the Australians at Cardiff and travelled there with fellow Irishmen Willie Duggan and Phil Orr. A wicked snowstorm across the whole south of England and Wales cancelled the match. However, we secured seats on the last train from Cardiff to London that weekend and I recall spending two hours chatting with the late Bill McLaren, Willie Duggan and Phil Orr, a memorable journey with rugby giants.

'In London, Phil Orr left us. Willie Duggan and I tried to find a hotel room as all Heathrow flights were cancelled due to the weather. Eventually we found a room in the London Tara Hotel. As a student, I had no money on me except the expenses cheque provided by the Barbarians. However, the hotel night staff would not cash it. So I was left to the munificence of Willie, who generously funded my whole night in London.

'The next day revealed we were going to be stranded a second night. Again I attempted to get my expenses cheque cashed. The young receptionist looked at me and said she would have to speak to the manager and rang him in front of me. I recall her saying, "Sir, Mr Duggan's son is here and he wants to cash a cheque." When I told Willie, he of course laughed. The incident provided much amusement, with my father joining in on the joke, often looking to Willie to cover some of the expense of funding me throughout my rugby career.

'Another angle to the story came about when, a couple of years ago, I bumped into Willie in an RTÉ studio in Dublin, both of us appearing on the same radio show. My son was with me and I introduced him to Willie with a joke that this was the grandfather who had never written, sent birthday presents or remembered any Christmas since he had been born.

'Again there was much humour around it, the sort of banter that brings nicknames and "in-jokes" guaranteed to cause a wry grin whenever you meet again. I couldn't believe it when my son's next birthday came around a couple of months later and a card and present arrived from the notoriously late Willie Duggan and his wife Ellen.

'Willie John McBride and Willie Duggan, both hard men, also had hearts of gold.'

SINCE I RETIRED

David Irwin
New Zealand 1983, 3 caps
Ireland 1980–90, 25 caps

I first met David Irwin when he was a wee boy playing for Royal Belfast Academical Institution (INST) under 13s who were coached by my great friend Mervyn Elder. I passed on some tips, but I might not have bothered if I'd known what a grown-up David Irwin would do to me about ten years later. I prided myself as a mauler of the ball and I wouldn't have minded if someone like Ballymena's Harry Steel had stripped me of the ball. However, in a club game against Instonians, I had the ignominy of being robbed of the ball by a back – David Irwin – and he still reminds me.

David, after retirement from the game, has served Ulster for many years as team doctor.

Always Speak Your Mind

'Don't be misled by the poeticism of "the land of the long white cloud",' warned David. 'Touring New Zealand with any team is tough. On a Lions tour it is even more so as there is exceptional intensity to everything, and although downtime is sparse, it is important to make the most of it when you can.

'In 1983, our twelve-week tour of eighteen matches included four Test matches against the All Blacks. Our party consisted of our manager (Willie John McBride), our first-time Lions coach (Jim "Creamy" Telfer), our doctor (Donald McLeod) and our physio (Kevin Murphy) plus, of course, a panel of 30 players – not quite the professional circus of more recent tours with up to 50 players and an unbelievable backroom staff of about 30 including chefs, lawyers and PR gurus!

'By the time we reached Dunedin for the third Test, having lost the first two narrowly 20–16 and 9–0, I found myself for the first time on the "dirt trackers" (players not playing or on the bench for the next match), a merry band of about ten including my fellow Ulsterman Trevor Ringland, Dr John O'Driscoll, Dusty Hare, Jim Calder and many more.

'Willie John, being a man of immense experience, realised our disappointment at non-inclusion and invited us all to a drinks party in his suite the night before the Test, and after – a meal out on the town in Dunedin. Prior to leaving the hotel in our bright-red Lions polo shirts and dickey bows, someone had a great idea of exiting via our team room in the middle of Jim Telfer's intense "night before Test" team talk. We duly interrupted, Seven Dwarf style, singing "Hi-ho, hi-ho, it's off to drink we go", marching merrily between and around our bemused team-mates and – in retrospect – a very non-amused coach. Off into the Dunedin night we marched, smug with our performance and had a great night's craic well into the wee small hours.

'Our return, much less vigorous than our departure, left me in the hotel foyer with Trevor Ringland (now MBE for some reason). Trevor stood beside the lift, looking vacant – as he tended to do while under the influence. The lift beside him pinged before the doors opened, which coincided with me spotting some cash on the floor. I bent down to pick it up, conveniently hidden behind a large potted rubber plant. Through the leaves I could see Jim Telfer stepping out of the lift and approaching a bemused Trevor. Despite my inebriation, I recognised it was a good time to stay concealed behind my jungle screen as he confronted Trevor in his broad Scottish Borders accent. "Ringland, d'you realise we've a Test match in the morn?"

'Realising he was in trouble anyway, Trevor quickly replied, "Jim, *you* may have a Test match in the morning, but *I* certainly don't."

'Stunned, and for once speechless, the coach stormed back into the lift muttering. It seemed opportune to come out from my hiding place and I congratulated Trevor on his bravado and stupidity. Grin. We headed to our beds and fell into deep slumber.

'Only a few hours passed when, at 7 a.m., a phone call from the duty boy for the day, "Ginger" McLoughlin, disturbed my room-mate, Dr John O'Driscoll (or maybe his "friend") and I. Ginger delighted in telling us to get up for training. John O'D informed him on our thoughts about the situation. Ginger rang again and repeated the earlier message in no uncertain terms. John slammed the phone down and left it off the hook so we could return to our prematurely interrupted sleep.

'Before long, our door rattled with vigorous knocking. John rose grudgingly to tell Ginger where to stick his training, only to be confronted by Jim Telfer, fully clad in Lions red tracksuit, announcing, "You're on the bus in five minutes." Somehow we managed to get our gear, still dressing as we went, meeting our fellow dirt trackers en route to the foyer and then the bus.

'Jim Telfer sat at the front, grinning as we headed off towards the local sand dunes for the training from hell. Anyone who had seen *One Flew Over the Cuckoo's Nest* might have thought the single-decker bus in which we sat was strangely familiar. The sad individuals that trooped from the bus were reminiscent of the patients of the local asylum featured in the film. After an hour of mental and physical torture, we headed back to the hotel for rehydration. Jim Telfer's wry smile glinted a hint of evil that ensured we knew he'd made his point. Thanks, Trevor.'

Hugo MacNeill
New Zealand 1983, 3 caps
Ireland 1981–8, 37 caps

I went with Hugo MacNeill on an Easter tour to Bermuda in 1981, a terrific location for any side but especially so for teams with Irish connections due to the organiser John Kane. The island's hospitality is unsurpassed and Hugo certainly embraced the atmosphere with a splendid attitude to the game and social responsibilities, singing Irish songs like his party piece 'Fiddlers Green'.

An Exile's Club

'How cool is it to be selected for a Lions tour?' asked Hugo. 'It's a rhetorical question really, but if I had to answer it, I'd say we'd need to measure it in Kelvin degrees – definitely cool. As a 25 year old having enjoyed club rugby, of course I aspired to playing in a top-level team and worked hard to that end. Something that struck me very early in my career, having played for London Irish, is how much responsibility a rugby player has to so many people. Exiled in London, supporters, family and work colleagues all got caught up in the excitement of an Irish match at Twickenham.

'The game was important to them in a way I was unable to fully appreciate when living at home. Support for Ireland was intense. In 1982, I remember fabulous scenes on the way from the dressing-room to the bus when Ginger McLoughlin's try and Ollie Campbell's kicks put us on the brink of a first Triple Crown and championship for decades. The joy and expectation was palpable. Disappointment and dumbstruck disbelief on an Irish supporter's face on the Sunday night in a pub in Belgravia after we were hammered in the Chris Oti hat-trick game of 1988 will forever stick in my mind too. He stood open-mouthed in front of me, his eyes pleading for an explanation. Neil Francis tells of supporters bending down to kiss the ground in front of him after their victory in 1994 when Simon Geoghegan blazed down the wing (something that never happened to Franno before or since!). These things really mattered to those of London Irish stock. Although London Irish, the club represented the Irish in England and many would travel great distances down to the city to catch a glimpse of the boys representing their homeland, north or south of the border. They gave massive support to the lads and made us determined to do them proud with our performances.

'Doubtless others will mention the camaraderie that develops within a team. It is an essential component and one that is the foundation of what is an amazing international brotherhood. For me, the most important thing that came from rugby was the incredible selflessness of players. This was epitomised in the overwhelming response to Neil Murphy's Rugby Legends Benefit.

'Neil Murphy was and is stoutly of the Irish stock mentioned earlier. I met him first in 1985 when I came down from Oxford to work and play rugby in London. A very talented player and comfortable in most positions across the back line, Neil played most of his career at centre, the hardest position in the back line to play really well in my estimation. That is due to the fact that you have so little space and are so dependent on the way that the people inside use you and present you with the ball. It is not difficult to be competent, taking the ball into contact and tackling your own man. Really good centres are those who play with intelligence, setting the direction of the line with an ability to glide and drift into spaces they help to create. Neil was definitely in this class, an elegant runner with magnificent distribution skills and solid in defence. He was terrific to play full-back outside; he always kept the line straight, fixing the opposition and not allowing them to drift off him onto you.

'Neil usually gave me a lift to training and we got to know each other well. I worked near Green Park and would take the Tube to Earls Court, meeting him at the exhibition centre side before heading off to Sunbury.

'Neil always loved his Irish roots and was so proud to play for London Irish. He loved the music, humour and banter and probably savoured the whole concept of the "craic" as much as anyone I knew. We had many great nights at Sunbury and back in town. He always had a great love of family and huge appreciation for his friends. His 21st birthday party was such a special occasion for those invited to share the revels; everyone will remember the unprecedented hospitality extended to the guests, many of whom were club-tie-wearing individuals, genuinely welcomed to a family affair.

'It is therefore entirely appropriate that the "family" of rugby should align itself with him as he meets the new challenges that the great game of life throws at him. (Neil was recently disabled by a severe brain haemorrhage. Showing that the spirit of rugby is still alive and well, his former colleagues and friends in the game, led by his former centre partner Simon Cooke, assembled a "Legends XV" to raise money for his benefit fund.) He was always a natural team player. It still remains one of the greatest aspects of the game of rugby football that it rallies to those in the "family" when they are in need. Neil did that for others. Now others are doing that for him. Sometimes he gave the scoring pass. Other times he took it and scored the try. It is a tribute to him that there have been so many today who are happy to make that pass to him.'

Donal Lenihan
New Zealand 1983; Australia 1989
Ireland 1981–92, 52 caps

I never really got a chance to meet the Irish players of the '80s, as I had moved to England, though I do remember seeing the Munster man's famous break that set up Michael Kiernan's drop goal in 1985. However, at Moss Keane's funeral there were ex-players from every era, including Donal Lenihan who went on two Lions tours without gaining a Test place. However, such was his loyalty he personally organised the Wednesday side 'Donal's Donuts' and this was a great source of support to the coaches Ian McGeechan and Roger Uttley. Donal captained Ireland 17 times during his career, the first occasion being in the inaugural World Cup in 1987, became manager of Ireland in 1998 and managed the 2001 Lions.

It's How You Say It
'Lions tours are special and in the amateur days represented the highlight of a player's career,' said Donal. 'When the 1986 tour to South Africa was called off on political grounds, a host of internationals lost out on one of life's great rugby experiences. Playing instead against a World XV in Cardiff, even if it did contain the best the southern hemisphere had to offer at the time, just wasn't the same.

'Bob Norster and I were the only survivors from the last Lions expedition to New Zealand in 1983. In the interim six years, faces had changed and all was fresh and new. That is why the tour to Australia in 1989 was so special. I will never forget the reaction of the squad when we pulled into the palatial surrounds of the Burswood Hotel in Fremantle on the outskirts of Perth for the opening game and a week of acclimatisation. The pyramid glass exterior of the hotel surrounded by two golf courses and a casino captivated us. We thought we had arrived in heaven.

'Ireland hadn't had a great season and as a consequence only four Irish players were selected, including me and Ballymena's Ulster hooker Steve Smith. The Troubles still had an impact on the North at the time, but it never affected relations between the players in the North and the South. We fully respected the sacrifices and pressures on the Ulster lads when playing for Ireland. After a few pints there was always a good bit of banter when songs from both cultures were sung freely by all without malice or offence.

'Steve and I roomed together on several occasions on international duty and always got on well. Smithy had a reputation for going a bit wild after a few pints and redecorated a few establishments in his time, not always at the owner's request. I decided I had better look out for him on this trip and told him as much. After a few days, I decided to go on reconnaissance in Perth and discovered a great pub called Finian's – according to the Australian accent I heard – like Finian's Rainbow. Irish bars were not the norm away from home in those days. I rounded up a posse including my Ulster Protestant friend along with that great Scottish back row at the time of John Jeffrey, Derek White and our tour captain Finlay Calder.

'After a few pints, we were getting on famously, despite the disparity in the accents from my Cork brogue to three different Scottish dialects. At one stage I was talking to White about the merits of Christy Moore – Ireland's top ballad singer – when he thought I was extolling the virtues of Chris de Burgh. Something lost in translation there.

'Smithy never says much at the best of times, but on this occasion he barely opened his mouth and looked decidedly nervous. Having encouraged him to mix and get to know everyone early on tour, I was a bit annoyed with this and pulled him aside for a quiet word.

'"What's up?" I asked.

'"Have you seen where you brought me?"

'"What do you mean? This is a great spot, a good traditional Irish pub."

'Stevie squirmed. "Have you seen the name?"

'Ticked off at his attitude and annoyed that he didn't seem to appreciate

196

my homework I answered sharply. "I have – Finian's bar."

"'It's not Finian's," he said, "it's *The Fenians.*"

'Now anyone familiar with the Troubles at the time will know Fenians was the derogatory term used in the North by Loyalists for Irish Republicans. Graffiti using the word could be seen in plenty of places up North, and pronounced in Ulster with such vehemence it exaggerated the insult. Entering into an establishment with such a name probably required a certain background in Smithy's eyes and explained just why he was so jumpy and kept his eye on the door. The Scottish trio on hearing this exploded in laughter while I assured Smithy he was in no danger. It was one of many nights I had reason to look after him, even if he was more than a little nervous with my early attempts to protect his best interests.'

Stevie Smith
Australia 1989
Ireland 1988–93, 25 caps

I met a man called Graham in a great pub in Deptford, South London, called the Dog and Bell. When he heard I had connections with Ballymena, he told me he had a friend in Broughshane and once, when visiting, he was invited to a BBQ near the village. 'A huge rugby player arrived,' he continued, 'hands like shovels, with a whole pig on one shoulder and a pint of beer in his free hand. God, could he drink beer.'

'I bet I know his name,' I replied. 'Steve Smith, my Saturday afternoon drinking partner in the Ballymena clubhouse.'

It's a small world, Stevie – you're well known, even in Deptford!

Donal's Donuts

'I toured with the Lions to Australia in 1989,' recalled Stevie. 'It's a rare privilege to be considered, given the infrequency of tours and the number of great players who have never had the opportunity to pull on the famous red jersey. Four different nations normally used to kicking lumps out of each other united under the same badge: it's a concept that probably shouldn't work but somehow it does, making the Lions a unique concept in world rugby.

'The 1989 tour was the first full tour of Australia undertaken by the Lions and, to be fair, Australia didn't have the depth of rugby at that time to host such a tour. Many midweek games especially were fairly meaningless affairs in exotic upcountry places where our arrival was the only significant happening since Ned Kelly robbed the local bank 100 years previously. In a country where rugby union struggles for recognition, media presence for the Lions was hard to find at times, though the *Dubbo Times* did carry a banner headline: "LIONS ARRIVE IN DUBBO". Closer inspection showed this denoted the arrival of a new pride of lions at the internationally acclaimed Dubbo Zoo, which we were later to visit as a publicity stunt at the behest of the real lions.

'I played in "Donal's Donuts" midweek team. Folk held a popular misconception we were named such because of our physical shape, but "Donut" was Roger Uttley's term of endearment for our captain Donal Lenihan. I have to say it did little to abate 800 years of simmering Irish resentment!

'Donal was a fine captain and a good lineout exponent who always encouraged his hooker, although I often wondered if he was cursing me under his breath in Irish if a throw didn't hit its intended spot. (I must find out the Irish translation of "useless fucker".) I would subsequently apologise in Ulster-Scots and we went to the next lineout neither of us any the wiser.'

Functions

'As part of the midweek team we were required to attend more than our fair share of functions so that the Test team could rest up back at the hotel in preparation for the Saturday game.

'We were the British and Irish Lions. In my experience of touring, any function that contained either the word British or Irish was to be avoided at all costs. "Irish" usually meant an Irish society function, which consisted largely of red-faced, bulbous-nosed, hairy-eared expats from Westmeath, Mayo, etc. telling you what a great place old Ireland was and "Wouldn't it be great if we could get rid of the border?" Given the delicacy of matters back home, these situations required diplomacy in response. "I respect your opinion, mate, but what the hell's it got to do with you living 10,000 miles away?" A hasty exit was usually recommended at this juncture.

'"British" usually meant a cocktail party at the British Governor's or British Ambassador's residence in which the Lions present were expected to mingle amongst their hosts, and inevitably meant being cornered by a J. Fotherington-Smythe type (think the major in *Fawlty Towers*) who regaled you at great length about his exploits for the Old Fartonian 3B's and also a ball-by-ball account of his 78 not out for the English Gentlemen against the Delhi Dagoes in 1938: ". . . one local chap had the temerity to appeal for LBW; of course we had him taken away and shot."

'Being a monosyllabic front row forward I never mastered the combined art of engaging in polite discourse whilst eating a hot mushroom vol-au-vent and so sought sanctuary with fellow front row Neanderthals in a darkened corner of the room where invariably could be found the Welsh gathered en masse anxiously awaiting the relief call from the duty boy of the day: "Right, boys, on the bus!"

'If you've ever played any rugby in the south of Wales you will appreciate that the concept of a cocktail party doesn't exist and, as exquisitely prepared canapés were being distributed, a Welsh voice could invariably be heard exclaiming, "Hey, Dai, I'm not eating that; them's fuckin' fish eggs!" followed shortly after by, "Have you any tomato ketchup, luv?" God bless the Welsh.'

Studs in the Back

'The tour was a great success from a playing point of view, winning all the games and the Test series 2–1. It has to be said that the Australians were sore losers, which ill-befits them, because of all the major rugby nations, admirably they have always been the most inventive and innovative. The midweek team was on the receiving end of this ingenuity in one of those "what happened next moments" which actually appeared on *A Question of Sport*.

'In the final midweek game of the tour against NSW Country, we were winning the game comfortably. A final push upfield meant the opposition won a scrum about 15 metres from our line in front of the posts with their out-half lined up directly behind for a drop goal to put some respectability on the scoreboard. The ball was heeled and I distinctly remember in the scrum at the time thinking, "Someone's just run over my back!" I dismissed it as the combined effects of too much sun and Bundaberg Rum over the previous eight weeks. But lo and behold, as the scrum broke up, their out-half touched down under the sticks having piggybacked his way to the line over the top of the scrum. The try was disallowed, of course, but you had to admire the two fingers to convention used in the move and this is why the southern-hemisphere teams dominate world rugby.'

Irish Rugby

'In my day "innovation" in Irish rugby was photocopying a New Zealand coaching manual and "vision" was distributing it amongst the coaches of Ireland. By the time we had worked out all the little grids and shuttles, New Zealand had moved on and were laughing at us in their wake.

'Times have moved on thankfully and Irish players now have the structures in place to compete on a world stage, though I wonder whether we'll ever win the truly big prize – encapsulated by our new stadium, 75 per cent world class with a bicycle shed at one end. Still, we should be thankful for small mercies; anything is an improvement on the old Lansdowne Road, quaint though it was: the only sports stadium in the world built round two cottages. I often wondered why we didn't reinforce the old stereotype and have a donkey and cart outside, peats stacked against the wall, with George Hook hanging over the half door dispensing his wisdom to all and sundry . . . on second thoughts, maybe not.

'The biggest challenge at the old ground wasn't on the field of play but as a spectator finding somewhere to have a half-time piss. This is where Irish rugby's real ingenuity and invention lay.

'I remember in a belated attempt to move with the times the Irish squad and peripheral players were summoned to the magnificently appointed UCL Limerick sports campus for a weekend of fitness and conditioning testing. Eminent people with white coats and clipboards supervised our every move, kind of a cross between a soap powder ad and an alien autopsy. At the end of the weekend they concluded we were neither fit nor well conditioned enough to play international rugby. This wasn't surprising given the last 20 minutes of most games were spent on our hands and knees gasping for air as the French, mostly, ran rings round us.

'On the final morning, we were summoned to one of the lecture halls at the university where an eminent sports scientist bamboozled us with information on sports nutrition, proteins and carbohydrates, both complex and simple. Being a humble front row forward I assumed all carbohydrates were simple, but this is not the case. Armed only with seven 'O' levels, a cycling proficiency badge and a 25-metre swimming badge from Cubs, most of this information flew over the top of my head.

'At the end of the lecture it was opened to the floor for any questions and our then team manager, a legendary former international, stepped forward to offer his opinion. "If I could give the lads one piece of advice," he said, "it would be on the morning of a big game I would always have an extra sausage and rasher of bacon for me breakfast." A silence ensued as we contemplated whether the previously explained, supposedly complex world of sports nutrition was in reality no more than an extra rasher of bacon and sausage and that the solution to the woes of Irish rugby were staring at us all along from the breakfast plate. If only life was that simple!

'The joke is no longer on Ireland, thankfully. Our current crop of players are great ambassadors for their country and have given us a lot to cheer in recent years. They say and do all the right things, but somehow in the midst of it all you wish a Moss Keane figure would emerge, somebody who took his rugby seriously but gave us all a laugh along the way and made you realise in the greater scheme of things rugby isn't all that important.'

Paul Dean
Australia 1989
Ireland 1981–9, 32 caps

I met Paul Dean in Dublin for the first time, but as he was with Terry (the Rat) Kennedy and J.B. Sweeney, things got a bit hazy and I ended up watching the Ireland v Wales game on television with the Rat. However, I sort of got the gist of a story which I must clarify the next time I see him. It was an Irish tour to South Africa and I do remember the ending, though, when Willie Duggan, clad only in underpants, with total malice in his heart chased the Rat through the foyer, thronged with hundreds of supporters, and tried to kill him. The only one to get injured was Willie. Anyway, it was all Paul Dean's fault, apparently!

The Kamikaze Move
'16 December 2010 at 16:41 my mobile rang with a UK number displayed, which I thought looked familiar. I answered:

Paul Dean: "Hi, Ian."
Stewart McKinney: "Deano! It's not Ian, it's me, Stewart McKinney. I need some stories from you for the book – great cause. No more than 800 words and email them before the end of Jan."
Paul Dean: "I'm fine, thanks, how've you been keeping?"

Stewart McKinney: "Yeah, great, now don't be late like Willie Duggan. Good luck!"
End of call 16:43.

'I learnt at an early age in rugby to respect big forwards!'

Paul said: 'One of the biggest and most wholehearted rugby forwards I played with was the late, great Maurice Ignatius Keane and also the nicest human one could meet. Just before Mossie left us I was helping at a charity fundraiser at the K Golf and Country Club where Mossie was the main celebrity. Our President of Ireland, Mrs Mary McAleese, arrived and explained to the hundreds in attendance that she knew Mossie because her husband attended the same college as he did. She recounted many stories of Moss in his earlier college days which were highly complimentary and very funny. Then in typical Irish style the President brought him down to earth with a few slags just to keep his head from swelling too much. Mossie was held in very high regard throughout Ireland. We all miss you!

'The first time I played against Moss was when I was 21. I clearly remember playing for my club St Mary's College RFC against Lansdowne RFC in Lansdowne Road. On that day I lined out in the centre position outside Tony Ward, and between the two teams we had a dozen internationals on duty.

'One particular play in that match came back to haunt me through later life. Wardie called a move named "Rangie" (after famous Australian brothers) and from an attacking scrum the centre (yours truly) takes the pass from the out-half on a diagonal run back towards the forwards *at full speed*. In hindsight we should have called it "Kamikaze".

'Wardie got the ball and ran across the pitch. I gathered a pop pass running at full tilt back towards the forwards slowly rising from a very stressful scrimmage.

'I remember gliding my 12 stones past the number 7 and to my horror I clearly remember Big (18½ stone) Moss being directly in my path. Thankfully he had just awoken from the scrum and was a little groggy. I put out my hand, purely in self-defence, caught him off guard and flush on the chest. He went reeling backwards and fell like a sack of spuds. I crossed the goal line and neatly placed the ball under the posts for a try.

'That hand-off was a Big Mistake. Mossie, one of those clever guys who sped through the *Irish Times* crossword, unfortunately for me, remembered everything. Payback came for me a number of times, the first when we played together in Rome with the Irish Wolfhounds. Having comfortably won the invitation game, mainly due to the backs, of course, we relaxed after the match and sampled the local Peroni beer and later ventured on to some cheeky Valpolicella. Terry 'the Rat' Kennedy accompanied us on that trip and, being the more experienced Tourist, he assured me "wine on beer is fine". Neither of the beverages on offer was to Mossie's or Willie's [Duggan] liking, so they decided to make their own fun.

'Because we were in the Holy City and because there was a convenient fountain close by, Moss and Willie thought it was only right that a back should be baptised. Mossie quickly selected me, they picked me up and completely submerged yours truly, blazer and all, in the fountain more times than I care to remember. Each time I came up for air I heard Mossie say, "Remember that hand-off?"

'Another memorable time on international duty we stayed in the beautiful Shelbourne Hotel in Dublin. The night prior to the match I shared a room with Mick (the Kick) Kiernan and Mossie normally shared with Willie Duggan. Everybody had retired early that night when a knock came to our door. I opened it and Moss brushed me aside, went into our bathroom and closed the door. Through the door I asked Moss as politely as possible, "Are you OK? What are you doing?"

'"Willie doesn't like me using our toilet when he is in the room, now be quiet!" He eventually left our room and whispered to me on the way out, "Try hand that off!"'

Little bit of trivia
Question: What do you call those types of people who constantly hang around with rugby players, follow them to the cool places and generally idolise their every move?
Answer: Forwards!

Andy Reed
New Zealand 1993, 1 cap
Scotland 1993–9, 18 caps

I met Andy Reed with the Judge (Paul Rendall) in Guernsey in 2011. They were on a Wasps Golden Oldies side and were having one hell of a weekend.

Although playing for Scotland and captaining them on a tour to

Argentina in 1994, Andy was a product of that fabulous rugby county, Cornwall. He made his way from Bodmin and Cambourne to Bath and finished his first-class career at Wasps.

The Orange Bus

'I played in the first Test of the '93 Lions tour to New Zealand,' recalled Andy, 'where we succumbed to a dubious late penalty from the ever reliable boot of Grant Fox. Unfortunately I had picked up a knee injury in the game, which kept me out of action for the following week and opened the door for a certain Mr Johnson to play against Taranaki and Auckland leading up to the second Test.

'We had just finished our team run at a local school on the Monday and I was thinking that a good match against Hawke's Bay on the Tuesday might keep me in the team for the second Test. Assistant coach Dick Best had taken the team run whilst Ian McGeechan and the remaining players trained alongside on another pitch. I think the schoolchildren gathered around the pitch where Geech was taking the session realised more than us that they were watching the Test team!

'Back in the changing-room we put our trainers on and made our way to the bus. It was normal to shower back at the hotel, which was a bit of a drive away so we were keen to get going. We waited on the bus whilst Geech continued with his session and as time passed the banter increased, as we were getting impatient with the wait.

'I think it was Richard Webster who suggested we should then fill up all of the seats from the back of the bus just to piss them off for keeping us waiting, them being the "Dream Team" as Webby put it! This may seem petty but there always will be an acknowledged seating order on a rugby bus dictated by the senior players. Dean Richards and Peter Winterbottom et al. occupied the back row on ours, with the less experienced such as me towards the front of the bus.

'We were still waiting when someone remembered there was a box of oranges in the changing-room, which one of the players fetched. The plan hatched was that once the Dream Team were on board and the bus moving we were to let them have it, *it* being the oranges we were armed with from our advantageous position at the rear.

'After what seemed an eternity, during which our frustrations grew, the Dream Team finally boarded the bus. Winters' and Deano's faces to name a few were a picture but even they realised we were pretty pissed off about the wait and took to the remaining seats.

'The bus pulled away and on cue we let fly with our ammo. Poor Martin Bayfield's head and shoulders were well proud of the seat back and presented a large target (it wasn't me!) but no one was safe. After the initial onslaught, oranges were raining to and fro. It must only have lasted a minute or two at most but came to an end when the driver had to stop the bus to clean the inside of the windscreen, as he couldn't see through it!

'It was all taken in good spirit but there was without doubt a little bit of underlying venom shown by the midweek boys!'

Brian O'Driscoll
Australia 2001, 3 caps; New Zealand 2005, 1 cap; South Africa 2009, 2 caps
Ireland 1999–present, 120 caps

There is nothing I can say to add to the millions of words written about Brian O'Driscoll except to thank him for the pleasure he has given to rugby spectators over the last 13 years. Apart from his undeniable skill and leadership, his sense of humour keeps him popular and down to earth. When I received Graham Price's email about the Nike ad re-done for YouTube with B O'D and Paul O'Connell I had a great laugh (check out the link: http://www.youtube.com/watch?v=zB5eu0EwK34).

I have played with geniuses like Mike Gibson and against the George Best of French rugby, Jo Maso, but Brian O'Driscoll will always be the king.

Making Parents Proud
'I was lucky enough to be part of a great Lions victory at the Gabba in 2001 and managed to score a try in that game,' said Brian. 'Tremendous euphoria enveloped the 20,000-plus Lions supporters and [there was] great singing at and after the game. The atmosphere, so far away from home, was magic. Buses provided free of charge got people away from the ground quickly and back into Brisbane. These were packed with our supporters and my mum and dad duly got on a bus. No one knew them from Adam.

'Shortly into the trip the entire bus load spontaneously burst into song singing "Waltzing O'Driscoll" with the adaptation, "And we sang and we danced as he waltzed thru the Wallabies, You'll come a waltzing O'Driscoll with me." It was something special for them.'

Jamie Heaslip
South Africa 2009, 3 caps
Ireland 2006–present, 50 caps

Jamie Heaslip is one of the professional-era players who still embraces the attitudes of the amateur players regarding camaraderie, fun and staying in touch with supporters. His Twitter and Facebook messages with updates of their pranks show that the lads still have time to have fun when they are away, which is such a relief after hearing tales of 'all work and no play'. The modern game is in good hands with characters like Jamie about and doubtless his uncle, former Irish international and 1971 Lion, Mick Hipwell encourages him.

The Bobby Cup

'My Lions tour of 2009 was full of great highlights and stories,' remembered Jamie. 'Some of these personal, some as a group and some that shall stay on tour. But one of my favourite moments of the tour was receiving the Bobby Cup.

'This prestigious trophy was in fact a little metal, travel coffee mug with a hand-written sticker on the front – "Bobby Cup". At the start of the tour, its purpose seemed a little bizarre, but it soon became an integral part of uplifting the camp mood. Bobby, our fitness trainer, handed it out the day after any game we won, to the player he thought had deserved it. It wasn't necessarily awarded to the man of the match, but the one he thought played a massive role in the game. There were also some entertaining videos that came along with the presentation, mostly taking the piss out of the management and players. This is where morale was lifted if it was at all down.

'The day after our last Test match against South Africa, the only one we won, there was a presentation. Now in this case, because there had been no Bobby Cup in the previous two weeks, everyone had forgotten about it and thought it was going to be a final few words from the management. However, in stepped Bobby. After a video, he announced his Bobby Cup winner, namely me. I was delighted as I thought Shane Williams would have got it for his man-of-the-match performance the day before.

'As I was the last one to receive it on tour, it is my obligation to make sure it manages to get to the next tour – be it with or without me. It currently sits proudly in my house in Dublin and I will be making sure that it goes on the next tour and hopefully I won't be far behind it.'

Joe Worsley
South Africa 2009, 1 cap
England 1999–2011, 78 caps

I don't get a chance to meet the younger, modern players too often, but I was lucky enough to meet Joe at a Wooden Spoon function in Guernsey in 2011. We also met at the Bengal Clipper Lunch for Esher Rugby Club.

He is a man who admits that the possibility of crunching contact attracted him to rugby as a boy. He is a much more rounded character than that, is a wonderful speaker and I'm sure everybody would wish him success in his new career of coaching after a serious neck injury. Good luck in Bordeaux Bègles.

Rugby Obsession

Joe said: 'One of my earliest rugby memories was getting up incredibly early to watch the Lions losing the Test in New Zealand, 1993, when Fox kicked a penalty at the death to win the match – I was annoyed with Dean Richards for months afterwards (God knows if the penalty was fair; I simply remember being pissed off with him).

'I don't remember exactly when I became so focused on rugby – before this stage in my memory life wasn't affected by huge men from the East Midlands; it had been more about bikes and Tonka trucks. From this point on my main concern in life wasn't bikes, Amiga 64, schoolwork, booze or women (I should add that that changed when I met my wife or she will be pissed!) but revolved around rugby.'

7

STEWART TELLS SOME TALES

Stewart McKinney
South Africa 1974
Ireland 1972–8, 25 caps

I'm often accused of being nosey, and I'm glad I am, otherwise I may not have come across as many stories as I have. Through club, provincial and international rugby I have had the opportunity to meet with players, referees, alickadoos and supporters in changing-rooms and clubrooms all over the world. Not only am I nosey, but I have also been told I have a terrific memory, and in writing this book many happy recollections were brought back to mind. I have included some of them that can be published; friendships are too strong to 'kiss and tell'.

Clohessey

Moss Keane had an excellent book, *Rucks, Mauls and Gaelic Football,* published. J.B. Keane was his ghost writer.

One day Moss ran into that great prop forward Peter Clohessey, who commented, 'I see you got J.B. Keane to write a book for you, Moss.'

'Really?' replied Moss. 'Who read it to you?'

For Ken Kennedy

On 24 July 1974, after enduring three months of a hard, physical tour, 15 of the 16 forwards were still available for selection for the final Test at Ellis Park, Johannesburg. (The late Gordon Brown, who had broken a knuckle in one of the many fights in the third Test in Port Elizabeth, was the only one off parade.) This was remarkable when considering previous and later tours.

Good luck? Perhaps. Good conditioning? Maybe. But the crucial factor was the daily clinic of Dr Ken Kennedy, who diagnosed, treated and cajoled his fellow team-mates throughout the tour. His diligence began in London when we assembled. Through blood tests he discovered that seven of the party were anaemic, a condition that would seriously affect performance when playing at altitude on the Highveld, so appropriate treatment was given at once.

The first major casualty was Mike Burton, who seriously injured a knee at the Stilfontein training camp. Ken aspirated a lot of blood from the knee in the middle of the night and by giving immediate treatment saved Mike's tour. Later on, in Rhodesia, Mike was extremely miffed when Ken declared him unfit to play because of an agonising eye condition, greatly aggravated by the fierce sunlight.

'I'll wear a patch over it,' declared an indignant Burton.

'And what would you do if your opposite prop was wearing a patch, Mike?'

'I'd hit him on the good eye,' replied Burton.

'I rest my case,' said Ken.

World-class hooker, world-class doctor; we '74 Lions owed him a lot.

A Chink in the Armour

Willie John was a powerful man in rucks and mauls. In those situations, no one, but no one, took the ball from him once his mighty arms were wrapped around it.

My first scrum-half when I played for Dungannon was the diminutive Micky McSwiggan. Micky was a Gaelic footballer of some note and he utilised some of his Gaelic skills on the rugby pitch. Sometimes, if the ball emerged quickly from the scrum, he wouldn't bother to pass it to the outside-half, but chip it to him instead, an art I saw him perform in an Ulster match with his half-back partner George Spotswood. Micky was talented, bold and cheeky, essential attributes of any scrum-half. He might have been small, but he was dynamite.

In the annual Dungannon v Ballymena Boxing Day match, Willie John took the ball into a maul situation. Somehow the delicate Micky had got caught up in the maul too. Suddenly, I heard a lot of giggling and the little scrum-half emerged with the ball. This was a miracle.

Micky had discovered a weakness in the mighty forward's capabilities – he had tickled him. To rub it in, Micky flexed his little biceps and retorted, 'Don't you think you'd ever get a ball off me, Willie John.'

Willie laughed, but the great Colin Meads or Frik du Preez might have got a different reaction if they had tried a similar play.

Cutting Corners

Mossie Keane had a huge fondness for company and people enjoyed his common touch. He loved life and was fun to be with. His repartee and wit were legendary. Mossie also never forgot those who had been his brothers in arms before he found fame in the international arena. Boys from UCC and Lansdowne, his relations and friends from his beloved Kerry, and everywhere else for that matter, all simply had to be fitted in after an international game before the formal part of the evening. So, he would disappear to some pub near Stephen's Green, sink pints with his pals and inevitably arrive back late at the Shelbourne Hotel to change into his dress suit.

Early on in his career I was rooming with him and was nearly changed when with a dash he burst into the room. I gave him a bit of a bollocking for keeping us late and continued the final touches to my attire. Imagine my amazement when, still struggling with my cufflinks, I noticed the giant resplendent in his finery. I don't know how he did it. 'Have you any deodorant?' he asked. I handed him an aerosol and he gave himself two shots through the armpits of his jacket.

'Come on, you Northern bastard, you're keeping me late!' he announced.

I wonder what he would have done if I'd reached him a roll-on deodorant?

Even in Chains

Kevin Lavelle, mentioned in the story by Peter Larter, was an amazing character. He never played for Ireland, although he was a travelling reserve before the advent of substitutes. However, he starred in the back row, alongside Tony O'Sullivan, in the brilliant Connacht team of the early 1960s. He considered himself a drop-goal expert and one of his proudest moments was playing for the Barbarians, when he attempted the feat many times without success.

When Kevin first arrived in Britain, he joined the navy and a friend of mine related a strange story of when HMS *Sea Urchin* docked in Bermuda. Both the local team and that from HMS *Sea Urchin* were on the pitch when the spectators could hear, 'left, right, left, right' and a rattle of chains. A manacled Kevin Lavelle was marched by the military police to the touchline, unlocked and released to play the game. After the final whistle, Kevin, who had dropped his obligatory goal, was once again shackled and marched away.

When I asked Kevin about the intrigue behind the misdemeanour that led to his ignominious appearance, he said he wasn't quite sure as there had been so many. But it may have been the time when he had tried to touch up the admiral's wife. The admiral had later said, 'I wouldn't have minded so much, Lavelle, but she told me she had thoroughly enjoyed it.'

Gareth as the Shadow

Choet Visser, our liaison officer in South Africa, was a wonderful rugby man who made sure we were looked after royally as he dedicated himself to the day-to-day running of the tour. No request was too much for him and he seemed to know everyone and certainly, the whole of South Africa seemed to know him. He stated from day one that he would love to see us win 17 of the 22 games and that his allegiance was to South Africa for the four Tests and his beloved Free State in Bloemfontein – understandably so. (The Orange Free State was within 20 seconds of making him a very proud man.)

Bloemfontein was Choet's home town and he had many business interests there. He also owned a jeweller's shop and we had by now a few rand in the kitty, through his effort I must say. He supplemented our £1.50 a day from other sources and informed us if we wanted to buy jewellery at wholesale prices he would arrange it.

Bobby Windsor intimated to Tommy David that this would be a wonderful opportunity to steal a large diamond. Tommy's imagination went wild and he had visions of a gem the size of the Cullinan being secreted to Pontypool. Tommy told Gareth Edwards of Bob's impending heist. Gareth was incensed and told Bobby in no uncertain terms that he was totally out of order to even think of stealing from Uncle Choet, who had smoothed our way and catered for our every whim.

Dai Morris, that great Welsh wing forward, was known as 'the Shadow' and from the moment we entered Choet's shop, Gareth assumed Dai's role. If you ever watched Gareth Edwards' eyes on a rugby pitch, they never stopped moving – scanning for gaps, looking for opportunity, but nothing compared to this. When Bobby moved, he moved; when Bobby stopped, he stopped; and where Bobby looked, he looked. And that's when he made his mistake. Bobby looked to his right; Gareth looked to his right and suddenly Bob's left hand shot down towards a jewellery case and back into his pocket.

Out the door he bolted, with Gareth in hot pursuit. When the scrum-half apprehended the hooker, he begged him to go back to the shop and replace the diamond. Bobby protested his innocence in his own inimitable way. 'You don't bastard trust me, Edwards. Do you think I'd steal from Choet Visser?' Gareth didn't and after a thorough search, realised he was the victim of the Duke's guile and his own imagination. It's the only time I ever saw Gareth Edwards take a dummy.

Icelander

Chris Lander, journalist from the *Daily Mirror*, accompanied us to South Africa in 1974. We trusted him and he was welcome to join us when we went carousing, as we knew he wouldn't report anything untoward in his paper. I only recently learnt that he had died some time back, which saddened me, as he was a very good friend. Chris was also a very determined individual. He joined Ian Botham on his first walk from Land's End to John O'Groats – he had intended only to accompany him during the first stage but ended up completing the lot.

He was also determined to get me drunk . . . in a very odd way. He'd heard that Chris Ralston and I were a bit down, as we had been injured and hadn't played for a while. He invited the two of us to join him for drinks on the roof bar at the Carlton Hotel in Johannesburg. Chris was good company, so Ralston and I accepted the invitation and looked forward to having a frosty brew or two.

When we arrived, he handed us each a bowl of ice-cream.

'What the hell is this?' I demanded. 'You asked us up here for a drink.' He smiled. 'It's C. Lander cocktails.'

He had mixed a bottle of whiskey with cartons of ice-cream and we had a 'jolly' good afternoon on the roof bar, smiling like little kids by the time we had finished our treat . . . well, several of them.

In Deep Water

Around 1978, Ian (Mighty Mouse) McLauchlan arranged for my club Dungannon to play his club Jordanhill in a pre-season friendly. It wasn't very friendly, with the likes of Richie Dixon, Hugh Campbell and Ian himself playing. Those guys could ruck, and so could we, but if you didn't come off the pitch in those days with your back striped, you weren't doing your job and neither were the opposition. I am so sad that 'proper rucking' has disappeared from the game. In my opinion, fast ruck ball was the best ball for the backs to deal with. During my era, the Scots were the best ruckers.

It was very friendly afterwards; a wonderful evening was spent with Jordanhill before we returned to our hotel somewhere off the Great

Western Road in Glasgow. I'd had misgivings when I'd seen its name – The Pond – and greater misgivings when I noticed as we boarded the bus for the game that there was a flotilla of rowing boats on the small lake that fronted the hotel. Perhaps in our probable state of inebriation late at night they would go unnoticed.

However, after many pints of 'heavy' the boats were all too visible and, indeed, becoming exceedingly attractive. There was one difficulty, though: they were moored about 30 yards out in the middle of the lake. As I was captain, I felt it was my responsibility and no less my duty (in case anyone got into difficulties in the water) to swim out and tow the boats to the bank. I stripped off, splashed in and set off feeling very noble and brave putting my body on the line for my team-mates. Except . . . I didn't get too far. It's extremely hard for someone my size to swim in a foot of water, the depth of the lake as I discovered. I felt a right eejit. Still, after I waded out and pulled the boats back we had great fun re-enacting the Battle of Trafalgar before the Scottish gendarmes arrived and suggested we retired to bed.

Jaws

In 1987, I was coach and steward of Askean's Rugby Club. At that time the landlady of the Coach and Horses public house in Greenwich Market was Heather Hill and a fine host she was too. Heather approached me one day on the possibility of using the facilities of Askean's to play a challenge game between the ladies of her pub and the Askean girls. She also insisted the women should have the use of the huge communal bath. I agreed, of course, to all her requests.

Modern-day players sadistically soak in ice baths, but in the 1980s some clubs like Askean's and Malone, in Belfast, did have communal baths, although the practice was dying out. This would I'm sure be frowned upon by modern-day sports science theorists, but it was a great way to luxuriate in hot water and discuss the previous 80 minutes with team-mates and opposition alike. Twickenham, of course, went one better – they had individual baths.

The great occasion arrived on a particularly muddy Sunday and the game was played with boundless enthusiasm and good humour. Few of them knew the rules, but this only added to the fun, and muddied, tired and bruised participants trooped off the pitch looking forward to the comfort of the communal bath.

Unknown to me, or anyone else for that matter, Heather Hill had purchased something interesting the day before in Deptford Market, which she added to the bath when she slipped away before full-time. Deposited in the bath was a monster, an evil-looking conger eel that had sunk to the bottom by the time the women plunged in. While they sat relaxing, drinking bottles of beer and singing bawdy songs, it got a bit livelier in the bath. The activity disturbed the conger eel and when it surfaced and began to disintegrate the ladies leapt from the bath and left the changing-rooms screaming. Never did a rugby club witness such scenes before. Shrieking women streaked through the bar in panic unconcerned about their nakedness. Nubile nudes scampered through the clubhouse to escape the beast of the bath. It took me two days to clean up the mess, but it was well worth the sight of that Sunday.

A Steady Run

Prior to the England v Ireland game of 1972, Mike Burton had (by devious and clandestine means) obtained the top-secret Irish scrum calls. As John Moloney our scrum-half addressed a vital scrum, Burton – in a perfect 'Ken Kennedy' Ulster accent – called 'banana', our signal for a quick put in. John Pullin took a strike against the head to much hilarity from the English pack. Ken Kennedy (our hooker) gave the innocent Moloney an awful bollocking. My friendship with Mike began that same evening, and even Kennedy laughed about the bogus 'banana' call.

Burton and I were both selected in 1973 for the Baa Baas Easter tour to Wales and once again Mike was somehow able to acquire crucial information ... The Baa Baas' committee by tradition would not divulge the make-up of the teams for the Penarth, Cardiff, Swansea and Newport matches until the eve of each game, when the selection would be pinned on the door of the team room. But Mike found out. 'Penarth Friday, Newport Tuesday,' Mike announced. 'You and I can plan the social arrangements for the next few days.' For the first time I heard him recommend a 'steady run', which we would do on Monday, to sweat out any weekend excesses.

On the 1974 Lions tour of South Africa, we were by now bosom friends and we needed to be as we were both injured and unavailable for selection for the first three games and tried to keep each other's spirits up. There is nothing worse than not being able to play on tour and we were really down in those first couple of weeks.

Our baptism in Port Elizabeth against Eastern Province was the first time on the tour that a South African side had tried to intimidate us in a game known as 'The Battle of Boet Erasmus'. They made one hell of a mistake. Burton felled Rowley Parker, who had the audacity to try and maim our captain of the day – the great Gareth Edwards – and I knocked out Van Eyk, who was trying to maim everyone. After the misery of the previous two weeks, we were at last Lions and our tails were swishing.

Mike and I roomed together, visited schools together, nearly ending up together in a school play when we got the staff drunk, not realising they were part of the cast. We even ran in the Kruger Park (something it turns out no sane person would do as 400 illegal immigrants are eaten each year, trying to enter South Africa through that wilderness) and we had quite a few extra 'steady runs' to sweat the beer out.

In August 1975, while on holiday in Hereford, Mike invited me to Gloucester and Kingsholm to train with the boys. 'We don't do much,' he informed me, 'just a "steady run", a few laps and then we'll have a few beers and reminisce afterwards.'

I duly arrived and we went to the house of John Parsons, a fanatical Gloucester supporter, to sign some programmes. I was fed a feast of elvers, tea and cake, but noticed Burton was not partaking. Perhaps he's on a diet, I thought.

There were dozens and dozens of players in the changing-room. That evening at Gloucester was Trials night and some of them were very nervous. I discovered by asking the twitchy ones a few polite questions that they were from local sides like Lydney, Berry Hill, Tredworth, Longlevens and Matson, all striving to achieve the honour of a place in the Gloucester squad.

I suddenly realised Burton had given me a 'bogus banana' call and, even worse, I was full of cake and elvers. Too late now: I was part of what Ivor Oakes called 'The Bash'. For the next two hours I never hated a man so much, especially as he put me in a group with John Watkins, a great, superfit England player. One guy from Lydney stopped to be sick and Oakes told him to bugger off and never come back as he would be no use to Gloucester at Pontypool on a Wednesday night in November. 'True Gloucester men never stop running, no matter what! You should have been sick as you ran.' I survived and even had a beer with the masochists in the club afterwards.

I didn't get the chance to even the score with Mike until Twickenham 1976. As he was my friend, I had only meant to wind him, but I broke his right floating rib – right in front of the Queen in the Royal Box. Mike Burton disguised the pain and played on with great courage for the remainder of the game, packing down in every scrum against Phillip Orr. In the words of Ivor Oakes, 'True Gloucester men never stop running, no matter what.'

Gotcha!

Harlequins' wonderful characters through the years include Mickey Skinner, one of my favourite people. When I was playing for London Irish in the early '80s, I heard of the colourful Caxton brothers, from west London, who all played for Harlequins. However, I never met them, as London Irish weren't on Harlequins' fixture list.

Metropolitan Police was also a very good team at that time with the likes of Tony Boddy, an English hooker, and John (Monty) Montgomery, a scrum-half who also played for Middlesex and London Scottish. Monty was a rare character and he once told me a story about Terry Caxton, the rough, tough, Harlequins prop.

Terry was driving a ramshackle scrap lorry on the Chertsey Road, the A316 in west London. Monty, then a motorcycle cop, recognised Terry and pulled him over. They were old friends and post-match drinking mates.

'How did you get on last Saturday against Richmond, Monty?'

'This is not about rugby, Terry' said Monty. 'I need to give the lorry the once-over.'

'Bollocks! You can't be serious.'

Monty kept on for half an hour as Terry Caxton grew more irate – tyres were checked, tax, MOT, etc. and when he finally drove off, Terry swore revenge.

One week later, he got his chance. On the same stretch of road at around the same time as the last encounter, Terry saw the motorbike with the traffic cop approaching from behind. Terry wound down his window and lifted a length of 4 by 2 timber. As the cop drew alongside, Terry leant out the window and struck him a hefty blow on the top of the helmet. There was only one problem – it wasn't Monty!

Off Season

Tony Bond and I ended our tenure as captain and coach at Askean's RFC in 1989. The next captain was Dylan Davies – mentioned and pictured in Brian Moore's book *Beware of the Dog* for his prowess at eating volcanic curries.

Dylan somehow came into possession of a large cheque meant for the club treasurer, Alan Eastick and no . . . he didn't return to his native Neath and spend it but strangely had a raft designed and built in Northern Ireland to enter the Portrush Raft Race, a huge event in the north-west of Ulster over the May Bank Holiday attracting 100,000 spectators each year.

The residue of the money was spent organising a tour for 20 players to participate in the raft race weekend tour. The rugby season had ended, so cricket and Gaelic games were organised at Rainey OBs and Coleraine RFC. As the Troubles were still continuing in the North of Ireland the wives and girlfriends of most of the party were strenuously opposing the raft adventure and the risks of a weekend in Ulster. Dylan, who had taught in Magherafelt, and I tried our best to appease their fears and after much heart searching the trip went ahead.

A very nervous group of players landed at Belfast International Airport and set off for Magherafelt in two minibuses. A few miles from our destination, two RUC (Royal Ulster Constabulary) Land Rovers pulled the vehicles into a lay-by beside a small wood. The jittery occupants were made to stand facing the hedge in a long line by the armed patrol officers. Some of the boys had never seen a gun before and some were discovering that adrenalin was a brown colour. One by one they were frisked and told to go around the back of the hedge into a forest clearing. What fate awaited?

Four members of Rainey OBs attired in dress suits as makeshift waiters dispensed champagne with great gusto for the next hour to give the south-east Londoners a proper Ulster welcome.

Before the great raft race, Dylan Davies had visited Deptford Market near Greenwich and purchased 20 pairs of garish Bermuda shorts. They looked ridiculous and with mighty protest the coach was forced to wear the compulsory, vulgar atrocities too. I would meet a lot of people I knew at home over the weekend, but at least there would be another 19 Askeans to be ridiculed also.

We had a splendid weekend with plenty of adventure. Our last port of call on the Sunday evening was to the Crown Liquor Saloon – my favourite pub in the world. The greatest example of Victorian style and architecture with original décor remains unscathed and protected now through ownership by the National Trust. Despite being located opposite Belfast's Europa Hotel, frequently bombed at the height of the Troubles, the Crown survives unharmed. It was in the Crown that it all went wrong.

I became nostalgic, recounting student days when the whole King's

Scholars' team would congregate in one of the roomy snugs to drink pints of porter. I decided I didn't want to go back, that I would stay one more day. Mark Hudson had played top-level rugby for the Maoris, Wellington and Otago and opted to remain too. The New Zealander had already caused a sensation two days earlier in the Bushmills Distillery by stripping, with great panache and flair, for a party from the Women's Institute who loved his performance.

We said our farewells to the lads, but to our horror discovered five minutes later we had forgotten to remove our bags from the minibus. Airline tickets, passports and most importantly – proper trousers – had all returned to London.

My great friend Mervyn Elder, who has rescued me from many a crisis, put us up for the night and liaised with Dylan to organise replacement tickets. We were due to fly to Luton in the evening so, with the afternoon free, spent the time in Belfast dressed in the ridiculous Bermuda shorts. I prayed I wouldn't meet anyone I knew, but Sod's Law meant I ran into many old friends that Monday afternoon. There was no strength in numbers now. 'Jesus, McKinney, you go to live in England and come back looking like an idiot,' was one of the milder remarks made. We skulked back to the snug in the Crown and hid until it was time to go to the airport.

As we approached the check-in desk, the ground staff were pointing at Mark and me. The shorts, probably, we thought. Then they approached us and took us to the front of the queue and informed us that we would be boarding first and asked us if we required wheelchairs. Wheelchairs? They led us across the tarmac before the rest of the passengers and seated us at the front of the plane where the air stewardesses treated us royally. We were totally bemused by the extraordinary service.

Early Tuesday morning, Dylan phoned to see if we had returned safely and innocently enquired if our treatment by the airline had been satisfactory. I explained the events at the airport and on the flight and he exploded into laughter.

'When I organised your replacement tickets, I told them that I was the head of a team of carers from a mental home and that we'd recently visited the Giant's Causeway with a party of patients. I told them that two had absconded, but had been found and would be on the evening flight to Luton. I also said they'd be easily recognisable as they were wearing outlandish Bermuda shorts, that they were normally placid but could become extremely violent if agitated.'

Bastard! Needless to say, I have never worn Bermuda shorts since.

Penal Servitude

Ireland toured Australia in 1979 under the captaincy of Fergus Slattery and the coaching of Noel 'Noisy' Murphy. It was an exceptionally successful tour. The boys won the series 2–0 and I was very proud watching in the BBC studio in Belfast, as I was in Jimmy Neilly's commentary team.

When the team arrived in Sydney, there were no problems at the immigration desk except for Moss Keane. As I never really understood what Moss was saying, I am sure the difficulties were caused by his Kerry accent. Anyway, things became very heated and the immigration officer asked Moss if he had any previous convictions. Moss thought for a second and replied, 'I didn't know it was compulsory any more to have a conviction to enter Australia.'

Ralston Takes the Pledge

In her excellent book *Thirty Bullies*, Alison Kervin exposes the drinking culture in English rugby and intimates that on an English tour to South Africa in 1984, some of the players were on the beer from night till morn for a full four weeks.

I had the privilege and honour to participate in two overseas tours, to South Africa with the '74 Lions and to New Zealand with Ireland in 1976. There were some legendary drinkers on both tours, but I can assure you the players took their responsibilities very seriously. The ethos and attitude of the management on both tours ensured that, particularly the '74 tour captain Willie John McBride and coach Syd Millar. There were no rules on what to eat or drink. 'You are grown men and we will treat you that way,' they said. Because we didn't overdo things, the fun we had on Saturdays was much more enjoyable. Training was so hard only a fool would have over-indulged. However, there was one exception.

Syd Millar's policy was to leave the match-day preparations to the captain of the day, should that have been Willie John, Gareth Edwards, Ian McLauchlan or whoever. On the morning of any game, after breakfast, he would drive the dirt trackers (those players not involved as a player or sub in the game) in a minibus to an adjacent sports ground – usually about eight of us. Syd always brought a net bag full of balls with him and we would complete an hour and a half session, always working with the balls. Despite hard, gruelling sessions, fatigue and pain were psychologically made easier by the inclusion of the ball work, a great dynamic that kept interest high and efforts strong.

They say familiarity breeds contempt and the eight dirt trackers, on the eve of the Boland game (having discovered a great pub in Wynburg, a suburb of Cape Town) had gone on the lash, secure in the knowledge that the next day's training would be made more bearable by the use of the balls. At nine o'clock next morning we climbed on board the minibus and Syd slung the balls into the front seat beside him. During the drive, I noticed that he looked at the passengers quite a lot through the driver's mirror. He didn't have to sniff much as the van smelt like a brewery, which even Chris Ralston's cigar failed to disguise.

We climbed out and Syd made his way to the middle of the pitch. Ralston stubbed out his cigar and drawled to Mike Burton, 'He's forgotten the balls, Micky. Tell him like a good chap, he's forgotten the balls.'

'I'm not telling him,' replied Burton.

'McKinney, you know him quite well; you're from Ulster, tell him he's forgotten the balls,' pleaded Ralston.

'Syd, shall I go back and fetch the balls?' I asked, trying to sound fresh and chipper.

Syd didn't glance back but marched on ahead. 'No balls today, lads,' he said matter-of-factly.

Ralston's face blanched. The subsequent 90 minutes were horrific. At one stage, Ralston crawled on his hands and was heard to murmur, 'If you go back for the balls, Syd . . . I promise – I'll never drink in my life again.'

The bag of balls returned for all further dirt-tracker sessions. A hard lesson had been learnt.

Retaliation

Willie John, in a concluding ritual before a game, would lock eyes with you and say, 'I want your best,' and tap you somewhere about the gut. The problem was the power in his paw. Acceptance of such a gesture made it imperative to stop jogging and brace firmly to the dressing-room floor. The short punch could have devastating effects on any unwary individual warming up.

In South Africa in 1974, all the Irish Lions knew exactly what to expect, having endured this pre-game assault for over two years. Not so Andy Irvine who, on his debut, ended up on the floor, having flown over the massage table and was only able to play after receiving medical attention.

The season after the Lions tour of '74, Ireland beat England at Lansdowne Road and although the changing-rooms were separate, the showers had to be shared. I had become great friends with Chris Ralston who had in South Africa attracted great misfortune. His was a tale of woe – dysentery in Port Elizabeth, flu in Cape Town, all the beds were too short, the removal of crowns because of severe toothache in Pretoria. To cap it all he was flattened by a punch aimed by the Leopard's prop in East London for the miscreant Mike Burton and woke up in hospital. I loved to sit with him over a beer as he described Jeremiah-style, between bouts of coughing, in his English public-school drawl the misery of a Lions tour. (He had quit cigarettes before leaving London and was now on 25 cigars a day.)

Anyway, that day at Lansdowne he was sharing a shower with Willie John and somehow, with great dexterity, managed to smoke a large cigar and keep it lit, coughing all the while.

'McBride,' he announced, 'it doesn't bloody work.'

'What doesn't work?' asked Willie John, thinking Chris was referring to the English tactics that afternoon.

'When I went back to Richmond after the tour, they appointed me captain of my great club. As the boys jogged on the spot before the first game of my captaincy, I looked them in the eye, told them I wanted their best and punched them in the stomach just like you. All the bastards punched me back.'

The Master

I had hoped my old PE teacher, Ken Armstrong, would contribute a story to my previous book; however, he unfortunately suffered from advanced Alzheimer's disease and was unable to do so. Ken was a superb all-round sportsman. He played soccer for Leicester City, rugby for Ireland, was an Irish basketballer, inter-provincial tennis player, single-figure golfer and unbeatable at table tennis. He could be awkward, obstinate and rigid, but to me he was 'the Master' and significant in my rugby development at school.

In February 1964, my school team, Dungannon, was on its way to Dublin on the Enterprise train. We had a fixture against St Columbus School that afternoon and we all anticipated the following day with great excitement as we had schoolboy tickets for the Ireland v Scotland match. Nine of us had never been to Lansdowne Road before and the prospect of seeing 'live' the likes of Tom Kiernan, Kevin Flynn, Bill

Mulcahy, Stewart Wilson, Norman Bruce and company was mouth-watering.

As we passed Dundalk, Ken Armstrong told me I wouldn't be required to represent the school against St Columbus. Before I could voice my indignation at being dropped, he continued, 'Because Dungannon requires you to play for them against Railway Union on Saturday morning. You will be my half-back partner.'

My last instructions before we took the field the next day were, 'You're only 16 and playing against mature men, so don't try to make any breaks, just pass the ball to me and above all – call me "Ken" on the pitch.'

He was soon sorry he had picked me . . .

'Go right, Mr Armstrong.'

'OK – but call me "Ken" on the pitch.'

'Go left, Mr Armstrong.'

'OK – but call me "Ken" on the pitch!'

'Pass it to me, Mr Armstrong.'

He grew more and more exasperated as both teams and the spectators were laughing. The last straw was near the end when we scored.

'Can I take the conversion, Mr Armstrong?'

'Take the bloody conversion – but call me "Ken" on the pitch!' he roared.

Never was Mr Armstrong so glad to hear a final whistle.

Warm-Ups

Usually if I go to an international these days, I arrive just a few minutes before the kick-off. However, on one occasion some years ago, my good friend John Murphy wasn't in good health and needed to get into Lansdowne Road before the crush as he'd just had a toe amputated.

I witnessed the most amazing sight. The Irish team at one end of the pitch performed elaborate drills and exercises and tore into padded bags and each other with immense vigour. And lo and behold the Scots did the same thing at the far end with equal intensity. How, I wondered, would they have enough energy left to pummel each other for another 80 minutes? After 45 minutes' frenzied activity they went inside – perhaps for a fag or at least a few minutes' kip before they re-emerged.

A strenuous warm-up in our day was reported to be three laps of Barry McGann, who always maintained he wasn't fat, but 'pleasantly built'. Roly Meates asked the aforesaid Barry to take our training warm-up on Lansdowne's back pitch one bitterly cold Sunday morning. 'Cup your hands,' he said, 'and blow into them five times.' He didn't like warm-ups, but in the heat of the battle he was one of the greatest footballing out-halves I ever played with.

Pre-match warm-ups usually consisted of stretching and jogging on the spot. Every so often the captain would shout, 'Ready, ready now!' and everyone sprinted to the count of five, shouting out numbers. Fit teams could even sprint to ten. After one or two of those sprints, Willie Duggan would disappear for a fag. Like Barry McGann, he didn't like training but was one of the all-time great number 8s, a world-class player.

I know of one team who recorded the sounds of a vicious warm-up, lots of swearing, shouting, threats and sprinting to ten and played the recording before kick-off knowing full well the opposition could hear the performance in the next changing-room. They themselves sat talking quietly, discussing the previous night and smoking cigarettes. Perhaps the opposition should have copied Tony O'Reilly, who took the wind out of an animated English warm-up by knocking on the door, entering and asking if anyone had a length of hairy twine as he had just broken his bootlace.

One Sunday in 1981, John Murphy was to pick me up at the World's End in Chelsea and drive me to Sunbury for a London Irish fixture against Blackheath. Late as usual, we were cutting it fine as we reached The Avenue. I was in the later stages of my career and I did need a few gentle stretches before kick-off. I had berated him throughout the journey for keeping me late, so at the approach to The Avenue he braked hard and told me to jump out. I thought there was some sort of emergency and automatically piled out. He threw the bag out behind me and drove off shouting, 'Run the last bloody half mile to the ground and you'll be well warmed up.'

Willie (No Joy) McCracken

The Bermuda Murphia consisted of Pat O'Riordan, Dave Lunn, John Kane and Tom Gallaher, and the first Bermuda Classic I was invited to was over Easter 1978. I had a superb time, especially in the company of the guy who looked after our day-to-day needs – Willie McCracken from Lurgan in Co. Armagh, a bit of a rogue, but if you needed anything, Willie would get it for you and nobody asked any questions. He was a representative for a California wine company and I believe that during the Classic week he'd given all his year's samples to us Tourists and got the sack for his troubles.

The following year I returned and this time Willie John McBride accepted the invitation on the promise of some deep-sea fishing for marlin and the like. Willie McCracken was by now a representative for a tobacco company and all the smokers were presented with Willie's promotional samples. As Willie John was a devoted pipe smoker – indeed he was voted 'Pipe Smoker of the Year', an honour shared with great pipe smokers like Harold Wilson – McCracken kept his bowl full during that week.

When we were leaving, McCracken gave Willie John some quality pipe tobacco for himself and some lesser quality stuff for his valued customers at the Northern Bank in Ballymena. Willie John duly dispensed the tobacco and it wasn't long before the phone was ringing with complaints about the tobacco. It wouldn't light. It would never have lit in a million years. McCracken had supplied Willie John with chewing tobacco – fine for spitting baseball players but not for Ballymena pipe smokers.

Don't Ask Too Much

Jammy Clinch was a wonderful character and I met him when I played for Dungannon and he was President of Wanderers.

Once, in a medical examination when he was at university, Jammy, following in his father's illustrious footsteps as a doctor, was shown a bone and asked what it was.

'A femur,' he replied.

'Right or left?'

'I'm not doing Honours!' he replied.